Clive Oxenden
Christina Latham-Koenig

New
ENGLISH FILE

Upper-intermediate
Student's Book

OXFORD
UNIVERSITY PRESS

Paul Seligson and Clive Oxenden are the original co-authors of
English File 1 (pub. 1996) and *English File 2* (pub. 1997).

Contents

Look out for Study Link
This shows you where to find extra material for more practice and revision.

G revision: question formation
V working out meaning from context
P intonation, stress, and rhythm in questions

1
A

Q and A

1 GRAMMAR   revision: question formation

a Complete the following questions with one or two question words or an auxiliary verb.

1   *How much*   do you earn?
2   ___*Are*___   you married?
3   _____   have you been learning English?
4   _____   do you prefer, small towns or big cities?
5   _____   do you go to the theatre a year?
6   _____   tall are you?
7   _____   religion are you?
8   _____   you want to have children?
9   _____   of music do you listen to?
10 _____   advice do you listen to most?
11 _____   you ever said 'I love you' and not meant it?
12 _____   did you vote for in the last election?

b Cross (✗) the questions above which you wouldn't ask a person you don't know very well. Are there any questions which you would not even ask a good friend? Which questions might you expect to find in a magazine interview with a famous person?

c Read the two interviews. Which question is…?

the most personal   the most boring   the most original.

d Read the interviews again and write **N** (Norah) or **L** (Lionel).

Who…?
1 never has enough time for what he / she wants to do   ___
2 has happy childhood memories   ___
3 avoids answering one of the questions   ___
4 feels guilty about something   ___
5 is probably a fan of the Rolling Stones   ___
6 is very proud about something   ___
7 says he / she is an insecure person   ___
8 needs help in his / her daily life   ___

e In pairs, look at questions 8–12 in the Lionel Richie interview. Find an example of…

1 a question where an auxiliary verb has been *added* to make the question.
2 a question where there is no auxiliary verb.
3 a question which ends with a preposition.
4 a negative question.
5 a question where the auxiliary verb and subject have been inverted to make the question.

f ⬦ **p.132 Grammar Bank 1A.** Read the rules and do the exercises.

Young star, old star

Every week the British newspaper, *The Guardian*, chooses people who have been in the news recently, and publishes a short interview with them called Q&A. The questionnaire often includes quite personal questions.

Q&A Norah Jones

Norah Jones was born in New York and is the daughter of the Indian sitar player and composer Ravi Shankar and the concert promoter Sue Jones; her half-sister is the musician Anoushka Shankar. A singer-songwriter, her debut album, *Come away with me*, sold more than 20 million copies worldwide and won her five Grammy Awards.

1 **Where would you like to live?**
   Barcelona.
2 **What do you most dislike about your appearance?**
   I am too short. I am 5ft 1in (155cm).
3 **Who would play you in the film of your life?**
   Maybe Christina Ricci.
4 **What's your favourite smell?**
   Onion, garlic, and butter cooking in a pan.
5 **What's your favourite word?**
   'No'.
6 **Which living person do you most despise, and why?**
   No comment!
7 **What single thing would improve the quality of your life?**
   Probably a housekeeper.
8 **Who would you invite to your dream dinner party?**
   All my friends and Keith Richards – I think he'd be great at a dinner pa
9 **What's the worst job you've done?**
   A waitressing job where I had the breakfast shift. It wasn't the jo
   that was so bad, just the hours. I had to go in at five in the mornin
10 **If you could go back in time, where would you go?**
   Summer camp in Michigan, aged 14.
11 **How do you relax?**
   A hot bath.
12 **What keeps you awake at night?**
   Music. A song will keep going round in my brain and keep me awake.

From *The Guardian*

Q&A Lionel Richie

Lionel Richie was born in Alabama, USA. He became famous in the 1970s as lead singer with The Commodores and again in the 1980s as a solo singer. He is best remembered for songs like *Three times a lady, All night long,* and *Say you (say me),* for which he won an Oscar.

What's your idea of perfect happiness?
Sunday by the pool, no phone calls.

What's your earliest memory?
My first day at pre-school. I was terrified. I'd never seen that many children in my whole life.

What's your most treasured possession?
My Oscar.

If you could edit your past, what would you change?
The Commodores never did a farewell tour. We just broke up and disappeared.

What has been your most embarrassing moment?
Forgetting the lyrics to my new single on a TV show.

What words or phrases do you most overuse?
'I'll call you back' or 'I'll see you soon'.

What's the most important lesson life has taught you?
Don't trust the smile, trust the actions.

What don't you like about your personality?
I'm an egotistical maniac with an inferiority complex.

What makes you depressed?
That there are 24 hours in a day and I need 36.

When did you last cry and why?
At the funeral of Milan Williams of The Commodores.

Who would you most like to say sorry to?
To my kids for not being there more.

What song would you like to be played at your funeral?
All night long and Stevie Wonder's *I just called to say I love you.*

2 PRONUNCIATION intonation, stress, and rhythm in questions

> Using the right **intonation** or tone helps you to sound friendly and interested when you speak English. **Stressing** the right words in a sentence helps you speak with a good rhythm. **Intonation** + **stress** = the music and **rhythm** of English.

a **1.1** Listen to questions 1–8. In which one does the speaker sound more friendly and interested? Write a or b.

1 ___ 2 ___ 3 ___ 4 ___ 5 ___ 6 ___ 7 ___ 8 ___

b **1.2** Listen and <u>underline</u> the stressed words in these questions.

1 <u>What's</u> your <u>favourite</u> <u>kind</u> of <u>music</u>?
2 Have you ever been to a health club?
3 How often do you go away at the weekend?
4 Do you know what's on TV tonight?
5 How long have you been living here?
6 What are you thinking about?
7 Are you a vegetarian?
8 What do you do to relax?

c Listen again and repeat the questions in **b**. Try to sound as friendly as possible. Then ask each other the questions.

3 SPEAKING

a Look at the answers other celebrities gave to some other questions in *The Guardian* interview series. In pairs, try to guess what the original questions were.

La Sagrada Familia basilica in Barcelona.

Natalie Imbruglia, singer and actress

When England went out of the World Cup.

Danny Jones, from the band McFly

For the Labour party.

Martin Freeman, actor

Paris in the first decade of the 20th century.

William Boyd, writer

Going from anywhere back to Copenhagen.

Helena Christensen, top model

Flying, especially since 9 / 11.

Shaznay Lewis, singer from All Saints

b Now choose six questions from the interviews to ask a partner. Only ask questions which you would be comfortable to answer yourself.

Three minutes to get to know the love of your life

4 READING & VOCABULARY

a Do you know what 'speed dating' is? Read the first half of the article to check, or to find out how speed dating works.

Working out meaning from context

When you are reading and you find a word or phrase you don't know, try to guess the meaning from the context (the other words around it). Think also about what part of speech the unknown word is (e.g. a verb, an adjective, etc.), whether it is similar to another English word you know, or whether it is similar to a word in your language.

If you still can't work out what the word or phrase means, either ignore it and carry on reading or use a good dictionary (or glossary if there is one) to help you.

---

b Read the first half of the article again carefully. With a partner, say or guess what the highlighted words and phrases mean. Then check with **Glossary 1**.

c Using your own words, answer questions 1–4 with a partner.
1 According to the writer, how did people use to get to know a prospective partner?
2 What kind of people is speed dating designed for?
3 Why does Adele Testani think three minutes is enough?
4 Why do you think that the journalist pretended to be a lawyer?

d Now read the second half of the article on page 7 and find out…
1 the advantages of speed dating (according to the participants).
2 if the journalist thinks speed dating is a good idea.

e Read the second half of the article again more carefully. With a partner, say or guess what the highlighted words and phrases mean.

Glossary 1

prospective partner someone who might become your partner in the future

courtship the period of time when two people have a romantic relationship before they get married

Mr or Ms Right (informal) the man / woman who would be the perfect partner for somebody

quick-fire (a series of things) done very quickly

a scorecard a card or paper where you write the points, e.g. in a game

a 'match' when two things or two people fit together

not your type not the kind of person who you would normally like or get on with

---

In recent years speed dating has become popular all around the world. Journalist, *Anushka Asthana* tried it out.

FINDING A PARTNER has always been a complicated process. It is a ritual which has evolved over the centuries; from a man taking food to a prospective partner in the Stone Age to young couples having tea together in Victorian times (under the watchful eye of an unmarried aunt) to dancing in a club to deafening music in the twenty-first century.

But now busy men and women who don't have the time for a slow, gentle courtship have a quicker way to find a partner: speed dating, where single people have exactly three minutes to decide if the person they are talking to could be Mr or Ms Right. The idea, which started in the USA, involves bringing together people for an evening of frenzied, 'quick-fire' dating. This is how it works.

Small tables are placed in a line and the women sit down at the one which has been given to them. They stay at their table all evening. The men take it in turns to sit next to each woman and have a very quick conversation. After three minutes a bell rings and, even if you are in mid-sentence, it is time for the man to move to the next table. If you like the person you have just spoken to, you put a tick in the 'yes' box on a scorecard. If the other person chooses you as well, this is called a 'match', and the organisers will send you the other person's email address a couple of days later and they will be sent yours too.

'Three minutes is enough time to talk to someone,' says Adele Testani, who runs a speed dating company, 'because you can get an idea of what a person is like in that time and you can eliminate them if you see immediately that they're not your type.'

Britain's largest ever speed dating evening took place this week at the Hydro Bar in London, so I decided to go along and see what it was all about. I pretended to be a single 24-year-old lawyer…

WHEN I ARRIVED at the Hydro Bar, the women, who were wearing fashionable dresses and smart suits, were giggling nervously as they put on badges with a number on them. 'Maybe my jeans are a bad idea,' I thought. I chatted to other people while we waited. People I spoke to said they had doubled the number of dates they had in a year with just one night of speed dating. The men included a chef, a banker, a photographer, an engineer, a management consultant, and a novelist. They were just pleased they could stop having to try to chat up strangers in bars: 'It's so hard to meet girls in London. With speed dating you meet 20 or 30 single girls in one night,' said one man. 'You can't talk to girls at salsa classes,' said another. Matt, 28, said, 'After doing this once I got several dates. There's a good atmosphere; it's safe and it's really good. It's like being at a party with lots of single women.'

Then it started. I made eye contact with the girl next to me so we could compare our opinions of the men; we raised our eyebrows for a possibility, exchanged a smile if the man was good-looking, and made a grimace if he made three minutes feel like three hours.

I thought it was boring just to ask questions like 'What do you do?' or 'Where are you from?' so I tried to think of more interesting and imaginative questions to ask, like 'If you could be an animal, what animal would you be and why?'

In the end I ticked six boxes. A couple of days later, I was told that four of the men had ticked me too. Four new dates. Not bad in 66 minutes.

Glossary 2

1 _____ a small piece of metal, plastic, or cloth with words or a design on it

2 _____ an expression on your face that shows you are in pain

3 _____ laugh in a silly way because you are amused or nervous

4 _____ move the line of hair above your eye upwards

5 _____ **pv** talk (to sb) in a friendly way because you are attracted to them

6 _____ talk in a friendly, informal way

---

f Complete **Glossary 2** with the correct word or phrase.

g Using your own words, answer questions 1–4 with a partner.
  1 Why did the journalist feel a bit uncomfortable at first?
  2 What kind of men went to this speed dating evening?
  3 What kind of signs did she make to the girl next to her? What for?
  4 What kind of questions did she think worked best?

h Do you think speed dating is a good way of meeting people? If you were looking for a partner, would you try it? What questions would you ask?

5 LISTENING

a **1.3** Listen to a radio programme about speed dating. A man and a woman who have both tried it talk about their experiences. How successful was it for them?

b Listen again. Then answer the questions with **E** (Emily), **A** (Alex), or **B** (both).
  Who…?
  1 preferred to ask normal questions ☐
  2 was asked an unusual question ☐
  3 was asked the same question again and again ☐
  4 got the fewest matches ☐
  5 had a disastrous date because he / she wasn't feeling well ☐
  6 was invited on a date which never took place ☐
  7 had a good date in spite of having had some bad news ☐
  8 realized on a date that his / her first impression was wrong ☐
  9 says he / she isn't planning to go speed dating again ☐

c Does hearing about Emily and Alex's experiences make you feel more or less positive about speed dating?

6 SPEAKING

GET IT RIGHT **reacting and asking for more information**
When you ask someone a question and they answer, it is normal to show interest, e.g. *Really?*, *Oh yes?*, *Yes, me too*, *Me neither*, *I know what you mean*, or by asking for more information, either with another question, e.g. *And what happened then?* or simply with a question word, e.g. *Why? When?*, etc.

---

a You are going to do 'speed questioning' with other people in the class. Before you start, think of five questions to ask.

b When your teacher says 'Start', you have three minutes to talk to the person next to you. Ask and answer each other's questions and ask for more information. When the teacher says 'Change', stop and go and talk to another student.

c Which questions were the best for finding out about other students?

G auxiliary verbs; *the...the...* + comparatives
V personality
P using a dictionary to check word stress; intonation and sentence rhythm

Do you believe it?

1 READING & SPEAKING

a Look at the signatures. Can you identify any of the people?

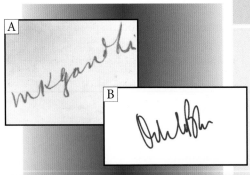

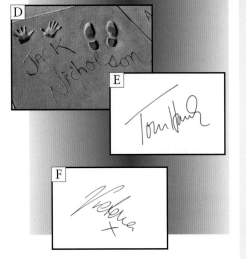

What your *signature* says about you

Your signature is the part of your handwriting that says the most about your personality. It is quite normal for your signature to change during your life, as your signature reflects how you evolve as a person. It is also common to have several signatures, for example a more formal signature (name and surname) when you sign a credit card or passport, and an informal signature (just your first name) when you sign a birthday card.

Your formal signature A signature usually contains either a first name and a surname, or initials and a surname, or, less frequently a first name and initials. Your first name represents your private or family self, and your surname represents your public self, how you are socially and at work.

If your first name is more prominent in your signature, this implies that you have positive feelings about your childhood and that your 'private' self is more important to you than your 'public' self.

If your surname is more prominent, this means that your 'public' self is more important to you. The more space there is between your name and surname, the more you wish to keep your public and private self separate.

If you use only initials either for your first name or your surname in your signature, this means that you are more secretive about this part of your personality (your private or public persona).

Legibility A legible signature, where names can be clearly read, implies that you are a person with clear ideas and objectives. The more illegible your signature is, the less assertive you are as a person, and the more you tend to avoid conflict.

Angle Most signatures are horizontal, rising, or descending. A rising signature means that you are the kind of person who, when faced with problems, will work to overcome them. Usually optimistic , you are in control and ambitious . A descending signature means that you have a tendency to get depressed and give up when faced with problems, and lack self-confidence . Some people's signatures go through a temporary phase where they go down, which shows that they are going through a hard time or an illness. A horizontal signature suggests an emotionally stable person who is well-balanced and generally satisfied with the way their life is going.

Size If your signature is bigger than the rest of the letter or document you have written, that means that you are self-confident and have quite a high opinion of yourself. Some people actually sign in capital letters, which suggests they are arrogant rather than self-confident. People whose signature is smaller than the rest of the text may be insecure and have low self-esteem .

b Read the first paragraph of an extract from a book about graphology. On a piece of paper, write the sentence *I look forward to hearing from you*, and then sign your name under the sentence.

c Now read the rest of the extract and answer the questions. According to the extract, which of the people A–F...?

1 has / had no separation between their public and private self, and is / was not very assertive

2 is / was more identified with their public self, optimistic, and ambitious

3 is / was more identified with their private self, and without much self confidence

4 is / was probably rather arrogant

5 keeps / kept their public and private life separate, is / was ambitious, and has / had positive feelings about their childhood

6 is / was secretive about their private life, and keeps / kept it very separate from their public life

d Try to guess the meaning of the highlighted words and phrases from the context. Check with your dictionary or the teacher

e Now look at your partner's piece of paper with his / her signature, and explain what it means.

f Did you agree with your partner's interpretation? Do you think graphology is a serious science? Why (not)?

2 VOCABULARY personality

a Without looking at the text, how many of the ten highlighted adjectives / phrases can you remember?

b ➲ p.146 Vocabulary Bank *Personality*.

c Add either a suffix or a prefix or both to the **bold** words to make an adjective that fits the sentence.

1 I don't think he's going to get very far. He's totally <u>unambitious</u>. **ambition**

2 You'll have a lively evening if Jane's coming because she's very _____. **talk**

3 You can't trust John to help. He's completely _____. **rely**

4 You look very _____. Have you had some good news? **cheer**

5 He's a bit _____. He said he liked my sister but he obviously doesn't. **sincere**

6 She's not very _____. She never has any good ideas. **imagine**

7 People say he's _____. You can't trust him with money. **honest**

8 She's so _____! She won't give me a hand with my homework. **help**

3 PRONUNCIATION using a dictionary to check word stress

In a dictionary, word stress is shown by an apostrophe before the stressed syllable, e.g. *begin* /bɪˈɡɪn/. Some words, especially compound words, have a primary (or main stress) and a secondary stress, e.g. *good-looking* /ˌɡʊdˈlʊkɪŋ/. Secondary stress is shown by a low apostrophe. It is less strong than primary stress.

a Use the phonetics to under<u>line</u> the *main* stressed syllable.

1 arrogant /ˈærəɡənt/
2 assertive /əˈsɜːtɪv/
3 bad-tempered /ˌbædˈtempəd/
4 creative /kriˈeɪtɪv/
5 considerate /kənˈsɪdərət/
6 conscientious /ˌkɒnʃiˈenʃəs/
7 possessive /pəˈzesɪv/
8 loyal /ˈlɔɪəl/
9 stubborn /ˈstʌbən/
10 impatient /ɪmˈpeɪʃnt/
11 unsociable /ʌnˈsəʊʃəbl/
12 immature /ˌɪməˈtʃʊə/

b **1.4** Listen and check. Are the negative prefixes or suffixes stressed?

c Practise saying the sentences below.

1 He's terribly bad-tempered – you need to be careful with him.
2 She's so conscientious – she always does her best in everything.
3 He's very easy-going – he never gets stressed.
4 His mother's really possessive – she doesn't want him to get married.
5 She's so immature – she behaves like a child.

4 SPEAKING

Talk in small groups. Give examples where you can of people you know or have known.

What kind of person makes…?
- a bad flatmate
- a bad travelling companion
- a bad boss
- a good teacher
- a good friend
- a good politician

MINI GRAMMAR
the…the… + comparatives

The more illegible your signature is, the less assertive you are as a person.

Use *the* + comparative adjective or adverb to show that one thing depends on another, e.g.
The sooner you do it, the easier it'll be = how easy it will be depends on when you do it.
The colder it is, the more clothes you need to wear.

Rewrite the sentences using *the…the…* + a comparative adjective or adverb.

1 If you study more, you learn more.
   The _____, the _____.
2 If we leave soon, we'll get there earlier.
   The _____, the _____.
3 If you are sociable, you have more friends.
   The _____, the _____.
4 If you are happy, you are nicer to other people.
   The _____, the _____.

5 **1.5** SONG ♫ *You gotta be*

6 LISTENING & READING

a Read the beginning of a magazine article. Do you know what a psychic is? Do you believe psychics have special powers or are you sceptical?

b You're now going to listen to Jane describing her visit to the psychic, Sally Morgan. After each part, discuss the questions with a partner.

Part 1 1.6
Answer the questions.
1 What was Jane's first impression of the room and of Sally?
2 What are the first questions Sally asked her?
3 Why is Jane surprised by two things Sally mentions?

Part 2 1.7
True or false?
1 Jane lived in Ireland when she was a child.
2 The psychic says Jane will meet someone new.
3 Jane is above average height.
4 She thinks Jane will be attracted to him by his looks.
5 Jane thinks she knows who the man is.

Part 3 1.8
Choose a, b, or c.
1 Sally says that, in the future, Jane ___.
  a will have the same health problems as her mother
  b will live longer than her mother
  c should have plastic surgery
2 According to Sally, ___ is good at reading and writing.
  a neither Jane's son nor her daughter
  b neither Jane's ex-husband nor her daughter
  c neither Jane's ex-husband nor her son
3 What Sally says about Jane's children makes Jane feel ___.
  a convinced that Sally is a genuine psychic
  b less sceptical about Sally being a psychic
  c sure that Sally is not a genuine psychic

c Read about some typical techniques used by psychics. Match the titles with the paragraphs.

A **Getting information from the client**
B **Using a name**
C **The flattering statement**
D **Identifying common medical problems**

d Listen to Jane talking about her visit again. Which techniques did Sally use?

e 1.9 Now listen to Jane talking a few weeks later. What was her final opinion about Sally's psychic abilities? What has happened since she went to see Sally?

f Do you know anyone who has been to a psychic? What happened?

Can psychics really see the future?
Jane Dickson investigates.

I am almost the only person I know who has never been to a psychic. Everyone I asked had a story about how key events in their lives had been predicted in some way. So I was really looking forward to my first visit to a psychic…

Tricks of the trade?
These are some of the techniques used by psychics…

1 Something psychics always do is say something that's true of almost anyone on the planet, preferably something positive. An all-time favourite is 'You're intelligent with a great sense of humour'. Who is going to answer, 'Well actually, I'm not. I'm really stupid and have no sense of humour at all'?

2 Statistics confirm that a headache is the most common female health problem and almost 50% of men have a scar on their leg, so it's not really surprising when a psychic 'sees' these problems.

3 A psychic can deduce a lot from your age and appearance, and most of them actually ask direct questions. It's difficult to avoid answering if you want results, because saying nothing is like going to the doctor and refusing to discuss your symptoms.

4 Coming up with a few names is always impressive. The usual method is to let the client work out who it might be. 'Does the letter *s* mean anything to you?' is a frequent strategy.

7 GRAMMAR auxiliary verbs

a Look at some extracts from the listening. Circle the correct auxiliary verb.

'Australia is very important in your life.'
'¹*Is / Isn't / Was it?* I've never been to Australia.'
'Another place which is very important in your life is Ireland.'
'Yes Ireland ²*is / does / has* play a big role in my life.'
'Let's see, your mother suffers from headaches, ³*doesn't / isn't / does* she?'
'Yes, she ⁴*is / does / has*, actually.'
'Well, you'll need to watch out for headaches, and so ⁵*is / does / will* your mother.'

b **1.10** Listen and check. <u>Underline</u> the auxiliaries which are stressed.

c In pairs, decide which auxiliary is used…
A as a short answer.   ☑ 4
B to add emphasis.   ☐
C to check information.   ☐
D to show surprise.   ☐
E to avoid repeating a verb or phrase. ☐

d ● **p.132 Grammar Bank 1B.** Read the rules and do the exercises.

8 PRONUNCIATION intonation and sentence rhythm

a **1.11** Listen to the conversation and circle the auxiliary verbs which are stressed.
A What's your sister like?
B Well, she's rather shy and quiet.
A (**Is**) she? So **is** my brother!
B **Isn't** your brother a doctor?
A That's right. And your sister works in a bank, **doesn't** she?
B No, she **doesn't**. She's a journalist.
A Oh yes, you **did** tell me, but I forgot. I think they'd probably get on well.
B **Do** you? But if my sister **doesn't** talk much and neither **does** your brother…
A Yes, you're probably right. We **won't** introduce them then.

b Listen and repeat the conversation copying the intonation and rhythm. Then practise it in pairs.

c **1.12** Listen and respond to the sentences you hear with an echo question, for example *Are you? Didn't you?*, etc.

d Complete the sentences on the left so that they are true for you. Then read them to your partner who will respond with an echo question and then say whether he / she is the same as you or different.

I'm not very good at _____ . (activity)	Aren't you?	Neither am I. / I am.
I'm very _____ . (adjective)	Are you?	So am I. / I'm not.
I hate _____ . (a food)	Do you?	So do I. / I don't. I like it.
I don't often _____ . (verb)	Don't you?	_____ .
I've been to _____ . (town / country)	_____ .	_____ .
My favourite season is _____ .	_____ .	_____ .

e ● **Communication** *You're psychic, aren't you? A p.116 B p.119.* Make guesses about your partner and then check if they are true.

1C

G present perfect (simple and continuous)
V illness and treatment
P consonant and vowel sounds

You're the doctor!

1 SPEAKING & VOCABULARY   illness and treatment

a Read about the two situations and work out the meaning of the highlighted words. Then decide which you think is the correct answer for each one.

You're the doc!

1 You're at home with some friends watching a football match on TV. In the excitement, one of your friends suddenly starts having a nosebleed .

DO YOU…?
a get some ice from the freezer and put it on his nose
b get some toilet paper, tell him to put it in his nose, and suggest that he goes to the doctor to check his blood pressure
c tell him to pinch the soft part of his nose for five minutes

2 You're having a barbecue with some friends on the beach. One of your friends accidentally picks up a very hot piece of wood and burns her hand. It hurts a lot and she has blisters on her skin.

DO YOU…?
a pour cold water on the hand and then cover it with a plastic bag
b cover the burn with suncream
c break the blisters and put on antiseptic cream

b ⟳ **Communication** *You're the doc! p.116.* Check your answers.

c ⟳ **p.147 Vocabulary Bank** *Illness and treatment.*

2 PRONUNCIATION   consonant and vowel sounds

> The phonetic symbols in a dictionary help you check the pronunciation of words which have an irregular sound–spelling relationship.

a **1.13** Use the phonetic symbols to help you pronounce these words. Then listen and check.

1 cough   /kɒf/
2 heart   /hɑːt/
3 asthma   /ˈæsmə/
4 bruise   /bruːz/
5 blood   /blʌd/
6 diarrhoea   /ˌdaɪəˈrɪə/

b How do you pronounce the sounds below? Write the words from the list in the correct column.

> ache infection ankle bandage specialist chemist
> choking GP allergy pressure rash check-up
> stomach temperature unconscious

ʃ	dʒ		k

c **1.14** Listen and check. Practise saying the words.

d ⟳ **p.160 Sound Bank.** Look at the typical spellings for these sounds.

e Ask and answer the questions below with a partner.
1 What are the main symptoms of…?
  a a cold
  b flu
  c a twisted ankle
  d a heart attack
  e an allergic reaction
  f food poisoning
2 What should you do if you have the illnesses or injuries above?

3 READING & LISTENING

a You are going to read an article about two people who found themselves involved in life or death situations. Work in pairs. **A** read the first article and **B** read the second.

Help! My friend's choking!

Library assistant, Mrs Johnson was having dinner with friends in a restaurant. They were all having steak and Mrs Johnson had just swallowed a piece of meat when she suddenly found that she couldn't breathe. Her friends hit her hard on the back, but the piece of steak remained stuck in her throat. She was starting to panic. One of her friends shouted out desperately, 'Excuse me, can anyone help my friend? She's choking.' At another table in the restaurant Trisha Goddard, a TV chat show presenter, saw what was happening and rushed over to try to help. She stood behind Mrs Johnson and put her arms round her waist, and then pulled hard inwards and upwards three times…

Trisha Goddard

The day my little boy swallowed a tomato

'Look at me, Mum,' giggled my three-year-old son. I could hardly understand him, as his mouth was full of cherry tomatoes. He had taken them out of the fridge while I was making lunch. 'Oh Peter, don't be silly,' I laughed. This was a big mistake. Peter tried to laugh too, and as he did so, one of the tomatoes got stuck in his throat. He tried to cough, but nothing happened. He was choking. I hit Peter on the back, but the tomato didn't move. Peter began to turn blue. I ran outside into the street, screaming for help, but the road was completely deserted. I was desperate. I put my whole hand in his mouth and pushed my fingers as far as I could down his throat…

b Take turns to tell each other your story. Explain…
  1 what the situation was.
  2 what the person who was giving first aid did.

c Discuss whether you think they did the right thing or not.

d (1.15) (1.16) Now listen to what happened next and answer the questions.
  1 What happened to Mrs Johnson in the end? Did Trisha Goddard do the right thing?
  2 What happened to Peter in the end? Did his mother do the right thing?

4 SPEAKING

> **GET IT RIGHT** **keep going!**
> Even when you know a lot of vocabulary connected with a topic, you may find that you don't know the exact word or phrase for what you want to say. If this happens, don't freeze! Paraphrase (use other words to say what you mean) and keep going!
>
> **Useful language**
> *What I mean is…*
> *I can't remember / I don't know the word, but it's…*
> *She had a sort of / kind of…*

Talk to a partner.

Have you ever had to give first aid?

YES
Who to? Why?
What happened?

NO

Has anyone ever had to give *you* first aid?

YES
What happened?

NO

How much do you know about first aid?
Where did you learn it?

What do you think you should do if…?
a someone is stung by a wasp
b someone has too much to drink and loses consciousness
c someone accidentally takes too many painkillers

5 GRAMMAR present perfect (simple and continuous)

a **Check what you know:** present perfect / past simple. Right (✔) or wrong (✘)? Correct the wrong highlighted phrases.

1 **A** Have you ever had an operation?
   B Yes, I've broken my leg two years ago.
2 **A** How long was your uncle in hospital?
   B Since last Tuesday. He's coming home tomorrow.
3 You haven't taken your medicine yet.

4 **A** Have you gone to see the doctor?
   B Not yet. I'm going this afternoon.
5 Ouch! I cut my finger! Have you got a plaster?
6 I know my doctor for ten years. She's very good.

Any problems? ⟳ **Workbook p.11**

b **1.17** **New grammar.** Read the jokes and use your instinct to cross out the wrong form (present perfect simple or continuous). Listen and check.

Patient Doctor, my son *has swallowed / has been swallowing* my pen, what should I do?
Doctor Use a pencil until I get there.

Doctor You look exhausted!
Patient Yes. *I've run / I've been running* after a cat.
Doctor After a cat?
Patient Yes, I think I'm a dog, doctor.
Doctor I see. How long *has this gone on / has this been going on* for?
Patient Since I was a little puppy.
Doctor OK. Just lie down here on the couch and we'll talk about it.
Patient I can't!
Doctor Why not?
Patient I'm not allowed on the furniture.

Patient *Have they sent / Have they been sending* you the results of my tests yet?
Doctor Yes. The news isn't good, I'm afraid.
Patient How long have I got to live, doctor?
Doctor Ten…
Patient Ten WHAT? Months? Weeks?
Doctor Nine, eight, seven, six…

c ⟳ **p.132 Grammar Bank 1C.** Read the rules and do the exercises.

d In pairs, use the prompts to ask and answer the questions. Is there anything you could do to improve your health?

1 / drink much water? How many glasses / drink today?
2 / do any physical exercise? What? How long / do it?
3 / eat a lot of fruit and vegetables? How many portions / have today?
4 / walk to school/work/university? How far / walked today?
5 / smoke? How long / smoke? How many cigarettes / have today?
6 / take any vitamins at the moment? How long / take them?
7 How many hours / sleep a night? / sleep well recently?
8 / allergic anything? / ever have a serious allergic reaction?

6 READING

a What symptoms do people have when they feel stressed?

b Which *three* of these things do you think are the most stressful? Number them 1–3 (1 = the most stressful) and compare with a partner.

- ☐ Packing for a trip at the last minute.
- ☐ Being stuck in a traffic jam when you have an appointment.
- ☐ Writing a report for your boss when you don't have much time to finish it.
- ☐ Running for a bus or train.
- ☐ Looking after a family member who has a chronic illness.
- ☐ Shopping in your lunch break.
- ☐ Programming a DVD player using the instruction manual.

c Read the article once quite quickly and then tick (✔) the activities that are bad for your health. What does the article say about the others?

d Read the article again more slowly. Circle the correct *main idea* for each paragraph.

1 a Being in traffic jams is bad for our health.
  b Some people think that not all kinds of stress are bad for us.
  c Doctors don't agree how we can reduce our levels of stress.

2 a Young people suffer more from stress than older people.
  b Alzheimer's is one of the illnesses many old people suffer from.
  c Good stress stops us from getting ill.

3 a Situations which produce good stress are always short term.
  b Some stress can make our cells stronger.
  c Too much protein can make us ill.

4 a We need some stress to exercise our cells' self-repair mechanism.
  b Doing physical exercise makes us feel less stressed.
  c Packing your suitcase in a hurry is an example of good stress.

e Complete the sentences using words from the article.

1 When we try to do less of something, we try to c_____ d_____ (paragraph 1).
2 An illness that you have for a very long time is called a c_____ illness (1).
3 Something which is good for us is b_____ (2).
4 The verb to make something stronger is s_____ (2).
5 Our body is made up of millions of c_____ (2).
6 When we treat our body badly we d_____ it (3).
7 Another word for illness is d_____ (3).
8 Something which is bad for us is h_____ (3).
9 Doing exercise helps to make our m_____ bigger and stronger (4).

f Use your dictionary to check the pronunciation of the words in **e**.

g Discuss these questions with a partner.

1 Do you agree with what you have read in this article? Why (not)?
2 What kinds of 'good stress' do you have in your life?
3 What other health stories have you heard about recently? Do you pay much attention to them? Do you believe them?

⊙ **p.157** *Phrasal verbs in context File 1.*

Get stressed, stay young

1 For decades doctors have warned us about the dangers of stress and have given us advice about how to cut down our stress levels. Everyone agrees that long-term stress, for example having to look after someone who has a chronic illness, or stressful situations where there is nothing we can do, for example being stuck in a traffic jam, is bad for our health and should be avoided whenever possible. However, some medical experts now believe that certain kinds of stress may actually be good for us.

2 Dr Marios Kyriazis, an anti-ageing expert, claims that what he calls 'good stress' is beneficial to our health and may, in fact, help us stay young and attractive and even live longer. Dr Kyriazis says that 'good stress' can strengthen our natural defences which protect us from illnesses common among older people, such as Alzheimer's, arthritis, and heart problems. He believes that 'good stress' can increase the production of the proteins that help to repair the body's cells, including brain cells.

3 According to Dr Kyriazis, running for a bus or having to work to a deadline are examples of 'good stress', that is situations with short-term, low or moderate stress. The stress usually makes us react quickly and efficiently, and gives us a sense of achievement – we did it! However, in both these situations, the stress damages the cells in our body or brain and they start to break down. But then the cells' own repair mechanism 'switches on' and it produces proteins which repair the damaged cells and remove harmful chemicals that can gradually cause disease. In fact, the body's response is greater than is needed to repair the damage, so it actually makes the cells stronger than they were before.

4 'As the body gets older, this self-repair mechanism of the cells starts to slow down,' says Dr Kyriazis. 'The best way to keep the process working efficiently is to 'exercise' it, in the same way you would exercise your muscles to keep them strong. This means having a certain amount of stress in our lives.' Other stressful activities that Kyriazis recommends as being good stress include redecorating a room in your house over a weekend, packing your suitcase in a hurry to reach the airport on time, shopping for a dinner party during your lunch break or programming your DVD player by following the instruction manual.

From *The Times*

So next time your boss tells you that she wants to see that report finished and on her desk in 45 minutes, don't panic; just think of it as 'good stress' which will have benefits for your long-term health!

THE INTERVIEW

a You are going to listen to an interview with Frank Clifford, an astrologer and palmist. Before you listen, read the glossary and look at how the words are pronounced to help you understand what he says.

> **Glossary**
>
> **birth chart** /bɜːθ tʃɑːt/ a map which shows the position of the planets when a person was born
>
> **unalterable** /ʌnˈɒltərəbl/ which can't be changed
>
> **destiny** /ˈdestəni/ what will happen to somebody in the future
>
> **genuine** /ˈdʒenjuɪn/ real, authentic
>
> **scared the life out of me** terrified me
>
> **curse** /kɜːs/ a word or phrase which has magic power to make something bad happen

b **1.18** Listen to part 1. Answer the questions with a partner.

1 What does an astrologer find out from a person's birth chart?
2 What does a palmist find out from reading someone's palm?
3 How can astrologers and palmists help people with their future?
4 Would Frank Clifford tell people if he 'saw' that they were going to have a serious illness? Why (not)?

c **1.19** Listen to part 2. Answer the questions with a partner.

What does he say about…?
1 choosing an astrologer or palm reader
2 a palmist he visited when he was 17
3 the kind of people who visit him
4 the different attitudes of men and women
5 predicting his own future

d **1.20** Listen and complete the phrases. What do you think they mean?

COMMON PHRASES

1 …or he may do a print and have _____ _____ at what is being shown in the hands now…
2 So it's our job really to encourage people to live their _____ _____ .
3 I'm not a doctor so I wouldn't _____ _____ . (informal)
4 …so I thought I'd learn this subject and understand _____ on earth she was talking about. (informal)
5 A lot of people would expect bored housewives, and people with _____ _____ to do, or…
6 …but in fact the truth is you tend to get _____ _____ of people. (informal)

e Listen to the interview again with the tapescript on page 121. Would you like Frank Clifford to read your palm or do you a birth chart? Why (not)?

IN THE STREET 🖥

a **1.21** Listen to five people talking about horoscopes. Write the number of the speakers next to their star sign. Which people believe strongly that star signs can influence people's personality?

Cherry   **Miles**   **Mike**   **Theresa**   **Kurt**

Aries /ˈeəriːz/
Taurus /ˈtɔːrəs/
Gemini /ˈdʒemɪnaɪ/
Cancer /ˈkænsə/
Leo /ˈliːəʊ/
Virgo /ˈvɜːgəʊ/

Libra /ˈliːbrə/
Scorpio /ˈskɔːpiəʊ/
Sagittarius /sædʒɪˈteəriəs/
Capricorn /ˈkæprikɔːn/
Aquarius /əˈkweəriəs/
Pisces /ˈpaɪsiːz/

b Listen again and write the name of the person.

1 Who thinks they are typical of their star sign?
2 Who thinks you can often know what someone is like if you know their star sign?
3 Who nearly forgets what star sign they are?
4 Who is the most sceptical about horoscopes and star signs?
5 Who sometimes enjoys reading his / her horoscope?

c **1.22** Listen and complete the phrases with one word. What do you think they mean?

COMMON PHRASES

1 _____ particularly, no.
2 I think it's _____ minimal . (informal)
3 You can definitely _____ their, sort of, personality straight away.
4 _____ whatsoever .

d Listen to the interviews again with the tapescript on page 1. Then answer the same questions with a partner.

Study Link MultiROM

If you are writing an email, it is more usual to start with *Hi*. If you are writing a letter you should start with *Dear*.

a Read the email from Chris. It has 12 mistakes: four grammar, four punctuation, and four spelling. With a partner, correct the mistakes.

b Read Chris's email again and find phrases that mean…
I haven't written or phoned.
I've been reading and replying to my emails.
Say hello to your family from me.

○○○   New Message

Send   Chat   Attach   Address   Fonts   Colors   Save As Draft

From: Chris
To: Eva
Subject: News

Hi Eva,

Sorry that I <u>havent</u> been in touch for a while but I've been ill. I got flu last week and I had a <u>temprature</u> of 39°C so I've been in bed <u>since</u> four days. I'm feeling a bit better today so I've been catching up on my emails. <u>Luckly</u> my classes at university don't start till next week.

How are you? What have you been doing? <u>Anything exciting</u>. Here everyone <u>are</u> fine – apart from me and my flu! My brother Ian has just started his new job with a <u>record-company</u> – I think I told you about it when I last wrote – anyway, he's really enjoying it. How are your family? I hope they're well.

I have <u>a</u> good news – I'm going to a conference in your town in <u>may</u>, from 16th to 20th. Could you <u>recomend</u> a hotel where I could stay in the centre of town? It needs to be somewhere not too expensive because the university is paying. I'll have a free half-day for <u>siteseeing</u>. Do you think <u>you'll can show</u> me around? That would be great.

Well, that's all for now. Please give my regards to your family.

I hope to hear from you soon.

Take care,

Chris

---

c You're going to answer Chris's email. Look at the **Useful language** expressions and try to complete them.

> **Useful language**
> **Opening expressions**
> Thanks ¹_____ your email / letter.
> It was great ²_____ hear from you.
> Sorry for ³_____ writing earlier / that I haven't been in touch for a while.
> I ⁴_____ you and your family are well.
>
> **Responding to news**
> Sorry ⁵_____ hear about your exam results.
> Glad ⁶_____ hear that you're all well.
> Good luck ⁷_____ the new job.
> Hope you ⁸_____ better soon.
>
> **Closing expressions**
> Anyway, / Well, that's all ⁹_____ now.
> Hope to hear from you soon. / Looking ¹⁰_____ to hearing from you soon.
> ¹¹_____ my regards (love) to…
> Take ¹²_____ / ¹³_____ wishes / Regards / (Lots of) love from…
> ¹⁴_____ (= something you forgot and want to add) Please send me the photos you promised.

> **PLAN** the content.
> 1 Underline the questions in the email that Chris wants you to answer.
> 2 Underline other places in the letter where you think you need to respond, e.g. *I've been ill.*
> 3 Think about how to respond to each of the things you've underlined.
>
> **WRITE** 120–180 words, in two or three paragraphs. Use informal language (contractions, colloquial expressions, etc.), and expressions from **Useful language**.
>
> **CHECK** your email for mistakes (grammar , punctuation , and spelling).

GRAMMAR

a Complete the sentences with one word.

1 What were you and Sarah talking ____?
2 You didn't like the film, ____ you?

THE END

3 My father loves opera, and so ____ my mother.
4 **A** I've been to India twice.
  B ____ you? I'd love to go.
5 What have you ____ doing since I last saw you?

b Circle the right answer, a, b, or c.

1 Could you tell me what time _____?
  a the bus leaves
  b leaves the bus
  c does the bus leave
2 How many people usually _____ to this class?
  a do come
  b come
  c did come
3 _____ at least three books so far this month.
  a I've been reading
  b I read
  c I've read
4 That was the best film _____!
  a I've ever seen
  b I've never seen
  c I've ever been seeing
5 The sooner you start, _____ you'll finish.
  a sooner
  b the sooner
  c the sooner than

VOCABULARY

a Word groups. <u>Underline</u> the word that is different. Say why.

1 vain   stubborn   possessive   wise
2 cheerful   loyal   insincere   conscientious
3 flu   blister   cold   asthma
4 GP   A & E   specialist   doctor

b Complete the sentences with a preposition.

1 Who were you talking ____ on the phone?
2 She's very good ____ listening to people.
3 Sam is a real pain ____ the neck.
4 She's allergic ____ milk.
5 What are you waiting ____?

c Complete the sentences with an adjective made from the word in **bold**.

1 Damien is very _____. He never remembers our anniversary.   **forget**
2 I'm _____ – I want to go far in my profession.   **ambitio**
3 My brother is very _____. I can always depend on him for anything.   **rely**
4 Luke is very _____ – happy one moment and sad the next.   **mood**
5 Madeleine is very _____. It's very easy to hurt her feelings.   **sense**

d Write words for the definitions.

1 **b**_____ (verb)   when blood comes out of, for example, your finger
2 **s**_____ (adj)   bigger than normal, especially because of an injury or infection
3 **b**_____ (noun)   a piece of cloth used to tie round a part of the body that has been hurt
4 **b**_____-**t**_____ (adj) (a person who) gets angry very easily
5 **b**_____ (adj)   (a person who is) always telling other people what to do
6 **a**_____ (adj)   (a person who) thinks he / she is superior to other people

PRONUNCIATION

a <u>Underline</u> the word with a different sound.

1	cheerful	headache	choking	stitches
2	sociable	unconscious	pressure	bossy
3	funny	impulsive	blood	flu
4	cough	open	swollen	throat
5	heart	calm	earache	arm

b <u>Underline</u> the stressed syllable.

arrogant   immature   injection   allergic   specialist

CAN YOU UNDERSTAND THIS TEXT?

a Read the article and choose a, b, or c.
1 The survey was paid for by ___.
   a Dr Petrie   b City University   c CentralNic
2 If your password is 'family oriented', you ___.
   a probably have a large family
   b probably don't use a computer very often
   c are likely to be an animal lover
3 If your password is 'Brad Pitt', you probably ___.
   a want to identify yourself with a famous person
   b watch a lot of TV
   c go to the cinema very often
4 People who belong to the 'cryptic' group ___.
   a worry about other people reading their emails
   b don't spend much time trying to invent a password
   c can't think of an interesting password
5 Passwords say something about our personalities
   because ___.
   a we think for a long time before choosing one
   b we choose words which we will remember easily
   c we choose something without thinking about it
     consciously

b Look at the highlighted words and phrases. Can you
  guess what they mean?

CAN YOU UNDERSTAND THESE PEOPLE?

a ▸ 1.23 Listen and circle the correct answer, a, b, or c.
1 How did the woman meet her current partner?
   a By speed dating.
   b Through a friend.
   c On an Internet dating site.
2 How does the man describe the girl he met?
   a shy
   b extrovert
   c hard-working
3 How will the man be travelling?
   a By train and taxi.
   b By bus and taxi.
   c By train and bus.
4 What does the doctor tell Mr Strong to do?
   a Take antibiotics.
   b Drink a lot.
   c Stay in bed.
5 What do the two commentators agree about?
   a That the player won't be playing in the next match.
   b That the player has twisted his ankle.
   c That the player won't be able to play again for
     two months.

Passwords reveal your personality

THE WORD OR PHRASE that you use to open your email account may provide a key to your personality as well as to your correspondence, according to a British psychologist. Helen Petrie, professor of human / computer interaction at City University in London, analysed the responses of 1,200 Britons who participated in a survey funded by CentralNic, an Internet domain-name company. The results were recently published on CentralNic's website.

Petrie identifies three main password 'genres'. 'Family oriented' respondents numbered nearly half of those surveyed. These people use their own name or nickname, the name of a child, partner, or pet, or a birth date as their password. They tend to be occasional computer users and have strong family ties. 'They choose passwords that symbolize people or events with emotional value,' says Petrie. One third of respondents were 'fans', using the names of athletes, singers, movie stars, fictional characters, or sports teams. Petrie says fans are young and want to ally themselves with the lifestyle represented by a celebrity. Two of the most popular names were Madonna and Homer Simpson. The third main group of participants are 'cryptics' because they pick unintelligible passwords or a random string of letters, numerals, and symbols such as 'Jxa+157'. Petrie says cryptics are the most security-conscious group. They tend to make the safest but least interesting choices.

Passwords are revealing for two reasons. First, because they are invented on the spot. 'Since you are focused on getting into a system, for example your email account, you're likely to write down something that comes quickly to mind,' says Petrie. 'In this sense passwords tap into things that are just below the surface of consciousness. Also, to remember your password, you pick something that will stick in your mind. You may unconsciously choose something of particular emotional significance.'

b ▸ 1.24 You will hear two women who visited a psychic talking about their experiences to a man from the Psychic Association. Answer the questions.
1 Why did Lorenna go to a psychic?
2 What did the psychic tell her?
3 Was it good advice?
4 What's the man's opinion of the psychic Lorenna saw?
5 Why doesn't Alice agree with Lorenna?
6 What did the psychic tell her?
7 How did the psychic's advice help her?
8 What advice does the man give Alice?

CAN YOU SAY THIS IN ENGLISH?

Can you…?

☐ ask questions with or without auxiliaries and with
   prepositions
☐ describe your and your friends' / family's personalities
☐ talk about health problems and describe symptoms to
   a doctor

2
A

G adjectives as nouns, adjective order
V clothes and fashion
P vowel sounds

National stereotypes: truth or myth?

1 LISTENING & SPEAKING

a You're going to listen to four people talking about the typical characteristics of people from their country (England, Ireland, Scotland, and the USA). Before you listen, with a partner try to predict what positive and negative characteristics the speakers might mention.

b **2.1** Listen and try to match the speakers 1–4 with their nationality. Use their accent and what they say about people from their country to help you.

English ☐		Scottish ☐	
Irish ☐		American ☐	

c Listen again. Write down at least one negative and two positive characteristics about each nationality. Does each person think they are typical or not? Why (not)?

d **2.2** Now listen to two extracts from each speaker. Try to write in the missing words. What do you think they mean?

1 a We think that if we work hard we can _____ anything.
   b I think I have _____ the typical optimism and drive.

2 a Historically there has always been a lot of _____.
   b It's probably because of our _____ and our history.

3 a It's difficult to generalize about us as a people, especially as our big cities now have such a _____ population.
   b Just think of our inability, or our _____, to learn foreign languages!

4 a There is also a negative _____ towards our neighbour.
   b I feel that we tend to focus too much on the _____ done to us in the distant past.

e In pairs or small groups, discuss the questions.
   1 What do you think are the strengths of your nationality?
   2 What are the weaknesses?
   3 In what way would you say *you* are typical?

2 GRAMMAR adjectives as nouns

a In many parts of the world there is a joke which is based on national stereotypes. With a partner, complete *Heaven* with five different nationalities. Then do the same for *Hell*. Compare your version of the joke with another pair.

Heaven
'Heaven is where the police are _____,
the cooks are _____,
the mechanics are _____,
the lovers are _____,
and everything is organized by the _____.'

Hell
'Hell is where the police are _____,
the cooks are _____,
the mechanics are _____,
the lovers are _____,
and everything is organized by the _____.'

b Read the article *Do we see ourselves as we really are?* and answer the questions.
   1 How was the research done?
   2 What does it tell us about national stereotypes?

c Read the article again. Which nationality / nationalities…?
   1 were friendlier than they thought
   2 were less extrovert than they thought
   3 were more hard-working than they thought
   4 knew themselves the best
   5 knew themselves the least
   6 thought they were calm and reasonable, but they weren't

d After reading the article, do you think any of the strengths and weaknesses of your nationality you mentioned before (in **1e**) may not be completely true?

Do we see ourselves as we really are?

A worldwide survey casts doubt on national stereotypes

The English are cold and reserved, Brazilians are lively and fun-loving, and the Japanese are shy and hardworking – these are examples of national stereotypes which are widely believed, not only by *other* nationalities but also by many people among the nationality themselves. But how much truth is there in such stereotypes? Two psychologists, Robert McCrae and Antonio Terracciano, have investigated the subject and the results of their research are surprising. They found that people from a particular country do share some general characteristics, but that these characteristics are often very different from the stereotype.

In the largest survey of its kind, a team of psychologists used personality tests to establish shared characteristics among 49 different nationalities around the world. They then interviewed thousands of people from these same groups and asked them to describe typical members of their own nationality. In most cases the stereotype (how nationalities saw themselves) was very different from the results of the personality tests (the reality).

For example, Italians and Russians thought of themselves as extrovert and sociable, but the personality tests showed them to be much more introvert than they imagined. The Spanish saw themselves as very extrovert, but also as rather lazy. In fact, the research showed them to be only averagely extrovert and much more conscientious than they thought. Brazilians were quite neurotic – the opposite of their own view of themselves. The Czechs and the Argentinians thought of themselves as bad-tempered and unfriendy, but they turned out to be among the friendliest of all nationalities. The English were the nationality whose own stereotype was the furthest from reality. While they saw themselves as reserved and closed, Dr McCrae's research showed them to be among the most extrovert and open-minded of the groups studied.

The only nationality group in the whole study where people saw themselves as they really are was the Poles – not especially extrovert, and slightly neurotic.

Dr McCrae and Dr Terracciano hope that their research will show that national stereotypes are inaccurate and unhelpful and that this might improve international understanding – we're all much more alike than we think we are!

e Right or wrong? Correct the sentences which are *grammatically* wrong.
  1 English talk about the weather a lot. ✘ *The English*
  2 English people often travel abroad.
  3 The Spanishs enjoy eating out.
  4 Chinese and Japanese have a different cuisine.
  5 I know an Italian who doesn't like spaghetti.
  6 My sister married a Polish.

f ⯁ **p.134 Grammar Bank 2A.** Read the rules for adjectives as nouns, and do exercise **a**.

g In pairs, say if you agree or disagree with the sentences below.

The British are usually less friendly than the Americans.
The Italians dress better than any other nationality.
The rich are always meaner than the poor.
The elderly are best looked after in residential homes.
The unemployed should not receive state benefits.
Small towns are better places to live than big ones.
It's better to buy expensive clothes if you can afford to, because
    they last longer than cheap ones.

3 READING

a Look at the photos on page 23. Do you think the people are typically English in the way they dress? Who do you think is dressed in the most eccentric way?

b You are going to read an article about how the English dress. Before you read the first part, discuss with a partner whether you think the following statements are true or false. Write T or F in the box.

1 The English dress badly. ☐
2 The English make very good suits. ☐
3 English people need rules to dress well. ☐
4 Punks and Goths wear a kind of uniform. ☐
5 The English person with the best fashion sense is the Queen. ☐
6 Young people around the world copy 'street fashion' invented by the English. ☐
7 The English don't like people who dress 'differently'. ☐

c Now read the first part of the text and find out if the writer agrees with your answers.

d Look at the photo below. What 'tribe' of young people does he belong to? Read the second part of the text and find out why the anthropologist spoke to this person and what she discovered.

e Look at the highlighted adjectives and work out the meaning from the context. Check with your dictionary or the teacher.

f Choose the best summary of the article. From what you know of English people, do you think it is true?

A The English often dress badly because they are insecure about what to wear. However, they often have a sense of humour about it.
B The English are a nation of individuals, who each dress in a rather eccentric way. The Queen and the Goths are good examples of this.
C The English love wearing uniforms and the more outrageous they are, the better.

4 VOCABULARY clothes and fashion

a Look at the photos on page 23 again. What are the people wearing?

b ➡ p.148 Vocabulary Bank Clothes and fashion.

c ➡ Communication Clothes quiz A p.116 B p.119.

Watching the English: how the English dress

Kate Fox, an anthropologist, spent twelve years researching various aspects of English culture in order to try to discover the 'defining characteristics of Englishness'. The following is an extract from her book _Watching the English_.

THE ENGLISH have a difficult and, generally speaking, dysfunctional relationship with clothes. Their main problem is that they have a desperate need for rules, and are unable to cope without them. This helps to explain why they have an international reputation for dressing in general very badly, but with specific areas of excellence, such as high-class men's suits, ceremonial costume, and innovative street fashion. In other words, we English dress best when we are 'in uniform'.

You may be surprised that I am including 'innovative street fashion' in the category of uniform. Surely the parrot-haired punks or the Victorian vampire Goths are being original, not following rules? It's true that they all look different and eccentric, but in fact they all look eccentric in exactly the same way. They are wearing a uniform. The only truly eccentric dresser in this country is the Queen, who pays no attention to fashion and continues to wear what she likes, a kind of 1950s fashion, with no regard for anyone else's opinion. However, it is true that the styles invented by young English people are much more outrageous than any other nation's street fashion, and are often imitated by young people all over the world. We may not be individually eccentric, apart from the Queen, but we have a sort of collective eccentricity, and we appreciate originality in dress even if we do not individually have it.

IN OTHER AREAS OF RESEARCH another 'rule' of behaviour I had discovered was that it is very important for the English not to take themselves _too_ seriously, to be able to laugh at themselves. However, it is well known that most teenagers tend to take themselves a bit too seriously. Would a 'tribe' of young people be able to laugh at the way they dress? I decided to find out, and went straight to a group whose identity is very closely linked to the way they dress, the Goths.

The Goths, in their macabre black costumes, certainly look as if they are taking themselves seriously. But when I got into conversation with them, I discovered to my surprise that they too had a sense of humour. I was chatting at a bus stop to a Goth who was in the full vampire costume – with a white face, deep purple lipstick, and spiky black hair. I saw that he was also wearing a T-shirt with 'Goth' printed on it in large letters. 'Why are you wearing that?' I asked. 'It's in case you don't realize that I'm a Goth,' he answered, pretending to be serious. We both looked at his highly conspicuous clothes, and burst out laughing.

5 PRONUNCIATION vowel sounds

| English vowel sounds are either short, long, or diphthongs (a combination of two short sounds). |

a Look at the sound pictures below. Which are short sounds, which are long, and which are diphthongs?

b **2.3** Put two words in each column. Listen and check.

collar   fur   high-heeled   loose   Lycra™   plain   put on   sandals   linen
sleeveless   shirt   slippers   striped   suede   suit   woollen

c Practise saying the phrases.

a loose linen suit   blue suede shoes   a pale grey suede jacket
pink silk slippers   a sleeveless white T-shirt   a tight Lycra™ skirt

d ➲ **p.159 Sound Bank.** Look at the typical spellings for these sounds.

6 SPEAKING

GET IT RIGHT *wear* and *dress*
Circle the right word.
1 The English don't *wear / dress* very stylishly.
2 The Goths *wear / dress* a lot of black clothes.

Talk in small groups.

How your nationality dresses

Do people in your country have a reputation for dressing well or badly?
Do you think women pay more attention to their appearance than men, or vice versa?
Are people generally very fashion conscious?
What is in fashion at the moment for men and women?
What are the current 'tribes' of young people? What do they wear?
   Do you like the way they dress?
Are there any celebrities in your country who dress in a very eccentric way?
   What do you think of them?
Do people tend to judge others by the way they dress?
Do *you* think you dress like a typical person from your country? Why (not)?

7 GRAMMAR adjective order

a Use your instinct. Complete each sentence with the **bold** words in the right order.
   1 The Goth in the photo has _____ .   **hair black spiky**
   2 For the wedding I'm wearing a _____ .   **suit linen beige**
   3 I want to buy a _____ .   **bag black big leather**
   4 I'm looking for a _____ .   **vest running nylon white**

b ➲ **p.134 Grammar Bank 2A.** Read the rules for adjective order and do exercise **b**.

c Imagine you were given two items of clothing for your birthday which
   you don't like. You have decided to sell them on eBay™. Write a detailed
   description, making them sound as attractive as possible.

d Now tell other students about your two items. Try to find someone who
   wants to buy them and agree a price.

8 **2.4** SONG ♫ *Englishman in New York*

2 B

G narrative tenses, past perfect continuous; *so / such…that*
V air travel
P irregular past forms

Air travel: the inside story

1 READING

a Read the back cover of a book about air travel. Can you guess the answers to any of the questions?

> *Air Babylon* is a best-selling book, co-written by Imogen Edwards-Jones and anonymous airline staff whose identities must remain secret. It tells the 'inside story' about flying and answers all these questions and many more…
>
> What are the check-in staff <u>really</u> doing when they type at their computers?
>
> Why is the heating often suddenly turned up halfway through a flight?
>
> Out of 1,000 passengers, how many will probably lose their luggage?
>
> Why do airport staff sometimes have a problem with wheelchairs?
>
> Why can you sometimes smell roast chicken in a plane when they are serving you fish?

ISBN 978-0-593-05457-4

9 780593 054574

b Now quickly read the extract from *Air Babylon*. Did you guess correctly?

c Now read the extract again. Complete each paragraph with one of the sentences below. Be careful, as there is one sentence you do not need to use.

A Wheelchairs are a big problem for us.

B It flies into the engine, totally destroying itself and the machinery.

C I'll never forget the last time it happened to me.

D So you can see, it really does pay to be nice to the person at the desk.

E This is mainly because the transport times between the terminals are so tight.

F And, as every flight attendant knows, a snoring plane is a happy plane.

d Do you believe everything you read in the extract?

Air BABYLON

Depending on what computer system the airline uses, check-in staff can talk to each other via simultaneous email. So when they seem to be taking a very long time to type your rather short name into the computer, they are probably sending one of their colleagues a message – usually about you or about someone in the queue behind you. These messages range from 'Have you seen this incredibly good-looking woman / man?' to 'I've got a really difficult passenger here – does anyone have a seat next to a screaming child?' 1 ☐

There is a sensible drinking policy on all airlines, which means that we are not supposed to serve passengers if they start getting noisy, but some air crew think that if you give them enough to eat and drink, they will eventually fall asleep and give you no trouble at all. 2 ☐ That's the reason, of course, why we like to turn the heating up halfway through a flight…

Some airports are notorious for losing passengers' luggage. Heathrow has a poor reputation – most airports lose about two in every thousand bags, but Heathrow loses eighty per thousand, which means for every five hundred people who check in, forty won't get their bags or suitcases at the other end! 3 ☐ When the airport is busy, which it always is, there is so much baggage being transported between the terminals and so little time to do it that a lot of the transferred luggage gets left behind.

4 ☐ Not only is there always a shortage of them for the people who really need them, but worse still, some of the people who request them often don't need them at all. I've lost count of the number of times I've pushed someone through the airport, taken them through customs and passport control, and got a porter to pick up their luggage, and then seen the person jump up in Arrivals and sprint towards their waiting relatives. One flight attendant I know gets so annoyed when this happens that as soon as the passenger gets out of the chair she shouts, 'Ladies and gentlemen! I give you another miracle, courtesy of the airline industry! After decades in a chair, he walks again!' The passenger is normally so embarrassed that he (and it's usually a *he*) disappears as quickly as he can.

Birds are one of the major problems for any airport when planes are taking off and landing. A swan or any large bird can easily cause an accident. 5 ☐ Smaller birds are less of a problem. In some cases they can do some damage, but more often than not they are just roasted. When this happens, there is often such a strong smell of roast bird that passengers on the plane think that chicken is being cooked, and they're often surprised when they are given a choice of fish or beef at dinner!

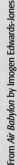

From *Air Babylon* by Imogen Edwards-Jones

2 VOCABULARY air travel

a Complete the column on the right with a word or phrase (all the words come from the *Air Babylon* extract).

At the airport

1 Most big airports have several different buildings called ▢▢. _terminals_
2 Passengers leave from Departures and arrive at ▢▢. _____
3 Two general words for bags and suitcases are ▢▢ and ▢▢. _____ / _____
4 When you arrive at the airport, you go to ▢▢ to get your boarding pass. _____
5 Before you get on the plane you have to show identification at ▢▢ ▢▢ and go through security. _____
6 After you have arrived you go to baggage reclaim to ▢▢ your luggage. _____
7 When you go through ▢▢, you may be asked, 'Do you have anything to declare?' _____
8 A person whose job is to carry your bags for you is called a ▢▢. _____
9 Ryanair and easyJet were two of the first low-cost ▢▢. _____

On the plane

10 The pilots and other people who work in the plane are the (air) ▢▢. _____
11 The people who have paid to travel in a plane are ▢▢. _____
12 The person who looks after you during a flight is the ▢▢. _____
13 You can usually ask for a window or aisle ▢▢. _____
14 The noun from the verb *fly* is ▢▢. _____
15 When a plane is going up into the sky it is ▢▢. _____
16 When a plane is coming down from the air it is ▢▢. _____

b Which of the words in **a** can also be used if you are travelling by bus or train?

c Cover the words on the right and read the definitions again.
   Can you remember all the words and pronounce them correctly?

MINI GRAMMAR *so / such...that*

The passenger is normally so embarrassed that he disappears as quickly as possible.
When this happens there is often such a strong smell of roast bird that passengers on the plane think that chicken is being cooked.

We often use *so / such... (that)* to express a consequence.

Use *so* + adjective / adverb	*The film was so good (that) we went to see it again.*
	He drives so dangerously (that) nobody wants to go with him.
Use *so much / so many* + noun	*There was so much traffic (that) we nearly missed our flight.*
Use *such a* + adjective + single countable noun	*It was such a good film (that) we went to see it again.*
Use *such* + adjective + uncountable or plural noun	*They played such awful music (that) nobody wanted to dance.*
	They were such beautiful shoes (that) I bought them.

Complete the sentences with *so*, *such*, or *such a*.

1 The flight was _____ long that I got really bored.
2 I had _____ noisy child sitting beside me that I couldn't sleep at all.
3 There was _____ long delay because of fog that we had to sleep at the airport.
4 My suitcase was _____ heavy that I had to pay excess baggage.
5 I slept _____ badly in the plane that it took me two days to recover.
6 We were served _____ terrible food that I couldn't eat a thing.
7 There were _____ many people at check-in that we had to queue for an hour.
8 We had _____ heavy cases that we had to ask for a porter.

3 GRAMMAR narrative tenses, past perfect continuous

a Read a newspaper story about an incident during a recent flight. What happened?
Do you think the flight attendant should lose her job?

We're going to crash!

Hysterical flight attendant causes panic on transatlantic flight

Everything was going smoothly on Virgin Atlantic flight VS043 from London Gatwick to Las Vegas. The 451 passengers were relaxing after lunch when the plane hit some turbulence over Greenland. There was no advance warning, so many passengers were out of their seats or were not wearing seat belts when the plane started dropping violently.

Suddenly one of the flight attendants screamed , 'We're going to crash!' Panic immediately broke out. In the 30 minutes of chaos, passengers desperately clung to their seats, as drinks and magazines flew around the cabin. Amid the terror, the flight attendant screamed every time the plane dropped.

Businesswoman Angela Marshall was travelling with her partner. 'Until then the flight had been fine,' she said afterwards. ' I'd been reading my book and my partner had been having a nap. But when the flight attendant started screaming, I was totally convinced that we were about to die.'

Another passenger said, 'It was unreal, like something from a film. People started crying and being sick. That woman shouldn't be a flight attendant. After we landed she was joking and laughing as if nothing had happened, but we all staggered off the plane in a state of shock.'

From Daily Mail

Glossary
turbulence sudden and violent changes in wind direction
break (broke, broken) out pv start suddenly
cling (clung, clung) hold on tightly to sb / sth
nap a short sleep especially during the day
be about to be going to do something very soon
stagger walk as if you are about to fall

b Copy the highlighted verbs into the chart.

past simple regular _____
past simple irregular _____
past continuous _____
past perfect _____
past perfect continuous _____

c In pairs, look at the sentences and circle the more logical verb form. Be prepared to say why.

When the plane hit turbulence…
1 …the passengers *screamed / were screaming*.
2 …the passengers *relaxed / were relaxing*.
3 …they *finished / had finished* lunch.
4 …they *had flown / had been flying* for two hours.

d ⊙ **p.134 Grammar Bank 2B.** Read the rules and do the exercises.

e In pairs or groups, try to complete the two sentences in four different ways using the four narrative tenses.

1 The police stopped the driver because he…
2 I couldn't sleep last night because…

4 PRONUNCIATION irregular past forms

a Match the sentences 1–8 with the correct sounds A–H according to the pronunciation of the vowel sound.

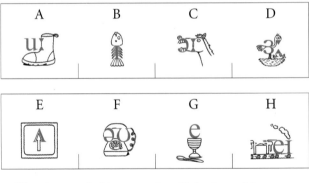

| A | B | C | D |
| E | F | G | H |

1 ☐ I thought he'd caught that flight. I saw him checking in.
2 ☐ The hotel was built in 1950. The date was written above the door.
3 ☐ The company had become successful since it won the prize for Best Airline.
4 ☐ I flew to Mexico City. I knew the city very well.
5 ☐ She read for a while before she fell asleep. Then she dreamt about her childhood.
6 ☐ We'd flown from New York that day. We'd chosen a bad day to travel.
7 ☐ I heard that they'd been hurt in the accident, but they weren't.
8 ☐ She said she'd paid for the train with money she'd taken from my wallet.

b ⏵ 2.5 Listen and check. Then practise saying the sentences.

5 LISTENING

a You are going to listen to an interview with two pilots. Before you listen, discuss questions 1–6 with a partner and guess how the pilots will answer them.

  1 What weather conditions are the most dangerous when flying a plane?
  2 Which is more dangerous, taking off or landing?
  3 Is it really worth passengers wearing seat belts?
  4 Is it worth listening to the safety instructions?
  5 Are some airports more dangerous than others?
  6 How important is it for pilots to speak English well?

b **2.6** Listen to the first part of the interview. How many of the questions did you answer correctly?

c Listen again for more detail. Then with a partner try to remember as much as possible about the pilots' answers.

d **2.7** Now listen to the second part. What three questions do they answer?

e Listen again and try to remember the anecdotes.

f Do you think you would like to work as a pilot? What are the main advantages and disadvantages?

6 SPEAKING

> **GET IT RIGHT** active listening
> When someone tells us a story or anecdote, we normally interact with the person who is telling the story.
> **Useful language**
>
> | ASKING FOR MORE INFORMATION | SHOWING SURPRISE | SHOWING APPROVAL | SHOWING SYMPATHY |
> |---|---|---|---|
> | *What happened next?* | *Really?* | *Wow!* | *Oh no!* |
> | *Then what happened?* | *You're joking?* | *That's great / fantastic!* | *How awful!* |
> | *How did you feel?* | *No! I don't* | | *What a pity!* |
> | *What was it like?* | *believe it.* | | |

a **Communication** *Flight stories A p.116 B p.119.* Read a newspaper story to retell to your partner.

b You are going to tell an anecdote. **The story can either be true or invented.** If it is invented, you must try to tell it in such a convincing way that your partner thinks it's true.

Choose one of the topics below and plan what you are going to say. Look at the **Story plan** below, and ask your teacher for any words you need.

Talk about a time when you (or someone you know)…

  • had a frightening / funny / unusual experience when travelling by plane / bus / train.
  • got ill or had an accident while travelling.
  • missed a bus / train / flight which caused serious complications.
  • arrived home from a trip and had a surprise.

Story plan

Setting the scene
This happened to me when I was…
I was …-ing when…
I …because I had / hadn't…

The main events
I decided to…because…
So then I…
Suddenly / At that moment…

What happened in the end?
In the end… / Eventually…
I felt…

c In pairs, A tell B your story. B ask A for more details and decide whether the story is true or not. Then swap roles.

2C

G adverbs and adverbial phrases
V confusing adverbs and adverbial phrases
P word and sentence stress

Incredibly short stories

Mini sagas

A mini saga is a story which must be told in exactly 50 words. The original idea came from science fiction writer Brian Aldiss and the British newspaper the *Daily Telegraph* has run several mini-saga competitions.

A [   ]

She recognized the writing on the envelope immediately . The Gypsy had warned her that she had no future with this man, yet here he was – five lonely years after their last meeting, begging her to join him in New York. She felt unbelievably happy as she stepped on board the *Titanic*.

B [   ]

He was worried. Unfortunately , since his wife's death his teenage daughter had become increasingly difficult.
They had agreed 2.00 a.m. as the latest return time from nightclubs. It was now 3.30.
He prepared himself for confrontation as the door opened.
'Dad!' she shouted angrily . 'I've been frantic. You're late again .'

C [   ]

'He always has dinner at six,' she told the maid. 'No beef. He has dessert in the garden. Fill the bath at eight – he goes to bed early .'
'When will I meet the master?' the maid asked, as she tripped over a sleeping poodle.
'You already have,' laughed the housekeeper.

D [   ]

My house looks as if it's been hit by a bomb. Since I'm hopeless at organizing, I bought a new book *Key to organizing your life*. I felt so proud.
I started cleaning the bookcase. Five minutes later I couldn't believe my eyes.
I'd bought the same book last year .

From *Mini Sagas*

Glossary

beg ask sb very strongly or anxiously for sth
confrontation a situation where there is angry disagreement
frantic very worried
maid female servant
master man who has people working in his house as servants
poodle a dog with very curly hair
housekeeper woman employee in charge of a house and its servants
hopeless very bad

1 GRAMMAR adverbs and adverbial phrases

a Read the four mini sagas and match them with the titles. You don't need to use one of the titles.

**Generation gap   The last laugh   Good intentions
Written in the cards   Meeting the boss**

b Read the mini sagas again. Some of them are quite cryptic and the story is not immediately obvious. In pairs, explain each story in your own words. Which story do you like most / least?

c Look at the highlighted adverbs or adverbial phrases in the stories. Think about what they mean and notice their position in the sentence. Write them in the correct place in the chart.

Types of adverbs
Time (when things happen, e.g. *now*) *immediately* _____
_____
Manner (how you do something, e.g. *slowly*) _____
Frequency (how often sth happens, e.g. *sometimes*) _____
Degree (describing / modifying an adjective, e.g. *very*) _____
_____
Comment (giving an opinion about a phrase, e.g. *luckily*) _____

d Use your instinct. Where should the adverb go in these sentences?

1	He speaks three languages.	**fluently**
2	I have breakfast during the week.	**hardly ever**
3	My brother was in a car crash, but he wasn't hurt.	**fortunately**
4	It's often hot in Greece in July and August.	**extremely**
5	When I know the date, I'll call you.	**straight away**

e ➡ **p.134 Grammar Bank 2C.** Read the rules and do the exercises.

f **2.8** Listen to some sound effects or short dialogues. Then use the adverb in **bold** to complete the sentence.

1	When he got to the bus stop, _the bus had just left._	**just**
2	They were having a party when…	**suddenly**
3	He thought he had lost his boarding pass, but…	**luckily**
4	The woman thought Andrea and Tom were friends, but in fact…	**hardly**
5	The driver couldn't see where he was going because…	**hard**
6	Alain couldn't understand the man because…	**incredibly**

2 VOCABULARY confusing adverbs and adverbial phrases

a Match each pair of adverbs with a pair of sentences.

at the moment / actually	5	in the end / at the end	☐
especially / specially	☐	late / lately	☐
ever / even	☐	near / nearly	☐
hard / hardly	☐	still / yet	☐

Adverb

1 a Her French isn't very good. She can   say anything. _____
  b He works very   – at least ten hours a day. _____

2 a My boss always arrives   for meetings. _____
  b We haven't seen Mary   . She's been very busy. _____

3 a   of the concert, everybody applauded. _____
  b I didn't want to go, but   they persuaded me. _____

4 a I love all sports, but   basketball. _____
  b All her clothes are   made for her in Paris. _____

5 a She looks younger than me, but   she's two years older. _____
  b He's unemployed   , but he's looking for a job. _____

6 a It's   stopped raining. We'll be able to leave soon. _____
  b Does your boyfriend live   here? _____

7 a Have you found a flat   ? _____
  b No, we're   looking. _____

8 a Have you   been to Texas? _____
  b I've been all over the USA – I've   been to Alaska! _____

b Now decide which adverb goes where and write it in the adverb column. Compare with a partner, and say what you think the difference is between the two adverbs.

c Cover the adverb column and look only at sentences 1–8. Try to remember the adverbs.

3 PRONUNCIATION
word and sentence stress

a Under<u>line</u> the main stressed syllable in these adverbs.

absolutely   actually   almost   apparently
definitely   especially   even   fortunately
ideally   incredibly   luckily
unfortunately

b **2.9** Listen and check.

> Remember adverbs, like other 'information' words, are normally stressed in a sentence.

c **2.10** Now <u>underline</u> the stressed words in each sentence. Listen and check. Practise saying the sentences.

1 There was a lot of traffic, and unfortunately we arrived extremely late.
2 We definitely want to go abroad this summer, ideally somewhere hot.
3 It's incredibly easy – even a child could do it!
4 I thought he was Portuguese, but actually he's Brazilian.
5 You said they'd already gone, but apparently they're still here.
6 I absolutely love Italian food, especially pizza.

4 WRITING

a You are going to write a mini saga.

> Your story must be 50 words exactly (not including the title) and you must include at least two adverbs. Contracted forms (e.g. *I'd*) count as one word. First choose one of the titles below.
>
> **A holiday romance**   **Revenge is sweet**
> **The lie**   **Never again**

b Think of a plot. Then write a first draft without worrying about the number of words.

c Now count the words and then try to cut or add words until the story is the right length. Write your final version.

d Read two other students' stories. Which do you like best?

5 SPEAKING

⊙ **Communication** *Reading habits p.117.*

6 READING & LISTENING

Reading for pleasure

When you read a longer text, e.g. a short story, you normally don't read once quickly for gist and then re-read. You read, perhaps at a slightly slower speed, and keep going, focusing on following the story. It is also especially important to try to guess words from context. Only look up a word while you are reading if it's holding you up or you really want to know what it means. Frequently looking up words may get in the way of your enjoyment. However, it can help to pause from time to time and look back, just to check you are clear about what is happening.

a Read and listen to an American short story. Answer the questions 1–13 in pairs.

Little Brother™

by Bruce Holland Rodgers

Peter had wanted a Little Brother™ for three Christmases in a row. His favourite TV commercials were the ones that showed just how much fun he would have teaching Little Brother™ to do all the things that he could already do himself. But every year, Mommy had said that Peter wasn't ready for a Little Brother™. Until this year.

This year when Peter ran into the living room, there sat Little Brother™ among all the wrapped presents, babbling baby talk, smiling his happy smile, and patting one of the packages with his fat little hand. Peter was so excited that he ran up and gave Little Brother™ a big hug around the neck. That was how he found out about the button. Peter's hand pushed against something cold on Little Brother™'s neck, and suddenly Little Brother™ wasn't babbling any more, or even sitting up. Suddenly, Little Brother™ was limp on the floor, as lifeless as any ordinary doll.

2.11

1 What kind of toy is Little Brother™? What does the ™ mean?
2 What do you think 'babbling' means?
3 What happened when Peter hugged Little Brother™?

"Peter!" Mommy said.

"I didn't mean to!"

Mommy picked up Little Brother™, sat him in her lap, and pressed the black button at the back of his neck. Little Brother™'s face came alive, and it wrinkled up as if he were about to cry, but Mommy bounced him on her knee and told him what a good boy he was. He didn't cry after all.

"Little Brother™ isn't like your other toys, Peter," Mommy said. "You have to be extra careful with him, as if he were a real baby."

She put Little Brother™ down on the floor, and he took tottering baby steps toward Peter. "Why don't you let him help open your other presents?"

So that's what Peter did. He showed Little Brother™ how to tear the paper and open the boxes. The other toys were a fire engine, some talking books, a wagon, and lots and lots of wooden blocks. The fire engine was the second-best present. It had lights, a siren, and hoses just like the real thing. There weren't as many presents as last year, Mommy explained, because Little Brother™ was expensive. That was okay. Little Brother™ was the best present ever! Well, that's what Peter thought at first.

2.12

4 How did Peter's mother stop Little Brother™ from crying?
5 What do you think 'wrinkled up' means?
6 What does the last line make you think?

Glossary

in a row /rəʊ/ one after the other
wrapped (up) covered with paper
pat hit lightly with your hand
limp not firm or strong
lap the top part of your legs that forms a flat surface when you are sitting down
bounce move (sb or sth) up and down, e.g. a ball
tottering walking like a baby, nearly falling over
tear /teə/ **(tore, torn)** to break sth by pulling it apart, e.g. paper, material
keep up pv to move at the same speed as sb or sth
stacked up placed one on top of another
swat /swɒt/ hit, (esp an insect) using your hand
howl /haʊl/ make a long loud cry, like a dog or wolf
calm down pv become quiet and calm
wad into balls /wɒd/ make e.g. paper into tight balls
let drop allow sth to fall

At first, everything that Little Brother™ did was funny and wonderful. Peter put all the torn wrapping paper in the wagon, and Little Brother™ took it out again and threw it on the floor. Peter started to read a talking book, and Little Brother™ came and turned the pages too fast for the book to keep up.

But then, while Mommy went to the kitchen to cook breakfast, Peter tried to show Little Brother™ how to build a very tall tower out of blocks. Little Brother™ wasn't interested in seeing a really tall tower. Every time Peter had a few blocks stacked up, Little Brother™ swatted the tower with his hand and laughed. Peter laughed, too, for the first time, and the second. But then he said, "Now watch this time. I'm going to make it really big."

But Little Brother™ didn't watch. The tower was only a few blocks tall when he knocked it down.

"No!" Peter said. He grabbed hold of Little Brother™'s arm. "Don't!"

Little Brother™'s face wrinkled. He was getting ready to cry.

Peter looked toward the kitchen and let go. "Don't cry," he said. "Look, I'm building another one! Watch me build it!"

Little Brother™ watched. Then he knocked the tower down.

Peter had an idea.

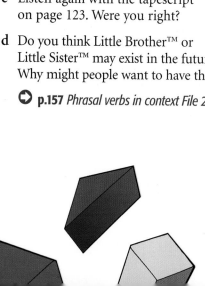

2.13

7 What funny things did Little Brother™ do at first?
8 What do you think 'grabbed hold of' means?
9 What do you think Peter's idea was?

When Mommy came into the living room again, Peter had built a tower that was taller than he was, the best tower he had ever made. "Look!" he said.

But Mommy didn't even look at the tower. "Peter!" She picked up Little Brother™, put him on her lap, and pressed the button to turn him back on. As soon as he was on, Little Brother™ started to scream. His face turned red.

"I didn't mean to!"

"Peter, I told you! He's not like your other toys. When you turn him off, he can't move but he can still see and hear. He can still feel. And it scares him."

"He was knocking down my blocks."

"Babies do things like that," Mommy said. "That's what it's like to have a baby brother."

Little Brother™ howled.

"He's mine," Peter said too quietly for Mommy to hear. But when Little Brother™ had calmed down, Mommy put him back on the floor and Peter let him toddle over and knock down the tower.

Mommy told Peter to clean up the wrapping paper, and she went back into the kitchen. Peter had already picked up the wrapping paper once, and she hadn't said thank you. She hadn't even noticed.

Peter wadded the paper into angry balls and threw them one at a time into the wagon until it was almost full. That's when Little Brother™ broke the fire engine. Peter turned just in time to see him lift the engine up over his head and let it drop.

2.14

10 Why didn't Peter's mother even look at the tower?
11 What makes Little Brother™ a different kind of toy?
12 Why did Peter feel annoyed with his mother?
13 What do you think is going to happen next?

---

b **2.15** Listen to the end of the story. In pairs, discuss what you think happened.

1 What did Peter do to Little Brother™ after he broke the fire engine?
2 How did his mother react?
3 What did Peter threaten to do?
4 How did Peter's mother punish him for his behaviour?

c Listen again with the tapescript on page 123. Were you right?

d Do you think Little Brother™ or Little Sister™ may exist in the future? Why might people want to have them?

➲ **p.157** *Phrasal verbs in context File 2.*

THE INTERVIEW

a You are going to listen to an interview with Hayley Levine, a flight attendant with *First Choice Airways*. Before you listen, read the glossary and look at how the words are pronounced to help you understand what she says.

> **Glossary**
>
> **immediate care** /ɪˈmiːdiət keə/ first aid, simple medical treatment given to passengers
>
> **sick bag** /ˈsɪk bæg/ a paper bag kept in the seat pocket in case somebody needs to be sick on a flight
>
> **gruelling** /ˈgruːəlɪŋ/ very difficult and tiring
>
> **emergency exit** /iˈmɜːdʒənsi ˈeksɪt/ the way out of a plane or building, etc. in a dangerous situation
>
> **aircraft** /ˈeəkrɑːft/ a general word for a vehicle which can fly and carries goods or passengers, e.g. plane, helicopter

b **2.16** Listen to part 1. Answer the questions with a partner.

1 Why did Hayley apply for a job as a flight attendant?
2 What did she learn in her first week of training?
3 What did she learn in the next four weeks?
4 What kind of person makes a good flight attendant?
5 What are the good and bad sides of the job?
6 What tips does she give for the problem of jet lag?

c **2.17** Listen to part 2. Answer the questions with a partner.

What does she say about…?

1 how to help passengers who are afraid of flying
2 how she can tell if a passenger is scared of flying
3 a passenger who had a panic attack
4 evacuating an aircraft
5 how she feels when she flies

d **2.18** Listen and complete the phrases. What do you think they mean?

COMMON PHRASES

1 (if something happens) …you need to be trained to _____ with it , quickly, efficiently.
2 …just someone who's a _____ _____ really.
3 Yeah, it's good. I wouldn't _____ _____ for the world . (idiom)
4 You do suffer a lot, but, you know, it's part of the job. You just sort of _____ _____ with it . pv
5 Poor guy, I felt really _____ _____ him .
6 I feel really safe up there, really safe, _____ I wouldn't do it.

e Listen to the interview again with the tapescript on page 12. Does Hayley make her job sound attractive to you?

IN THE STREET

a **2.19** Listen to four people talking about air travel. Match the speakers to what they most <u>dislike</u> about air travel. Are any of the speakers afraid of flying?

Anne

Jordan

Jeff

Ben

not enough space to stretch your legs	☐
bad weather conditions	☐
what you are given to eat	☐
not being able to control what happens to them	☐

b Listen again. Who …?

1 enjoys not being able to use their phone
2 had a problem at an airport in the USA
3 only talks about general frustrations
4 had a problem with excess baggage

c **2.20** Listen and complete the phrases. What do you think they mean?

COMMON PHRASES

1 But it wasn't _____ on the plane.
2 Yeah, one _____ they lost my baggage. (NAmE, informal)
3 Air travel, _____-wise , is very frustrating. (informal)
4 _____ major , no.

d Listen to the interviews again with the tapescript on page 12. Then answer the same questions with a partner.

It was only a small mistake, but it changed my life.

I had been working at JB Simpson's for ten years. It was a small ¹_____ company which exported garden furniture. I was ²_____ happy with my job – I got on ³_____ with the owner, Arthur Simpson but not with his wife, Linda. She was a loud, ⁴_____ woman, who ⁵_____ used to turn up at the office and start criticizing us for no reason. Everyone disliked her.

One afternoon Mrs Simpson came in while I was finishing writing a report. She looked at me and said, 'If I were you, I wouldn't wear that colour. It doesn't suit you at all.' I was wearing a ⁶_____ pink shirt that I was ⁷_____ fond of, and her comment really annoyed me. I typed a ⁸_____ email to Alan Simmonds in Sales. 'Watch out! The old witch is on the warpath!' and pressed 'send'. A couple of minutes later I was surprised to receive an email from Mr Simpson asking me to come to his office ⁹_____. When I opened the door, I saw his wife glaring at the computer screen, and I realized, to my horror, what I had done. I had clicked on Simpson instead of Simmonds. ¹⁰_____ I was packing my things. I had been sacked!

a Read the story. What was the 'small mistake'? What happened?

b Using adverbs and adjectives helps to make a story come alive and makes it more enjoyable to read. Complete the story with an adjective or adverb from the list below.

aggressive an hour later extremely family-run frequently immediately new reasonably quick well

c You may want to write some dialogue as part of your story. Rewrite the following with the correct punctuation. Use the dialogue in the story to help you.

sit down mr simpson said coldly i want to talk to you about an email you sent

'*Sit* _____

_____

_____

d You are going to write a story beginning with the sentence *It was three o'clock in the morning when the phone rang.* Look at the time expressions in **Useful language** and correct one word in each.

Useful language
Time expressions
¹ In that moment , the door opened. *At*
² As soon than I saw him, I knew something was wrong.
³ Ten minutes after , I went back to sleep.
⁴ A morning in September I got to work early.
We got to the station ⁵ just on time to catch the train.

PLAN the content.
1 Invent a plot and write what happened simply, in about 50 words.
2 Then think about how you could improve your story by adding more details, e.g. with adjectives and adverbs.
3 Think about what tenses you need for each part of the story, e.g. how to set the scene, what significant events happened before the story starts.

WRITE 120–180 words, organized in two or three paragraphs. Use a variety of narrative tenses and adverbs and adjectives to make your story more vivid.

CHECK your short story for mistakes (grammar , punctuation , and spelling).

GRAMMAR

Circle the right answer, a, b, or c.

1 Some people think that _____ don't pay enough tax.
   a the rich
   b the rich people
   c rich

2 **A** Which shoes do you like best?
   B I like _____.
   a the reds
   b the red
   c the red ones

3 I got a _____ bag for my birthday.
   a beautiful leather Italian
   b Italian leather beautiful
   c beautiful Italian leather

4 We _____ for about five hours when we decided to stop and rest.
   a were driving
   b had been driving
   c have driven

5 When we got to Terminal 2, the flight from London _____.
   a had already landed
   b had already been landing
   c already landed

6 As soon as we arrived at the airport, we _____.
   a had checked in
   b were checking in
   c checked in

7 Her father _____.
   a speaks very fluently English
   b speaks English very fluently
   c speaks English very fluent

8 I just need another five minutes. _____.
   a I've nearly finished
   b Nearly I've finished
   c I've finished nearly

9 The driver _____ in the accident.
   a seriously was injured
   b was injured seriously
   c was seriously injured

10 It was _____ boring film that we left in the middle of it.
   a a so
   b such a
   c a such

VOCABULARY

a Word groups. Underline the word that is different. Say why.

1	striped	spotted	hooded	patterned
2	silk	cotton	fur	smart
3	station	flight	land	pilot
4	backpack	scarf	vest	cardigan
5	to fit	to suit	to hang up	to match
6	lately	slowly	nearly	friendly

b Complete the sentences with one word.

1 The plane took ___ at 7.15.
2 I've just found ___ that my boss is going to work for another company.
3 You'd better walk a bit faster if you don't want to get left ___.
4 People here dress ___ a lot for weddings – long dresses and suits.
5 We checked ___ as soon as we got to the airport.
6 My new jeans fit ___ a glove – they're so comfortable.
7 I live quite near here, ___ the end of this road.

c Circle the right word.

1 We haven't seen each other much *late / lately*.
2 The skirt doesn't *fit / suit* me. It's a bit too big.
3 The view is awful! You can't *even / ever* see the sea!
4 I've been working so *hard / hardly* that I think I need a holiday.
5 How much *cases / luggage* have you got?
6 I love all pasta, *especially / specially* lasagne.
7 Can I go in jeans? I don't feel like *getting dressed / getting changed*.

PRONUNCIATION

a Underline the word with a different sound.

1	aisle	flight	linen	striped
2	nearly	early	heard	fur
3	wear	airline	carefully	weren't
4	crew	loose	suit	took
5	crashed	missed	changed	dressed

b Underline the stressed syllable.

stylish	undressed	arrivals	passenger	actually

CAN YOU UNDERSTAND THIS TEXT?

a Read the article and fill the gaps with a sentence A–E.

A 'You see how safe it is,' he smiled.

B Apparently, they thought that was what would work best for me.

C It was an experience I would rather not go through again.

D Like many fearful fliers, I often experienced a heightened sense of hearing, noticing small changes in noises and amplifying them dramatically in my mind.

E Which is unfortunate, because as a foreign journalist I can't exactly stay at home.

b Look at the highlighted words and phrases. Can you guess what they mean?

CAN YOU UNDERSTAND THESE PEOPLE?

a **2.21** Listen and circle the correct answer, a, b, or c.

1 What did the woman buy in the sales?
 a A black sweater.
 b A blue jacket.
 c A black jacket.

2 How did the man feel?
 a embarrassed
 b offended
 c confused

3 What is the man's criticism of the book?
 a It's too long.
 b It's boring.
 c It's complicated.

4 The flight to Budapest will leave from ____.
 a Gate B 50
 b Gate P 50
 c Gate B 15

5 The man is stressed because ____.
 a his friends have a problem with their luggage
 b his friends may think he isn't there
 c his friends' flight was late

b **2.22** Listen to a Swede talking about people from his country. Answer the questions.

1 What does he think is the stereotype of the Swedes?
2 How much of the stereotype does he think is true?
3 Why does he mention the Swedish army?
4 What three other aspects of the Swedes does he mention?
5 What does he say about Swedish men?

CAN YOU SAY THIS IN ENGLISH?

Can you…?

☐ describe the strengths and weaknesses of people from your country
☐ describe what someone in the room is wearing
☐ describe a trip you have taken by train or plane

How I conquered my fear of flying

Journalist and documentary maker Sean Langan talks about his irrational phobia of flying.

My fear of flying is not just a mild case, but a real, oh-my-God-I'm-going-to-die-any-second kind of fear. ¹☐ My job has taken me to dangerous places such as Afghanistan and Iraq, but I'm far more worried about flying planes than by flying bullets. After an awful flight earlier this year on a small plane, I decided I would either have to stop flying altogether or I could try to overcome my fears. Which is why, a few weeks later, I agreed to take the flight to end all fears.

The plane was going almost vertically upwards before moving sharply to the left. To make matters worse, my seat was shaking violently because of severe turbulence. My stomach was turning. The captain, sensing my fear, took his hands off the controls and turned to face me. ²☐ In fact Captain Keith Godfrey had designed the flight, or rather the terrifyingly realistic flight simulator, to my needs.

In the two years Virtual Aviation have been running the course at Heathrow, they had never put the plane through such extreme flying before. ³☐ And they were right. By showing me just how far you can push a plane, and still keep it safely within its limits, they allayed my fears. I had to experience things for myself before I was able to convince myself of the truth. That planes, generally speaking, do not fall out of the sky like rotten apples.

In their careful pre-flight questioning with a therapist called Susie, they focused on what lay beneath my fear. ⁴☐ Something moving in an overhead locker could sound to me like an engine about to fall off. But Susie focused on my heightened sense of movement as my main problem, which is why during the flight the captain flipped the plane over like a pancake.

⁵☐ But by facing my worst fear, I'd overcome it. And fellow sufferers will be glad to know that I got through my next real flight safe and sound.

3A

G passive (all forms), *it is said that…, he is thought to…*, etc.
V crime and punishment
P the letter *u*

The one place a burglar won't look

1 SPEAKING & LISTENING

> **GET IT RIGHT** agreeing and disagreeing
>
> Use a variety of expressions for agreeing and disagreeing:
>
> | | |
> |---|---|
> | *I think it must be…* | *That's what I was thinking.* |
> | *Do you agree with that?* | *Exactly!* |
> | *Don't you think…?* | *I don't think that's true.* |

a Do the quiz in pairs. Give reasons for your answers.

BEAT THE BURGLARS!

1 **How long do you think a burglar normally takes to search someone's house?**

  a 10 minutes
  b 20 minutes
  c 30 minutes

2 **Which of these are the most common things burglars steal?**

  a TVs, digital cameras, etc.
  b paintings and antiques
  c money and jewellery

3 **Which of these is more likely to stop a burglar coming into your house?**

  a a dog
  b a burglar alarm

4 **Which three of these would most influence a burglar to choose a particular house or flat?**

  a It looks expensive.
  b There is no one at home.
  c There aren't many other neighbours nearby.
  d There are good places to hide around house.
  e They have burgled the house before.

5 **How are burglars more likely to get into a house?**

  a through an open door or window
  b by breaking a door or window

6 **What is the best place to hide your valuables? Number these rooms in the order that burglars usually search them.**

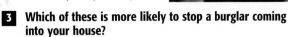

  ☐ the living room   ☐ the main bedroom
  ☐ the kitchen   ☐ a child's bedroom
  ☐ the dining room   ☐ the study

From *The Sunday Times*

b ➡ **p.117 Communication** *There's only one place burglars won't look…* Read the answers to the quiz – provided by ex-burglars themselves!

c Look at the photos. Have you seen the film *Oliver Twist* or read the book by Charles Dickens? What is the old man teaching the boys to do?

d (3.1) James Freedman, an ex-magician, worked as the 'pickpocket consultant' for Roman Polanski's film *Oliver Twist*. Listen to him being interviewed on the radio and answer the questions.

1 What is the main trick pickpockets use when they steal from someone?
2 Why are tourists particularly at risk from pickpockets?

e Listen again for more detail. Then answer with a partner.

What does he say about…?
1 training boys
2 Prague
3 Roman Polanski's watch
4 Fagin
5 'misdirection'
6 some keys
7 the journalist's wallet and pen
8 a map
9 Westminster tube station and Big Ben.
10 'Watch out! Pickpockets about!'

f What have you learned to do or *not* to do…?
a to protect your house
b if you are on holiday in London

2 VOCABULARY   crime and punishment

a Match the words for people who steal with the definitions in the list.

pickpocket	mugger	burglar	robber	shoplifter	thief

1 A _____ is someone who breaks in and steals from a private house.
2 A _____ is someone who breaks in and steals from e.g. a bank or business.
3 A _____ is someone who steals something when he / she is in a shop.
4 A _____ is someone who steals from you in the street, often without you noticing.
5 A _____ is someone who uses violence to steal from you in the street.
6 A _____ is the general word for someone who steals.

b (3.2) Listen and check. <u>Under</u>line the stressed syllable.

c ➲ p.149 **Vocabulary Bank** *Crime and punishment.*

3 PRONUNCIATION   the letter *u*

a Look at the words in the list, which all have the letter *u* in them. Put them in the right column below according to how the vowel sound is pronounced.

accuse	burglar	caught	community	court	drugs	fraud	guilty
judge	jury	manslaughter	mugger	murderer	punishment	smuggling	

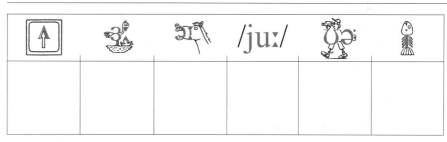

⬆	🐦	🐴	/juː/	🚶	🐟

b (3.3) Listen and check. Which two words are pronounced exactly the same? What happens to the pronunciation of *u* in *guilty*?

c Practise saying the sentences.
1 He was accused of smuggling drugs.
2 'Murderers must be punished,' said the judge.
3 The burglar is doing community service.
4 It wasn't murder, it was manslaughter.
5 The jury said he was guilty of fraud.
6 The mugger was caught and taken to court.

d Talk to a partner. Find out as much information as possible.

What are the most common crimes in your town or city?
What crimes have been in the news recently?
Do you have trial by jury in your country? Do you think it's a good system?
Do you know anyone…?
• who has been burgled
• who has been mugged
• whose car has been stolen
• who has been unfairly accused of shoplifting
• who has been stopped by the police while driving
• who has been robbed while on holiday
• who has been offered a bribe
• who has been kidnapped

4 GRAMMAR passive (all forms), *it is said that…, he is thought to…*, etc.

a **Check what you know.** You are going to read two true crime stories. In *World Cup thief's own goal* complete the article with the verb in brackets in the past simple active or passive. Then in *Parrot held in prison*, circle the right form.

Any problems? ➲ **Workbook p.25**

World Cup thief's own goal

A thief who ¹_____ (steal) a World Cup ticket from a woman's handbag ²_____ (catch) after he sat down to watch the game next to the victim's husband.

Eva Standmann, 42, ³_____ (mug) as she was going to the Munich stadium for the game between Brazil and Australia. The thief, a 34-year-old man, ⁴_____ (discover) the ticket in her bag and he decided to use it.

But when he ⁵_____ (take) the woman's seat in the stadium, he ⁶_____ (meet) by her husband Berndt, 43, who immediately called the police on his mobile.

A Munich police spokesman said, 'The thief ⁷_____ (find) the ticket in the bag and decided to watch the game. When he sat down next to his victim's husband, officers on duty at the stadium ⁸_____ (inform) of the situation and the thief ⁹_____ (arrest).'

Parrot held in prison

A parrot has spent five days ¹*interrogating / being interrogated* by police in a prison in Argentina.

A judge ²*ordered / was ordered* the parrot, which ³*calls / is called* Pepo, ⁴*to hold / to be held* in custody until he told police who his real owner was. Two neighbours, Jorge Machado and Rafael Vega, were disputing who the bird ⁵*belonged / was belonged* to.

Judge Osvaldo Carlos decided the parrot should ⁶*send / be sent* to prison until he said the name of his owner. After five days, Pepo said Jorge's name and also sung the anthem of his favourite football team, San Lorenzo. Mr Machado said, 'I knew he wasn't going to let me down. He is a real friend and we ⁷*support / are supported* the same football team.'

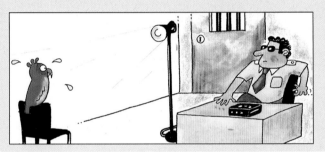

b **New grammar.** Read another true story. How does the hypnotist rob banks?

Hypnotic bank robber

Bank clerks in Moldova have been told by the police not to make eye contact with customers after a series of robberies. The robber is believed to be a trained hypnotist from Russia.

He is said to put cashiers into a trance before making them hand over tens of thousands of dollars' worth of notes.

It is thought that the criminal begins talking to bank tellers and gradually hypnotizes them. After getting them to give him money, he then brings them back out of the trance and leaves them with no memory of handing over the cash. It is believed that the man has robbed at least three banks in the last month.

c Look at the highlighted phrases. Do people *know* this information for sure about the robber or do they only *suspect it*? How is the structure different after *he* and after *it*?

d ➲ **p.136 Grammar Bank 3A.** Read the rules and do the exercises.

e Complete the newspaper crime story using the words in brackets.

Britain's most polite armed robber

Police in Stockport in the UK are looking for a man who ¹_____ (believe / be) Britain's most polite armed robber.

The robber, who always says 'please' and 'thank you' when he orders shop staff to give him the money in the till, ²_____ (say / be) a tall man in his early forties.

He wears a mask and washing-up gloves during robberies. It ³_____ (think / he / rob) at least four shops in Stockport in recent weeks.

A police officer said, 'He ⁴_____ (report / be) polite to his victims, but there is nothing polite about armed robbery. Last week this man used a knife to threaten shop staff. They were terrified. Saying "please" and "thank you" cannot change that.'

5 READING

a What do you think would be an appropriate punishment for…?

1 a woman who abandoned some kittens in a forest
2 people caught speeding in a residential area
3 a man who was caught carrying a loaded gun in the street
4 some teenagers who vandalized a school bus
5 noisy neighbours who play rock music very loudly at all hours

b Read the first four paragraphs of the article. What sentence did Judge Cicconetti give these people? Why? Do you think his sentences would be more effective than yours?

> Sometimes when you read a newspaper article for detail, the information is not given in a chronological order. You may need to re-read the article to clarify in your mind information about people and events.

c Read through the questions below. Then read the whole article to find the information.

1 **The judge**
What was his early life like? How successful has he been professionally?

2 **The punishments**
Which three creative punishments get the offenders to learn from a personal experience?
Which two punishments get them to do something for other people?

3 **The reasons behind his system**
What inspired his system of creative punishments?
Why does he think they are better than conventional punishments?
What evidence does he have that the punishments are successful?

d What do you think of his system? Would you like to have a judge like Cicconetti in your town?

6 SPEAKING

> **GET IT RIGHT** giving your opinion
> When we are giving our opinion about the right way to punish someone, we often use *should* + passive infinitive:
> *I think they should be made to…*
> *I don't think they should be allowed to…*

a In groups, decide on creative punishments for these crimes or offences.

• An arsonist who sets fire to a local beauty spot, for example, a forest.
• A 15-year-old who is caught drinking and smoking.
• Someone who parks illegally causing major traffic delays.
• A group of teenagers who paint graffiti all over walls in a small town.
• A couple whose dogs bark incessantly and bother the neighbours.
• A young person who creates a computer virus which infects thousands of computers.

b Compare with other groups and decide which you think are the best solutions.

Making the punishment fit the crime
– Mike Cicconetti, a US judge with a difference

Judge Cicconetti

Michelle Murray

1 When Michelle Murray was arrested for abandoning some kittens in a forest, she expected to get a fine or a short prison sentence. Instead she was sentenced to spend the night in the same cold, dark forest. In the end it was so cold that she only had to spend three hours in the woods, but Judge Mike Cicconetti had made his point. He wanted the 26-year-old Ohio housewife to feel the same pain and suffering as the animals she had abandoned, many of which later died.

2 Judge Cicconetti's unusual ruling was just the latest example of his unique brand of 'creative justice' which has won him national acclaim. He was elected unopposed to serve another six years in Lake County, Ohio last month, and this year won the presidency of the American Judges Association.

3 Cicconetti allows offenders to choose between jail, and an alternative, 'creative' sentence. For example, people accused of speeding are offered a choice between having their licence suspended for 90 days, or having it suspended for a shorter period and spending one day working as a school crossing guard. The judge says that offenders who spend a day helping school children across the street never appear in his courtroom for speeding again.

4 The judge also sent a man who was caught with a loaded gun to the mortuary to view dead bodies and ordered teenagers who let down tyres on school buses to organize a picnic for primary school children. He has ordered noisy neighbours to spend a day of silence in the woods, or to listen to classical music instead of rock.

5 Cicconetti attributes his unusual approach to his tough family background. He was the oldest of nine children and had to work part-time collecting rubbish to pay his way through college. He studied law at night school. 'I didn't go to a prestigious law firm,' he says, 'I had to get to where I am the hard way. It makes you understand what the working man has to go through, and why some of them commit crimes. I want to give people a positive lesson, not a negative one.'

6 A drawer in his cramped office in the Painesville Municipal Courthouse is full of thank-you letters from both victims and criminals. 'Some people will say that my punishments are cruel or unusual,' the judge said. 'OK, it's a little bit of embarrassment and humiliation. But when you have people fulfilling these sentences, you are doing it for them and the victims and the community. And above all, I can remember only two people who have been sentenced to alternative punishments and who have reoffended.'

3

B

G future perfect and future continuous
V weather
P vowel sounds

Stormy weather

1 READING

a Look at the three photos, and read extracts from three blogs. In pairs, guess which country / city the people are writing from.

b Read the blogs again and tick (✔) the right box(es). In which blog does someone…?

	1	2	3
1 go out in spite of a severe weather warning	☐	☐	☐
2 seem to be a foreigner living abroad	☐	☐	☐
3 have fun in spite of the weather	☐	☐	☐
4 complain about how the weather makes him / her feel	☐	☐	☐
5 talk about problems with transport	☐	☐	☐
6 describe how surprised people are by the weather	☐	☐	☐
7 criticize some people for doing something	☐	☐	☐
8 talk about the damage caused by the weather	☐	☐	☐
9 complain that people are not well prepared to cope with the weather	☐	☐	☐

c Look at the highlighted words in the blogs and discuss what they mean with a partner.

d Would any of these three types of weather be surprising where you live? Have you had any surprising weather where you live recently?

1

Posted: Tuesday 4th September

Yesterday was unbelievable. Though we were warned there was going to be a terrible storm , no one really expected or could possibly have visualized hurricane-force winds destroying bus stops and ripping trees out of the wet soil. They told us not to cycle anywhere and to stay indoors, but I had a job interview in the centre so I had to go out.

Thank God I did manage to get there, but I had to grab hold of traffic lights so I wouldn't be blown into the road. I saw some crazy people on bikes –

some of them got blown over and one even seemed to be going backwards. The canals were full of rubbish bins that had got blown in and there were piles of bikes in the streets and broken umbrellas everywhere, which people obviously thought they were going to be able to use and then couldn't. What a mess!

Comments **8**

2

Posted: Sunday 22nd July

Yet another scorching , sunny day…

I never knew this kind of heat was possible here. Last Wednesday was the hottest day ever in this country. The roads were melting in some areas, and the underground was a total nightmare — it was like being slowly cooked in an oven.

The main problem is that people here don't seem to understand the need for air conditioning during the summer. There is no escaping the heat and if you actually want to go anywhere, you have to be prepared to sweat and learn to enjoy your task sweating. Please tell me, how do you shop? Try on clothes? No thank you. Even going for an ice-cold beer can be uncomfortable if the pub isn't at least equipped with a large fan .

So I sit here sweating in my living room. The French windows are open but the coolest room in the apartment is the bathroom and sadly, there is no Internet connection so I can't work there!

Comments **22**

3

Posted: Thursday 8th November

I got woken up today by my daughter screaming, 'Dad…it's snowing… it's snowing!' She just couldn't believe it – not surprising as they said on the news that it hasn't snowed here for nearly fifty years! We decided not to send her to school and we had a great time – we even made a snowman in the yard. We used dried cranberries for the eyes and a baby carrot for the nose because it was a baby snowman. People are so amazed by the 'totally awesome' weather that I've seen some people just standing there staring as if they were in a trance. You kind of feel it's the work of a clever set decorator for a high-budget movie.

It was chaos, though, for people going to work – Interstate 5 was closed in some parts and a whole load of trucks were stuck in the snow. And it's been very bad news for the citrus trees – they're all frozen . Even if it thaws tomorrow, the damage is already done. So I'm afraid we won't be eating any local oranges this year!

Comments **104**

2 VOCABULARY weather

a ○ p.150 Vocabulary Bank *Weather.*

b Talk to a partner.

1 What kind of weather do you think is good or bad for…?
   a camping
   b going for a walk in the mountains
   c running a marathon
   d sailing
   e sightseeing

2 What cities or countries do you associate with…?
   a fog
   b smog
   c heavy snow
   d floods
   e hurricanes

3 PRONUNCIATION vowel sounds

Most vowels, or combinations of vowels, can be pronounced in more than one way. If you are unsure what the vowel sound is in a new word, check with your dictionary.

a Look at the groups of words below. Circle the word with a different sound.

1 blow   snow   showers   below
2 weather   sweat   heavy   heat
3 drizzle   blizzard chilly   mild
4 hard   warm   yard   farm
5 flood   cool   monsoon   loose
6 fought   ought   drought   brought
7 muggy   sunny   hurricane humid
8 scorching tornado   world   storm

b **3.4** Listen and check.

c **3.5** Dictation. Listen and write down five sentences. Then practise saying them.

4 LISTENING

a **3.6** You're going to listen to Martin Cinert from Prague talking about the night the River Vltava flooded. Mark the sentences T (true) or F (false).

1 His office wasn't at risk, but his flat was.
2 He took his wife and child to his parents' house.
3 He went back to the flat because he was excited by the situation.
4 Martin went to a place near his flat to watch the water level rising.
5 He looked out of the window and saw that his car park was starting to flood.
6 He was the last person to leave his block of flats.
7 All of the roads he tried were flooded now.
8 He decided to follow another car through the water.
9 Martin's car broke down as he drove through the water.
10 All the flats in his building were seriously damaged.

b Listen again. Then in pairs, correct the false sentences.

c What do you think you would have done in Martin's situation?

5 SPEAKING & WRITING

GET IT RIGHT modifiers

Cross out the wrong form. Tick (✔) if both are correct.

1 It's very cold! / It's very freezing!
2 It's really windy! / It's incredibly windy!
3 It's really boiling today! / It's incredibly boiling today!
4 I was absolutely frightened! / I was absolutely terrified!

a In small groups, talk about a time when you were somewhere when…

• there was a flood.
• it was very foggy or there was bad smog.
• it was unbearably cold.
• it was pouring with rain for days on end.
• there was a gale or hurricane.
• there was a terrible heatwave.
• you were caught outside in a thunderstorm.

What were you doing at the time?
What did you do to protect yourself from the weather?
Did you ever feel scared or in danger?

b Write a short blog (like the ones in 1) describing what the weather has been like recently. Talk about how it has made you feel and how it has affected what you have been doing.

6 **3.7** SONG ♫ *It's raining men*

7 GRAMMAR future perfect and future continuous

a Check what you know. Put the verb in brackets in the right future form (*will / shall* + infinitive, *going to* or present continuous). Sometimes more than one form is possible.

Future forms

1 **A** It's freezing in here!
   B _____ I _____ the window? (**close**)
2 The sky is really clear! I'm sure it _____ a lovely day tomorrow. (**be**)
3 **A** Do you think _____ while we're in London? (**rain**)
   B I don't know, but I _____ my umbrella just in case.
      I've already put it in my case. (**take**)
4 **A** _____ we _____ lunch in the garden? (**have**)
   B I'm not sure if it's warm enough. What do you think?
   A I think it's fine. I _____ the table outside. (**lay**)
5 **A** What time _____ you _____? (**leave**)
   B Soon, in about ten minutes. It's very foggy, but don't worry. I _____ (**drive**)
      really slowly, I promise. And I'm sure there _____ too much traffic. (**not be**)

Any problems? ➡ **Workbook p.28**

b New grammar. Read some of the predictions scientists are making about climate change and complete them with a word from the list below.

become   closed down   doubled   having (x2)   melted   risen (x3)   suffering

c Read the predictions again. Which ones worry you most? Have you noticed the effects of climate change in your country?

Storm clouds on the horizon

Climate change is now something that we cannot close our eyes to, and governments all over the world have finally realized that they have to sit up and take notice. These are some of the things that many scientists predict will happen if we carry on polluting the atmosphere with CO_2 emissions.

Short term: by the year 2050

- More than a third of the world's plant and animal species will have [1]_____ extinct.
- The ice in the Arctic Sea will melt every summer, causing the extinction of polar bears, and many glaciers, for example on Mount Kilimanjaro, will have [2]_____ completely.
- 50% of the worlds ski resorts will have [3]_____ due to lack of snow.

Mid term: by the year 2100

- Sea levels will have [4]_____ by between 16cm and 69cm. This means that low-lying islands like the Maldives will no longer be habitable.
- The number of serious coastal storms and tsunamis will have [5]_____.
- Northern European cities, e.g. Paris and London will be [6]_____ 50 days a year of heatwaves when temperatures are over 30ºC (there are currently 6–9 days).

Long term: by the year 3000

- Temperatures will have [7]_____ by about 15ºC.
- Sea levels will have [8]_____ by more than 11 metres, flooding large areas of Bangladesh, and many low-lying cities, such as London. Hundreds of millions of people will be displaced.
- One third of the world will be [9]_____ from extreme droughts, and half the world will be [10]_____ moderate droughts. Tens of millions of Africans will have to emigrate.

d Match the sentences A–C with pictures 1–3.

A This time tomorrow it will be snowing.
B By tomorrow evening it will have snowed.
C It will snow tomorrow.

 1
 2
 3

e ⮕ **p.136 Grammar Bank 3B.** Read the rules and do the exercises.

f What do you think? Explain why (not). What are the alternatives? Talk to a partner.

In 20 years' time…
we'll all be using solar power to heat our houses.
low cost airlines will have disappeared and tickets will be extremely expensive.
private swimming pools and golf courses will have been banned.
everyone will be using public transport to get to work.
we'll have stopped using petrol and we will be using electric cars.
people won't be going on skiing holidays anymore.

> I think it will have become so warm that we won't need any heating.

> I disagree. I think we'll be using nuclear power.

8 LISTENING & SPEAKING

a **3.8** Listen to the first part of a news story about a woman called Barbara Haddrill. What did she do? Why?

b Listen to the first part again and answer the questions.

1 What was Barbara's dilemma? Why?
2 What changes has she made to her lifestyle over the last six years? Why?
3 How did Barbara travel? Through which countries?
4 How was she able to take such a long holiday?

c **3.9** Listen to the second part and complete the information in the chart.

Barbara Haddrill

UK TO AUSTRALIA ONE-WAY

	Cost	Distance	Time	CO_2 emissions
Barbara	£_____	_____ miles	_____ days	_____ tonnes
plane	£_____	_____ miles	_____ hours	_____ tonnes

d What do you think of Barbara's trip?

e Read *What can you do to help?* about what *you* can do help prevent climate change. Talk to a partner or in small groups.

Which of the tips below…?   a do you already do   b are you prepared to try to do   c are you not prepared to try

What can YOU do to help? The top tips

1 Fly less. Use buses or trains instead where possible. If you have to fly, give money to an organization like Carbon Footprints to compensate for the CO_2 emissions of your flight.

2 Drive as little as possible. Use bikes, or public transport. And if you need to drive, buy a hybrid, a car which has an extra electric motor which charges up when you brake. You could also car share with a friend.

3 Use only energy-saving light bulbs.

4 Plant trees. Two or three dozen trees can absorb a whole household's emissions of CO_2.

5 Don't keep your TV or other electrical appliances on standby. Switch them off completely.

6 Use the cold water wash on your washing machine, and use a dishwasher, on the economy programme, which uses less energy and water than hand-washing dishes.

7 Try to buy organic food, if possible which has been grown locally. Take your own shopping bags when you go to supermarkets.

8 Turn your heating down and wear a sweater if you're cold. If you use air conditioning, don't have it at less than 25°C.

9 Have showers not baths.

10 Support an environmental organization, for example Friends of the Earth or Greenpeace.

11 Regularly recycle paper, glass, plastic, and household waste.

12 Vote for the political party which is doing the most to combat climate change.

G conditionals and future time clauses; *likely* and *probably*
V expressions with *take*
P sentence stress and rhythm

Taking a risk

1 READING

a Which of these things scares you more?
- being shot or drowning
- mad cow disease or bacteria in the kitchen
- flying or driving
- terrorist attacks or heart disease

b Read the article once quite quickly and find out which of the things in **a** is riskier.

c Read the article again and answer the questions.

1 Molly's parents…
   a worry too much about their daughter.
   b are scared of the wrong thing.
   c don't take danger seriously.

2 Having bacteria in our kitchen doesn't worry us because…
   a it isn't really dangerous.
   b we can keep our kitchen clean.
   c we are too worried about mad cow disease.

3 People are more afraid of flying than driving because…
   a they are in a situation where they can't do anything.
   b more people die in plane crashes than car crashes.
   c flying is more dangerous.

4 People…
   a believe that terrorism is more of a threat than heart disease.
   b shouldn't worry so much about heart disease.
   c are less worried about dangers in the near future.

5 People tend…
   a to worry too much about danger.
   b to confuse terror with danger.
   c not to do enough to stop accidents.

The **risk** factor

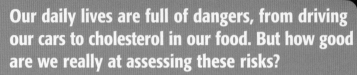

Our daily lives are full of dangers, from driving our cars to cholesterol in our food. But how good are we really at assessing these risks?

Not very good at all, according to Steven Levitt and Stephen Dubner in their best selling book *Freakonomics*. Parents, they say, take danger very seriously but they often worry about completely the wrong things. The authors give as an example the fictional case of a little girl they call 'Molly'. Her parents know that the father of one of her friends keeps a gun in their house, so they decide that Molly is not allowed to play there. Instead, they feel that Molly would be much safer spending time at another friend's house, where there are no guns, but there is a swimming pool. You may think this is the right choice, but according to the statistics, you would be wrong. Every year, one child per 11,000 private swimming pools is drowned in the United States. However, only one child is killed by a gun for every million guns. This means that a child is 100 times more likely to die in a swimming accident than because of playing with a gun.

Molly's parents are not unique. Generally people are just not very good at assessing risk. Peter Sandman, a risk consultant at Princeton University, New Jersey, says 'The risks that scare people and the risks that kill people are very different things.' He compares the dangerous bacteria in our kitchen and diseases such as mad cow disease: the first is very common, but for some reason not very frightening; the second is extremely rare, but it terrifies us. 'Risks that you can control are much less worrying than risks you can't control,' says Sandman. 'We can't tell if our meat is infected, whereas we can control how clean our kitchen is.'

This 'control factor' probably explains why flying tends to scare people more than driving. Levitt argues, 'Their thinking goes like this: " since I control the car, I am the one keeping myself safe; since I have no control of the aeroplane, I am at the mercy of external factors."' Actually, the question of which is more dangerous is not as simple as many people think. Statistics for the United States show that, although many more people die each year in road accidents than in plane crashes, driving isn't necessarily more dangerous. This is because generally people spend far less time flying than driving. In fact statistically, the number of deaths for each hour of driving compared with each hour of flying is about the same. So flying and driving carry a very similar risk. It is just our lack of control when flying that makes it seem more scary.

Levitt also says that people tend to be much more scared of short-term dangers than long-term ones. The probability of someone being killed in a terrorist attack is infinitely smaller than the probability that this same person will eat too much fatty food and die of heart disease. 'But a terrorist attack happens now,' says Levitt. 'Death from heart disease is a distant, quiet catastrophe. Terrorist acts lie beyond our control – French fries do not.'

Finally there is what Peter Sandman calls 'the dread factor', that is how horrific we consider something to be. We are horrified by the thought of being killed in a terrorist attack, but for some reason we are not horrified by the thought of death from heart disease. Sandman uses the following equation: for most people risk = hazard (or danger) + outrage (or horror). 'When the hazard is high but the terror is low, people underreact. When the hazard is low and the outrage is high, people overreact.' Which is why so many parents will do more to protect their children from a gun accident than from a swimming pool accident. A gun horrifies us, but a swimming pool does not.

d Look at the highlighted words and phrases in the article and use them to complete these sentences.

1 Motorbikes are much cheaper than cars. _____, they are more dangerous.

2 _____ doctors it isn't a good idea to go swimming straight after lunch.

3 The open-air concert was a success, _____ it rained a bit.

4 People worry about terrorists, but _____ the risk of an attack is quite small.

5 John loves meat, _____ his wife is a strict vegetarian.

6 _____ the weather forecast is awful I think we should cancel the trip.

7 There was nothing on at the cinema, so we went out for a meal _____.

e Is there anything *you* are scared of? Do you think this is a real risk to you?

2 LISTENING

a You are going to listen to an American risk expert talking about the risks of driving in the USA. Before you listen, in pairs, predict which option you think is correct.

1 The most dangerous thing to be on the road is _____.

  a a pedestrian
  b a driver
  c a motorcyclist

2 Most accidents happen because drivers _____.
  a fall asleep at the wheel
  b are drunk
  c drive too fast

3 Driving at night is _____ as dangerous as driving during the day.
  a three times
  b four times
  c ten times

4 You're most likely to have a non-fatal accident on a _____.
  a Tuesday morning
  b Friday afternoon
  c Saturday night

5 Most fatal accidents happen on _____.
  a motorways
  b A-roads
  c country roads

6 Kilometre for kilometre, women have more _____ than men.
  a minor accidents
  b serious accidents
  c fatal accidents

7 The age at which a driver is most at risk is _____.
  a over 75
  b between 21 and 25
  c under 25

b 3.10 Listen once and check your answers.

c Listen again for more information.

d Talk to a partner.
  1 Would these statistics probably be similar in your country?
  2 Do you often travel at dangerous times and on dangerous roads?
  3 Do you think punishments for dangerous driving should be more severe?

3 VOCABULARY expressions with *take*

a Complete the questionnaire with the words in the list.

advantage   after   care   decisions   easy   notice
part   place   seriously   risks   time   up

The *take* questionnaire

1 Are you a cautious person or do you enjoy **taking** _____?
2 Are you a decisive person? Do you find it easy to **take** _____?
3 Do you **take** climate change _____? What are you doing about it?
4 Are you like your father or your mother? Who do you **take** _____?
5 Are you a busy, nervous person or do you **take** things _____?
6 Are you a stubborn person or do you **take** _____ of what other people tell you?
7 Do you worry about your health? Do you **take** _____ of yourself?
8 Do you get up very quickly in the morning or do you **take** your _____?
9 Have you ever not **taken** _____ of a good opportunity (and regretted it)?
10 Have you ever **taken** _____ in a demonstration?
11 Have you **taken** _____ a new sport or hobby recently?
12 Has any big sporting event ever **taken** _____ in your city?

b In pairs, take turns to ask and answer the questions. Ask for more information.

MINI GRAMMAR *likely* and *probably*

A child is 100 times more likely to die in a swimming accident than because of playing with a gun.

This 'control factor' probably explains why flying tends to scare people more than driving.

Likely and *probably* are very similar in meaning, but they are grammatically different. *Likely* is an adjective and *probably* is an adverb.

Use *be* + *likely* + infinitive, e.g. *She's likely to be off work for a long time.*

Use *probably* before the main verb in a [+] sentence, e.g. *She'll probably be off work for a long time*, but before the auxiliary verb in a [−] sentence, e.g. *He probably won't come.*

Complete the sentences with *likely* or *probably*.
1 I don't think the boss is very _____ to agree.
2 They _____ won't be here before 6.00.
3 That isn't _____ to happen in the near future.
4 I'll _____ be home late tonight.

4 GRAMMAR   conditionals and future time clauses

a **Check what you know.** Circle the right verb form.

1 If *I like / I'll like* the car when I see it, I'll buy it.
2 I *don't go / won't go* to work tomorrow unless I feel better.
3 We'll carry on playing until it *gets / will get* dark.
4 If it rains tonight, we *won't have to / don't have to* water the garden tomorrow.
5 I won't take a decision before *I have / I'll have* all the information.
6 I'll tell you when *I hear / I'll hear* from him.

Any problems? ➲ Workbook p.31

b **New grammar.** Match the sentence halves.

Main clause

1 Don't walk too near the river   ☐
2 You are more likely to have an accident ☐
3 They'll call us   ☐
4 You're going to be late   ☐
5 I'll probably be driving   ☐
6 I'll call back later   ☐
7 Take your umbrella   ☐
8 Please put everything away   ☐
9 I'll have already had lunch   ☐
10 I'm not starting the car   ☐

Other clause

A in case it's raining when you finish work.
B if you don't hurry up.
C if you're having supper now.
D if you've finished cooking.
E if you come at two.
F in case you fall in.
G when you call me so leave a message.
H until everybody has put their seat belt on.
I as soon as they've landed.
J if you drive too fast.

c Answer the questions with a partner.

1 Which sentence is a zero conditional and refers to something which always happens, not a future possibility?
2 In the other sentences, what tenses can be used in the main clause? What tenses can be used in the other clause after *if, in case, when*, etc.?
3 What does *in case* mean in sentences 1 and 7?

d **➲ p.136 Grammar Bank 3C.** Read the rules and do the exercises.

e In pairs, complete each sentence to make some useful safety tips.

1 Don't let children play near a swimming pool unless…
2 Never leave a dog locked up in a car if…
3 Keep a first aid kit in your house in case…
4 You shouldn't leave children alone in the house until…
5 Always unplug electrical appliances (e.g. a hairdryer) as soon as…
6 Always keep medicines in a safe place in case…
7 Don't allow strangers into your house unless…
8 If you are frying something and the oil catches fire, …

5 PRONUNCIATION   sentence stress and rhythm

a **3.11** **Dictation.** Listen and write six future sentences into the dialogues.

1 **A** If we <u>rent</u> a house in <u>Italy</u> in <u>June</u>, will you <u>come</u> and <u>stay</u>?
  B *I'll tell you…* _____

2 **A** Do you <u>think</u> you'll be <u>able</u> to <u>repair</u> them <u>soon</u>?
  B _____

3 **A** <u>How</u> will I <u>know</u> where to <u>find</u> you?
  B _____

4 **A** <u>What</u> <u>time</u> did <u>Mandy</u> <u>say</u> she was <u>coming</u>?
  B At 8.00. But _____

5 **A** What have you got in that bag?
  B _____

6 **A** Will it <u>be</u> a <u>problem</u> if they <u>stay</u> for <u>lunch</u>?
  B _____

b Listen again and <u>underline</u> the stressed words.

c In pairs, practise the dialogues. Try to say the sentences as fast as possible with the right rhythm.

6 LISTENING

a Look at the photo and read an extract from an article about a children's nursery in Japan. What are the main safety measures? What do you think of them?

Risk-taking nursery is a breath of fresh air

b 3.12 Now listen to an interview with Sue Palmer, head of Farley Nursery School. How is her attitude different from that of Mr and Mrs Suzuki?

c Listen again and complete the information about the school with a word or phrase.

1 The nursery is in a _____ in southern England.
2 Children spend most of their time _____, even in the _____.
3 They learn about the world by _____.
4 Sue thinks children today don't have enough _____.
5 They need to be allowed to _____ when they play.
6 She thinks that schools are obsessed with eliminating risk because if children _____ their parents will sue the school.
7 Parents at her school are _____ about what the school is doing.

d Do you agree with Sue Palmer's philosophy about young children and risk?

Japan's children play safe

When Ryosuke and Taemi Suzuki take their 18-month-old daughter to Fantasy Kids Resort in Japan they are guaranteed total peace of mind. Fantasy Kids Resort is one of several similar playgrounds in Japan that provides for the growing number of parents who constantly worry about possible dangers threatening their children such as disease and accidents.

First-time visitors to the playground must provide proof of identification before they enter, and shoes must be removed at the door, because they carry germs. Even the wheels of baby buggies are sprayed with an antibacterial solution.

Inside, children are watched over by about 20 staff dressed in bright yellow uniforms and more than a dozen security cameras are mounted on the ceiling. Although pets are banned from the playground, its large sandpit contains sterilized sand which is cleaned daily to remove any potentially harmful objects. Most of the bigger toys are inflatable to reduce the risk of injury. This is to protect the resort as much as the children, because parents of a child injured while at the playground might easily sue the resort.

'We've been here before and we'll definitely come again,' says Mr Suzuki. 'This place has everything under one roof, but most importantly, it puts absolute priority on safety.'

Mr and Mrs Suzuki are not alone in wanting to remove just about every element of risk from their children's lives. According to a recent government survey…

7 SPEAKING

Talk in small groups.

GET IT RIGHT   **comparing past and present**

Cross out the wrong form. Tick (✔) if both are correct.
1 I *must* / *had to* walk to school by myself when I was little.
2 I *was allowed to* / *could* play in the street.
3 I *used to* / *use to* go to the park alone when I was *a child* / *young*.
4 *Nowadays* / *Today* parents think this is too risky.
5 They don't let children *go* / *to go* on the bus by themselves.

Did you use to do the following things when you were younger?

• play in the street
• walk to school
• go to a nearby park or playground alone or with friends
• use public transport on your own or with friends
• stay at home alone
• go swimming without an adult supervising
• use the Internet
• choose what TV programmes you want to watch
• travel in a car without a seat belt

Do you think it was safe?

Do you think it is safe for children to do them today?

Are there any other things you used to do as a child that you think would be risky today?

➡ p.157 *Phrasal verbs in context File 3.*

THE INTERVIEW

a You are going to listen to an interview with EZ, a 'free runner' who started the organization Urban Freeflow. Free runners use obstacles in a town or city to create movement by running, jumping, and climbing. Before you listen, read the glossary and look at how the words are pronounced to help you understand what he says.

> **Glossary**
>
> **the South Bank** /saʊθ bæŋk/ the area of London on the south side of the River Thames
>
> **lamp post** /læmp pəʊst/ a tall post with a lamp on top used to illuminate the street
>
> **PE** physical education, especially as a school subject
>
> **skateboard** /skeɪtbɔːd/ a short narrow board with small wheels at each end, which you stand on and ride as a sport
>
> **BMX** a kind of mountain bike
>
> **calluses** /ˈkæləsɪz/ areas of thick hard skin on a hand or foot.

b **3.13** Listen to part 1. Answer the questions with a partner.

1 Can you do free running anywhere?
2 Does EZ usually do it alone or with other people?
3 What sport did he do before free running?
4 Why did he take up free running?
5 How many athletes are there in the Urban Freeflow team? What kind of work do they do?
6 How is free running helping youth offenders and schoolchildren? Why do they like it?

c **3.14** Listen to part 2. Answer the questions with a partner.

What does he say about…?

1 being safety conscious
2 the sense of freedom
3 blisters and sprained ankles
4 a tree
5 gymnastics and football

d **3.15** Listen and complete the phrases. What do you think they mean?

COMMON PHRASES

1 …but generally the people who practise would go to _____ _____ _____ …
2 …someone leading _____ _____ and the rest following.
3 …and had to just change my life around and become sensible all of _____ _____ .
4 _____ _____ _____ of it what we do seems to be quite dangerous.
5 To _____ _____ , the risk element played a part.
6 As _____ _____ you start out very small scale…

e Listen to the interview again with the tapescript on page 125. Do you think free running is a good thing for young people to do? Why (not)?

IN THE STREET

a Look at this list of high-risk sports. Do you know what they all are?

bungee jumping ☐☐   potholing / caving ☐☐
climbing ☐☐   skiing ☐☐
horse-riding ☐☐   snowboarding ☐☐
parachuting ☐☐   white-water rafting ☐☐

b **3.16** You're going to listen to four people talking about high-risk sports. Write the number of each speaker next the risk sport(s) they have done.

| 1 | 2 | 3 | 4 |
| Agne | Anne | Mark | Ray |

c Listen again. Who…?

1 isn't quite sure what is / isn't a risk sport
2 wasn't very good at the activity they tried
3 talks about a risk sport they would like to try
4 is the most enthusiastic about their experience

d **3.17** Listen and complete the phrases. What do you think they mean?

COMMON PHRASES

1 It was just _____ a fool of myself .
2 That was in my _____ days .
3 Oh, it was _____ ! (NAmE, informal)
4 Do _____ count?

e Listen to the interviews again with the tapescript on page 1 Then answer the same questions with a partner.

Study Link MultiROM

a Read the title of the composition. Do you agree or disagree? Then quickly read the composition and see if the writer's opinion is the same as yours.

b Complete the composition with a word or phrase from the list below. Use capital letters where necessary.

> finally   firstly   in addition   in conclusion
> in most cases   ~~nowadays~~   secondly   so   whereas

c You're going to write a composition titled *There is nothing that we as individuals can do to prevent climate change.* Look at the **Useful language** expressions and make sure you know how to use them.

Useful language

Ways of giving your opinion
(Personally) I think / I believe…
In my opinion…

Ways of giving examples
There are several things we can do, for example / for instance / such as…
Another thing we can do is…
We can also…

PLAN the content.

1 Think about the introduction. This should state what the current situation is and why it is important. Decide what the effects of climate change are now in the world and in your country.

2 Decide whether you agree or disagree with the title. Try to think of at least two or three good reasons to support your opinion, including examples of why you think the alternative point of view is wrong.

3 Think of how to express your conclusion (a summary of your opinion). This should follow logically from the examples you have given.

WRITE 120–180 words, organized in four or five paragraphs (introduction, reasons, and conclusion). Use a formal style (no contractions or colloquial expressions). Use the phrases in **b** and in **Useful Language**.

CHECK your composition for mistakes (grammar , punctuation , and spelling).

Community service is the best punishment for young people who commit a minor offence.

¹ *Nowadays* in the UK when a young person commits a minor offence he or she is normally sentenced to prison, a fine, or community service. ²_____ I believe that community service is the best option.

³_____, community service often persuades a young person not to reoffend. Working with sick children or old people makes young offenders realize that there are people who have more difficult lives than they do. So, community service can be an educational experience, ⁴_____ going to prison or paying a fine is not.

⁵_____, spending time in prison results in young people meeting other criminals and learning more about the criminal world, which may tempt them into committing more crimes. ⁶_____, in prisons many of the inmates take drugs and this is a terrible example for young offenders.

⁷_____, I do not think that a fine is a suitable punishment for young people. They do not usually have much money themselves ⁸_____ it is often their parents who pay the fine for them.

⁹_____, I believe that community service has important advantages both for minor offenders and for the community.

GRAMMAR

a Complete the second sentence so that it means the same as the first.

1 The accident happened when they were repairing the road.
The accident happened when the road _____ repaired.

2 They'll probably never find the murderer
The murderer will _____ found.

3 People think the burglar is a teenager.
The burglar is thought _____ teenager.

4 They say that crime doesn't pay.
It is _____ crime doesn't pay.

5 He isn't likely to come.
He probably _____ .

b Complete the sentence with the right form of the verb in **bold**.

1 Imagine! This time tomorrow we _____ on the beach. **lie**

2 The match starts at 7.00. By the time I get home, it already _____ . **start**

3 You mustn't use your mobile phone until the plane _____ . **land**

4 Many people have problems sleeping if they _____ coffee after midday. **drink**

5 I want to spend a year travelling when I _____ university. **finish**

VOCABULARY

a Word groups. Underline the word that is different. Say why.

1	robber	burglar	pickpocket	kidnapper
2	fraud	smuggler	theft	terrorism
3	evidence	judge	jury	witness
4	chilly	cool	scorching	freezing
5	hurricane	mist	blizzard	flood

b Complete the sentences with a verb in the past simple.

1 They **c**_____ a terrible crime.
2 The police **c**_____ the burglar at the scene of the crime.
3 The judge **s**_____ him to five years in jail.
4 They **k**_____ the politician's son and asked for a million dollars ranso▮
5 Jack the Ripper **m**_____ seven women in London in the 19th century▮
6 The wind **b**_____ so hard that two trees fell down.
7 I **sw**_____ so much when I was at the gym that my T-shirt was soaking wet.
8 It **p**_____ with rain last night and we got soaked coming home.
9 We had six centimetres of snow when I woke up but it **m**_____ duri▮ the morning.
10 We **t**_____ advantage of the good weather and spent the day at the beach.

c Complete the sentences with one word.

1 The woman was charged ____ drug dealing.
2 Are you planning to take ____ a new sport when you go to university?
3 Who do you take ____ most, your mother or your father?
4 Watch ____! You nearly hit that cyclist.
5 It's very hot here. Let's move and sit ____ the shade.

PRONUNCIATION

a Underline the word with a different sound.

1	θ	thaw	weather	theft	thunder
2	ɜ	burnt	jury	murder	burglar
3	dʒ	jail	charge	guilty	changeable
4	aɪ	mild	slip	icy	hijack
5	iː	steal	dealer	sweat	heatwave

b Underline the stressed syllable.

accuse   blackmail   community   blizzard   seriously

CAN YOU UNDERSTAND THIS TEXT?

Read the article and choose a, b, or c.

1 Mr Green did not fight the burglar because _____.
   a he was wearing his best clothes
   b he knew he would lose
   c the burglar was too quick

2 'Flat' (line 6) means _____.
   a broken
   b not round
   c without air

3 Mr Green used to be _____.
   a an artist
   b a footballer
   c a journalist

4 'Cruised' (line 15) means _____.
   a drove around slowly
   b looked everywhere
   c went at top speed

5 According to the police, _____.
   a crime victims should take photos
   b a drawing can be better than a photo
   c mobile phone photos cannot be used in court

6 'Assault' (line 23) means _____.
   a attacking someone
   b stealing property
   c breaking into someone's house

CAN YOU UNDERSTAND THESE PEOPLE?

a **3.18** You will hear five people talking about teenage crime. Match each speaker with the people A–F. There is one person you don't need.

A a journalist ☐   D a police officer ☐
B a lawyer ☐   E a teacher ☐
C a parent ☐   F a victim of teenage crime ☐

b **3.19** You will hear part of an interview with two mountain climbers. Write **D** next to what Dan says, **M** next to what Marion says, and **N** next to what neither of them says.

1 Climbing is safer than driving.
2 I try to control the element of risk when I climb.
3 Avalanches are a climber's worst enemy.
4 Climbing helps me do my job better.
5 My job is quite boring.
6 My partner is not happy that I go climbing.
7 People with young children shouldn't go climbing.
8 Accidents are usually a climber's own fault.

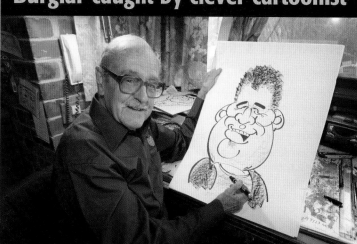

Burglar caught by clever cartoonist

WILLIAM ELLIS GREEN, aged 82, was making his breakfast when he heard somebody in his garden. 'I went out of the back door and suddenly I saw this bloke running towards me. He pushed me out of the way and took my bicycle from the garden shed.' Mr Green did not resist,
5 as he knew he would come off second best in a fight with the intruder. The burglar tried to cycle away, but the tyres on the bike were flat so it was difficult to ride. 'He kept falling off the bicycle,' said Mr Green, 'at least three or four times.' After the man had fled, Mr Green called the local police.

When they arrived, officers asked him to describe the man, but instead
10 he offered to draw them a picture. 'When Mr Green started drawing,' said one of the police officers, 'I knew straight away who the burglar was.' In fact, Mr Green had worked for more than 20 years in daily newspapers doing caricatures of Australian footballers. 'I had no difficulty in remembering the man's face because he was so close to me,' he said.

15 Police cruised the neighbourhood in a patrol car with the sketch in search of the alleged burglar and they found him within half an hour. 'The cartoon was a perfect likeness of the burglar,' said another police officer.

Police believe that this is the first time they have ever caught a suspect with a cartoon sketch. Phil Rushford, a senior police constable, said that
20 in the past some victims had used their mobile phones to take photographs at crime scenes, but they had not been as effective.

A 34-year-old man is expected to be charged with theft, burglary, and assault. The missing bike was later found in a road nearby.

From The Times

CAN YOU SAY THIS IN ENGLISH?

Can you...?
☐ talk about appropriate punishments for different crimes
☐ describe things we can do to reduce the effects of climate change
☐ talk about whether life is riskier today than it was in the past

G unreal conditionals
V feelings
P sentence rhythm

4 A Would <u>you</u> get out alive?

HOW TO GET OUT ALIVE

1 SPEAKING & READING

a Answer the questions with a partner.

1 How do you think *most* people react in a life or death disaster situation?
  a They panic and become hysterical.
  b They act coolly and calmly.
  c They 'freeze' and can't do anything.

2 What do you do when you are on a plane and the flight attendant starts to explain the safety procedures?
  a I don't listen. I've heard it so many times!
  b I listen but I don't take it very seriously.
  c I pay attention and also read the safety information in the seat pocket.

3 What would you do if you were in a hotel on the 5th floor and the fire alarm went off in the middle of the night?
  a I would pick up essential things like my passport and mobile and find the quickest way down to the lobby.
  b I would follow the emergency instructions on the back of the door, which I had read when I arrived.
  c I wouldn't pay any attention. I would think it was probably a fire drill.

b Read *How humans behave when the worst thing happens*, and check your answer to question **1** above. Then answer the questions below with a partner.

  1 What two reasons are given to explain why a lot of people freeze in a crisis?
  2 Is it possible to predict how people will react in a crisis?
  3 What do you think *you* would do?

c **A** read about a survivor of the World Trade Center, and **B** read about a survivor from the Tenerife air crash. Then use the questions below to tell each other about what you read.

  A 1 Where was Elia on 11th September 2001?
    2 How did she react when the plane hit the World Trade Center?
    3 What saved her life?
    4 How quickly did she leave?
    5 How could more lives have been saved?

  B 1 Where was Paul Heck on 27th March 1977?
    2 How did the accident happen?
    3 How could more passengers have survived?
    4 Why did Paul Heck survive?
    5 What previous experience influenced Paul?

d Read the whole article and in pairs, mark the sentences true (T) or false (F).
  1 Elia Zedeño's first instinct was to run.
  2 If her colleague hadn't shouted, she might not have reacted how she did.
  3 She took her time to leave because she didn't know where the exit was.
  4 Some people who died in the World Trade Center could have survived.
  5 The 1977 Tenerife air crash happened in bad weather conditions.
  6 The Pan Am passengers had plenty of time to escape.
  7 Heck always worried about how he would be able to escape from places.
  8 People don't read safety information because they aren't worried about crashing.

e Look at the highlighted words related to disasters. In pairs, try to work out the meaning from the context of the ones you didn't know.

f What survival tips have you learned from this article? Which were the best options in questions 2 and 3 in **a**?

How humans behave when the worst thing happens…

WE ALWAYS THINK 'it will never happen to me' but disasters can strike any time anywhere – from hotel fires to train crashes to terrorist attacks. How would you cope if the unthinkable happened?

According to experts, people caught up in disasters tend to fall into three categories. About 10% to 15% remain calm and act quickly and efficiently. Another 15% completely panic, crying and screaming and obstructing the evacuation. But the vast majority (70%) of people do very little. They are 'stunned and confused,' says British psychologist John Leach.

Why is this? Research suggests that under great stress our minds take much longer to process information. So, in a crisis many people 'freeze' just at the moment when they need to act quickly. It also seems that a person's personality is not a good guide to how they might react – a normally decisive person may not act at all quickly in a crisis and vice versa. 'Most people their entire lives without a disaster,' says Michael Lindell, a professor at Texas A&M University. 'So when something bad happens they are so shocked they just think, "This can't possibly be happening to me," instead of taking action.'

A

WHEN THE PLANE hit the World Trade Center on 11th September 2001, Elia Zedeño was working on the 73rd floor. She heard an explosion and felt the building actually move, as if it might fall over. Zedeño first shouted out, 'What's happening?' You might expect that her next instinct was to run. But she had the opposite reaction. 'What I really wanted was for someone to scream back, "Everything is OK! Don't worry."'

Luckily, at least one of Zedeño's colleagues responded differently. He screamed, 'Get out of the building!' she remembers now. Years later, she still thinks about that command. 'My question is what would I have done if that person had said nothing?'

Even then Zedeño still did not immediately run. First she reached for her bag, and then she started walking in circles. 'I was looking for something to take with me. I remember I took my book. Then I kept looking around for other stuff to take. I felt as if I was in a trance.' When she finally left, she went slowly. 'It's strange because the sound of the explosion and the way the building shook should have made me go faster.' But Zedeño made it to safety. Experts have estimated that at least another 130 people would have got out of the World Trade Center alive if they had tried to leave the building sooner.

Office workers flee the collapsing towers on 11th September 2001.

B

ON MARCH 27 1977 a Pan Am 747, which was waiting to take off from Tenerife airport, collided with a Dutch KLM 747 that was taking off in the fog. It was the worst air crash in history. Everyone on the KLM plane was killed but 62 passengers on the Pan Am plane survived. Many more would have survived if they had got off the plane immediately.

One of the survivors was 65-year-old Paul Heck. He led his wife Floy towards the exit and they got out just before the plane caught fire, just 60 seconds after the collision. Why Paul Heck and not others? In the hours just before the crash Paul did something highly unusual. While he was waiting for the plane to take off, he studied the 747's safety diagram. He looked for the nearest exit and he pointed it out to his wife. He had been in a theatre fire as a boy, and ever since then, he always checked for the exits when he was in an unfamiliar environment. When the planes collided, Heck's brain had the data it needed. He could work on autopilot, whereas other passengers froze, their minds paralysed by a storm of new information. Why don't more people read safety information on aeroplanes and fire escape information in hotels? The answer, according to research, is that people think it's 'cool' to do so. So next time you fly or stay in a hotel or find yourself in any new environment forget about 'being cool' and take a few seconds to find out where the nearest emergency exit is. It may just save your life.

Tenerife air crash 27th March 1977. The accident led to research into why people sometimes freeze when they need to flee.

2 VOCABULARY feelings

a Look at *How humans behave when the worst thing happens* and find adjectives which mean…

1 unable to think clearly or understand what's happening. _____
2 not excited or nervous. _____
3 very surprised by something unpleasant. _____
4 so surprised that you can't move or react. _____

b ⊙ **p.151 Vocabulary Bank** *Feelings.*

c Look at the pictures. Try to remember an adjective and an idiom to describe how each person feels.

d Choose two adjectives from below and tell your partner why you felt like that.
Can you remember a time when you felt…?

- amazed
- delighted
- exhausted
- furious
- grateful
- homesick
- terrified
- really fed up

3 GRAMMAR unreal conditionals

> 1 What would you do if your school caught fire?
> 2 What would you have done if you had been on the Pan Am plane in Tenerife?

a Look at 1 and 2 above. Which one refers to a hypothetical situation in the past? Which one refers to a hypothetical situation in the present or future?

b Underline the verb forms in 1 and 2. Which forms are they?

c Without looking back at pages 52 and 53, try to complete 1–4 below.

  1 What would do if you _____ (be) in a hotel and the fire alarm went off in the middle of the night?
  2 Another 130 people _____ (get out) of the World Trade Center alive if they had tried to leave the building sooner.
  3 Many more people would have survived if they _____ (get off) the plane immediately.
  4 If a fire alarm went off at work, I _____ (not pay) any attention.

d ⊙ **p138 Grammar Bank 4A.** Read the rules and do the exercises.

4 PRONUNCIATION sentence rhythm

a ⟨4.1⟩ Listen and write down the beginning of six sentences. Then match them with the sentence endings A–F.

  1 _____
  2 _____
  3 _____
  4 _____
  5 _____
  6 _____

  A I would have died. ⑤
  B if my husband wasn't afraid of flying. ☐
  C if I were you. ☐
  D I wouldn't have acted so quickly. ☐
  E if I'd been in that situation. ☐
  F you wouldn't believe me. ☐

b ⟨4.2⟩ Listen and check.

c Listen to sentences 1–6 again and underline the stressed words. Practise saying the sentences.

d Write conditional chains. For each chain, you must write two third conditional sentences.

  If I hadn't read the safety information, *I wouldn't have known where the emergency exit was.*
  If I hadn't known where the emergency exit was, I wouldn't have survived the crash.

  1 If I hadn't accepted the invitation, …
  2 If I hadn't got up so late, …
  3 If I had remembered to switch my phone on, …
  4 If I had known we had an exam, …

5 READING & LISTENING

a If you were going to go backpacking in the Amazon rainforest, what do you think would be the biggest dangers?

b Read the beginning of a true survival story and then answer the questions below.

  1 What was the three friends' original plan? How did this change?
  2 What caused tensions between…?
    a the three men and the guide
    b Kevin and Marcus
  3 Why did they finally separate?
  4 Which pair would you have chosen to go with? Why?
  5 How would you have felt if you'd been in Marcus's situation?

Escape from the Amazon

Four young men went into the jungle on the adventure of a lifetime. Not all of them would come out alive…

THE AMAZONIAN RAINFOREST is roughly the size of Europe or Australia. It is the home of more than half the plant and animal species known to man, many of which are lethal.

In 1981 three friends went backpacking in a remote area of Bolivia: Yossi, 22, and his two friends Kevin, 29, and Marcus, 29. They hired an experienced guide, an Austrian called Karl, who promised that he could take them deep into the rainforest to an undiscovered indigenous village. Then they would raft nearly 200 kilometres down river before flying to the capital, La Paz. Karl said that the journey to the village would take them seven or eight days. Before they entered the jungle, the three friends made a promise that they would 'go in together and come out together'.

The four men set off from the town of Apolo and soon they had left civilization far behind. But after walking for more than a week there was no sign of the village and tensions began to appear. The three friends began to suspect that Karl, the guide, didn't really know where the indigenous village was. Yossi and Kevin began to get fed up with their friend Marcus because he was complaining about everything, especially his feet, which had become infected and were hurting.

Eventually they decided to abandon the search for the village and just to hike back to Apolo, the way they had come. But Kevin was furious because he thought that it was Marcus' fault that they had had to cut short their adventure. So he decided that he would raft down the river, and he asked Yossi to join him – he didn't want Marcus to come with them. Karl and Marcus agreed to go back to Apolo on foot. The three friends agreed to meet in a hotel in La Paz in a week's time.

Early next morning the two pairs of travellers said goodbye and set off on their different journeys…

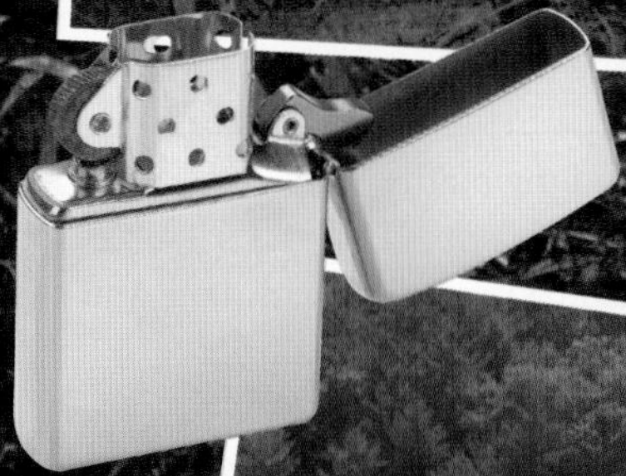

c Now listen to the documentary. When the recording stops, answer the questions with a partner.

4.3

1 What happened to Kevin and Yossi on the raft?
2 Why was Yossi really lucky?
Whose situation would you rather have been in?

4.4

3 How were Kevin and Yossi feeling?
4 What happened to Yossi on his first night alone in the jungle?
What would you have done if you had been in his situation?

4.5

5 Why did Yossi's spirits change from desperate, to optimistic, and then to desperate again?
Do you think you would have given up at this point? What do you think had happened to Kevin?

4.6

6 What had Kevin been doing all this time?
7 Why was he incredibly lucky?
If you had been Kevin, would you have continued to try to look for your friend?

4.7

8 How did Kevin first try to get help?
9 Why was it unsuccessful?
10 What was his last attempt to find his friend?
What do you think had happened to Yossi?

4.8

11 How long had Yossi been on his own in the jungle?
12 What did he think the buzzing noise was? What was it?
What do you think might have happened to Marcus and Karl?

d Listen again with the tapescript on page 125. Underline any words that were new for you, or words you knew but didn't recognize.

e Do you think you would have survived if you had been in Kevin or Yossi's situation? Would you have done anything differently?

6 4.9 SONG ♫ I will survive

4

B

G past modals; *would rather, had better*
V verbs often confused
P weak form of *have*

How I trained my husband

1 GRAMMAR past modals

a **Check what you know.** Look at the photo and then answer the questions using *must be*, *might be*, or *can't be*.

1 What time do you think it is?
  a 2.00 p.m.   b 8.00 a.m.   c 6.00 a.m.
2 What day of the week do you think it is?
  a Friday   b Saturday   c Sunday
3 What country do you think it is?
  a Brazil   b the UK   c the United States
4 What do you think the man is looking for?
  a his glasses   b his car keys   c his briefcase

Any problems? ➲ **Workbook p.37**

b **4.10** Listen to check your answers to **a**. What was the problem?

c **4.11** Now listen to two more conversations. What are they arguing about?

d **New grammar.** Listen again to all three conversations and complete the extracts with *must have*, *may / might have*, *can't have*, or *should have*.

Conversation 1
1 You _____ left them in your jacket pocket. ☐
2 I _____ put them there – I wasn't wearing a jacket. ☐
3 Someone _____ moved them. ☐

Conversation 2
4 We _____ taken the wrong turning again. ☐
5 We _____ turned left at the last traffic lights. ☐
6 OK, I _____ said 'right'. ☐

Conversation 3
7 Yes, but I think you _____ used less sugar. ☐
8 You _____ read it properly. ☐

e Look at the extracts in **d** again. In pairs, put A, B, C, or D in the box after each sentence. Which phrases (*may have*, *can't have*, etc.) mean…?

A you are sure about something that happened or something that somebody did
B you think it's possible that something happened or somebody did something
C you think it's impossible that something happened or somebody did something
D you think somebody did something wrong

f ➲ **p.138 Grammar Bank 4B.** Read the rules and do the exercises.

2 PRONUNCIATION weak form of *have*

a **4.12** Listen to the extracts from the dialogues in **1d** again. Underline the stressed words. How is *have* pronounced?

b **4.13** **Dictation.** Listen and write down six sentences.

c In pairs, complete B's responses with your own ideas. Then practise the dialogues.

1 **A** It was my birthday yesterday!
  B You should have *told me*.
2 **A** I can't find my glasses anywhere.
  B You can't have _____
3 **A** I gave Peter a map but he hasn't arrived.
  B He may have _____
4 **A** I have a terrible stomach ache.
  B You shouldn't have _____
5 **A** I thought the meeting was this morning but no one came.
  B _____
6 **A** I failed my maths exam.
  B _____
7 **A** I was in a restaurant with Jane and she suddenly walked out.
  B _____
8 **A** Sarah didn't come to the party last night.
  B _____
9 **A** We're going to be late. There's so much traffic.
  B _____

3 READING

a You're going to read an article by Amy Sutherland, a writer who wanted to cure her husband of some irritating habits. What do you think they might have been?

b Read the article paragraph by paragraph, using the glossary to help you. After each paragraph, stop and answer the questions with a partner.

1 What did Amy use to do when her husband couldn't find his keys? What does she do now?

2 Why and how did she learn about animal training? What idea occurred to her? What is the main principle of animal training?

3 What is the technique called 'approximations'? How did she apply it to her husband?

4 What behaviour did the bird trainer want to stop? How did he do it? How did she apply this technique to her husband?

5 What did she learn from the dolphin trainer? How did she apply this to her husband?

6 What often happens when animals learn a technique? What technique did her husband use on her, and how?

c What do think of Amy and the way she trained her husband? Is there anyone you would like to train? What technique do you think would work best?

Glossary

(1) **snarl** make an angry noise, like an animal does

(1) **faucet** tap (NAmE), the thing you turn to let water come out

(1) **join the hunt** take part in looking for sth (i.e. her husbands keys)

(2) **reward** give sth to sb because they have done sth well, e.g. worked hard

(2) **nag** talk to sb continuously in a complaining or critical way

(3) **hamper** clothes basket (NAmE)

(3) **praise** say sth positive about sb

(4) **African crested cranes** tall thin birds with very long legs

(4) **parsley** a herb commonly used in cooking

(5) **fuel** (v) increase sth, make sth stronger

(5) **mackerel** a kind of oily fish

(6) **be up to sth** pv be doing sth, often secretly

(6) **fall** autumn (NAmE)

(6) **braces** a metal plate worn over the teeth to correct dental problems

(6) **excruciating** very painful

(6) **tirade** a long angry speech

(6) **acknowledge my rant** show that he'd heard my angry words

(6) **do the trick** succeed

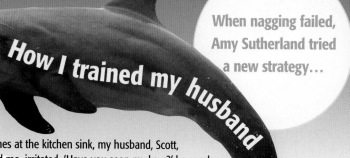

When nagging failed, Amy Sutherland tried a new strategy…

How I trained my husband

1 As I wash dishes at the kitchen sink, my husband, Scott, paces behind me, irritated. 'Have you seen my keys?' he snarls and stomps from the room with our dog, Dixie, at his heels. In the past I would have turned off the faucet and joined the hunt while trying to soothe my husband. But that only made him angrier, and a simple case of missing keys soon would become a full-blown drama starring the two of us and our poor nervous dog. Now, I focus on the wet dish in my hands. I don't turn around. I don't say a word. I'm using a technique I learned from a dolphin trainer.

2 For a book I was writing about a school for exotic animal trainers, I started spending my days watching students do the seemingly impossible: teaching hyenas to pirouette on command and chimps to skateboard. I listened, rapt, as professional trainers explained how they taught dolphins to flip and elephants to paint. Eventually it hit me that the same techniques might work on that stubborn but lovable species, the American husband. The central lesson I learned is that I should reward behaviour I like and ignore behaviour I don't. After all, you don't get a sea lion to balance a ball on the end of its nose by nagging. The same goes for the American husband.

3 I began thanking Scott if he threw one dirty shirt into the hamper. If he threw in two, I'd kiss him. I was using what trainers call 'approximations,' rewarding the small steps toward learning a whole new behaviour. You can't expect a baboon to learn to flip on command in one session, just as you can't expect an American husband to begin regularly picking up his dirty socks by praising him once for picking up a single sock. With the baboon you first reward a hop, then a bigger hop, then an even bigger hop. With Scott the husband, I began to praise every small act every time: if he drove just a mile an hour slower, tossed one pair of shorts into the hamper, or was on time for anything.

4 On a field trip with the students, I listened to a professional trainer describe how he had taught African crested cranes to stop landing on his head and shoulders. He did this by training the leggy birds to land on mats on the ground. This, he explained, is what is called an 'incompatible behaviour,' a simple but brilliant concept. Rather than teach the cranes to stop landing on him, the trainer taught the birds something else, a behaviour that would make the undesirable behaviour impossible. The birds couldn't alight on the mats and his head simultaneously. At home, I came up with incompatible behaviours for Scott to keep him from crowding me while I cooked. I piled up parsley for him to chop or cheese for him to grate at the other end of the kitchen island. Soon I'd done it: no more Scott hovering around me while I cooked.

5 I followed the students to SeaWorld San Diego, where a dolphin trainer introduced me to least reinforcing scenario (L. R. S.). When a dolphin does something wrong, the trainer doesn't respond in any way. He stands still for a few beats, careful not to look at the dolphin, and then returns to work. The idea is that any response, positive or negative, fuels a behaviour. If a behaviour provokes no response, it typically dies away. It was only a matter of time before he was again searching for his keys, at which point I said nothing and kept at what I was doing. It took a lot of discipline to maintain my calm, but results were immediate. I felt as if I should throw him a mackerel.

6 Professionals talk of animals that understand training so well they eventually use it back on the trainer. My animal did the same. When the training techniques worked so beautifully, I couldn't resist telling my husband what I was up to. He wasn't offended, just amused. Then last fall, firmly in middle age, I learned that I needed braces. They were not only humiliating, but also excruciating. One morning, as I launched into yet another tirade about how uncomfortable I was, Scott just looked at me blankly. He didn't say a word or acknowledge my rant in any way, not even with a nod. I started to walk away, then I realized what was happening, and I turned and asked, 'Are you giving me an L. R. S.?' Silence. 'You are, aren't you?' He finally smiled, but his L. R. S. had already done the trick. He'd begun to train me, the American wife.

4 LISTENING

a **4.14** What's the difference between a discussion and an argument? You're going to listen to a psychologist giving some tips to help people when they disagree with somebody about something. Listen once and tick the six things she says.

1 Think carefully what to say when you begin a discussion.
2 Try to 'win' the argument as quickly as you can.
3 Say sorry if something really is your fault.
4 Never avoid an argument by refusing to talk.
5 Don't say things which aren't completely true.
6 Don't shout.
7 Don't talk about things which aren't relevant to the argument.
8 Use another person to mediate.
9 Postpone the argument until later when you have both calmed down.
10 It's a bad thing for a couple to argue.

b Listen again and, with a partner, try to add more detail to the tips you ticked.

c With a partner, decide which two of the psychologist's tips you think are the most useful.

d Look at these sentences and try to work out what the missing words are.

1 But of course this is **easier said** _____ _____.
2 If you're the person who is _____ _____ **wrong**, just admit it!
3 It is important to _____ **things** _____ **control**.
4 Raising your voice will just make the other person _____ **their temper** too.
5 Stop for a moment and _____ **a deep breath**.
6 It is also very important to _____ _____ **the point**.
7 There is much more chance that you will be able to _____ **an agreement**.
8 _____ _____ **conflict** is an important part of any relationship.

e **4.15** Listen and check.

5 SPEAKING

a ○ **Communication** *Argument! A p.117 B p.120.* Roleplay two arguments with a partner.

b Did you follow any of the psychologist's advice about how to argue? Was there anything you should / shouldn't have done?

6 VOCABULARY   verbs often confused

a Circle the correct verb in each pair of sentences.

1 a When I saw my wife's face, I *noticed / realized* that I had bought the wrong size.
   b My husband never *notices / realizes* when I've been to the hairdresser's.
2 a The water level in the river is *raising / rising*.
   b Don't *raise / rise* your voice when you are having an argument.
3 a I think we need to *argue / discuss* our new marketing plan.
   b Teenagers often *argue / discuss* with their parents.
4 a There is a new road safety campaign to *avoid / prevent* accidents.
   b We took the ring road to *avoid / prevent* going through the city centre.
5 a Please *remember / remind* to lock the door before you go out.
   b *Remember / Remind* me to phone my mother later – it's her birthday.
6 a I *expect / hope* she'll come to the party. I'd really like to see her.
   b My driving test is next week, but I'm not *expecting / hoping* to pass – I've only had ten lessons.
7 a Mandy hasn't invited me to her party, but I don't *mind / matter*.
   b It doesn't *mind / matter* if we're a bit late.
8 a Oh no! Somebody's *stolen / robbed* my bike!
   b A 40-year-old man has been charged with *robbing / stealing* a bank in the High Street.
9 a I woke up in the night because I *heard / listened to* a noise.
   b If you had *heard / listened to* what I was saying, you'd know what the problem was.
10 a Your brother *seems / looks* exactly like your father – he's got the same eyes.
   b When I spoke to him on the phone, I thought he *seemed / looked* quite friendly.

b Compare your answers with a partner, and try to explain what the difference is between the verbs in each pair.

c Complete the questions with one of the verbs from each pair in **a** in the right form. Then ask and answer with a partner.

1 Do you usually _____ what colour eyes people have?
2 What would your boss do if you asked him / her to _____ your salary?
3 Do you often _____ with people in your family? Who with? What about?
4 What do you think is the best way to _____ catching colds in winter?
5 Are you good at _____ people's birthdays?
6 Are you _____ to pass or fail your next English exam?
7 Do you think it _____ if a wife earns more than her husband?
8 Has your car or bike ever been _____?
9 Are women really better at _____ than men?
10 Who do you _____ like in your family?

MINI GRAMMAR   *would rather, had better*

a Look at two sentences from the listening. Which of the highlighted phrases means *should*? Which means *would prefer to*? Do you know what *'d* refers to in each case?

I'd rather talk about this tomorrow when we've both calmed down.

I think we'd better have another look at how we divide up the housework.

b Now read the rules for using *had better* and *would rather*.

• Use *had better* with the infinitive (without *to*), e.g.
  You'd better hurry up. Your train leaves in ten minutes.
  You'd better not tell your parents – they'll be furious.
  NOT ~~You hadn't better tell…~~

  ⚠ *had better* is stronger and more immediate than *should* and is often used as a warning.

• Use *would rather* with the infinitive without *to*, e.g.
  I'd rather go on holiday in July this year, not August.
  Would you rather stay in or go out tonight?
  I'd rather not come to the meeting this afternoon. I'm really busy. NOT ~~I'd not rather.~~

c Rewrite the **bold** phrases using *had better* or *would rather*.

1 I think **I should go now**. It's very late.
2 **I'd prefer to go out** on Friday instead of Saturday.
3 **You shouldn't walk home.** It's a bit dangerous here at night.
4 Ana said **she'd prefer to meet** on Thursday afternoon.
5 James **should be careful**. If the boss finds out, he'll sack him.
6 **Would you prefer not to go to the party** if David is going to be there?
7 **You shouldn't leave your bag there** – someone will steal it.
8 **My wife would prefer not to fly.** She had a bad experience once.

4
C

G verbs of the senses
V the body
P silent letters

Let your body do the talking

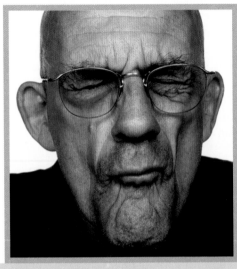

1 GRAMMAR verbs of the senses

a Look at the photo. In pairs, choose the best description of the man.

1 He looks…
   a angry. b in pain. c depressed.

2 He looks like…
   a a teacher. b a bank manager. c a builder.

3 He looks as if…
   a he has just eaten something nasty.
   b he has just been told some bad news.
   c he is listening to something that sounds awful.

b Now read about a book called *In character: actors acting* and check your answers.

1 Who is the man in the photo?   2 What's he doing?

In character: actors acting

The photographer Howard Schatz had a very unusual idea for a book. He invited actors into his studio, and asked them to 'be' certain characters in certain situations, and he then photographed them. For example, he told the actor Christopher Lloyd to be 'a violin teacher who is listening to his pupil massacre a Mozart piece'.

c ➲ **p.138 Grammar Bank 4C.** Read the rules and do the exercises.

d Look at the photos of Alan Cumming and Michael Cumpsty from the book and describe the actors. Use *looks*, *looks like*, and *looks as if*.

e Match the faces A–D with situations 1–4, and the faces E–H with situations 5–8.

1 You realize you have been betrayed by your best friend. ☐
2 You are a four-year-old letting the family's pet parrot out of its cage. ☐
3 You are a man begging your partner to come with you to visit your parents. ☐
4 You are a young child trying not to listen as your mother tells you off. ☐
5 You are a young driver telling a police officer that you haven't had anything to drink. ☐
6 You are a police officer leaning on the door waiting for a driver to show his license. ☐
7 You are a young driver admitting that you've had maybe a small beer. ☐
8 You are a police officer looking into a car filled with teenagers. ☐

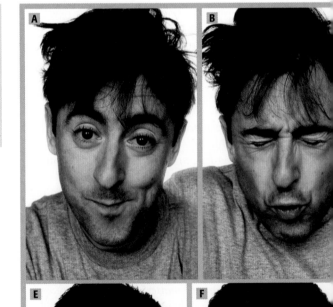

f **4.16** Listen to these sounds. What do you think is happening? Use *It sounds as if…* or *It sounds like…*

g Make pairs of opposites from the adjectives in the list. Do they usually describe how something feels or how something tastes / smells?

hard	loose	rough /rʌf/	smooth /smuːð/	soft	sour / bitter	strong	sweet	tight	weak

h Use *feels*, *smells*, or *tastes* + an adjective or + *like* + noun, etc. to describe one of the objects below for your partner to guess. Then swap.

a full ashtray

hair which has just been washed

cigar smoke

cheap wine

cabbage being cooked

a marble statue

a silk scarf

a lemon

a baby after its bath

a cat's tongue

espresso coffee without sugar

a two-day beard

Mexican food

jeans which are too small for you

2 LISTENING

a **4.17** You are going to listen to a radio quiz show *Use your senses*, where contestants have to identify the mystery food and the mystery drink, a mystery object, and a mystery sound. Listen once and write what you think the answers are.

1 _____

2 _____

3 _____

4 _____

b Listen again and complete the phrases.

Mystery drink

It smells _____.

It smells a bit _____.

Mystery food

It tastes a bit _____.

It tastes quite _____.

Mystery object

It feels like _____.

It definitely feels _____.

Mystery sound

It sounds like _____.

It sounds _____.

c Discuss your answers to **a** with a partner.

d **4.18** Now listen to the answers. Were you right?

3 VOCABULARY the body

a Look at a photograph of the actress Judi Dench. Match the words in the list with 1–8 in the photo.

cheek   chin   eyebrow   eyelashes
forehead /ˈfɔːhed/   lips   neck   wrinkles /ˈrɪŋklz/

b ➲ **p.152 Vocabulary Bank** *The body.*

c Do the *Body quiz* with a partner.

BODY QUIZ

A Which part of the body?

1 The place where you wear a watch.
2 The two places where you might wear a belt.
3 You can easily twist this when doing sport.
4 These are often red after you've been out in the cold or if you're embarrassed.
5 You use these to breathe.
6 Doctors sometimes listen to this to see if you have a breathing problem.

B Which idiom do you use...?

1 when you are very nervous (stomach)
2 when you can't quite remember something (tongue)
3 when you can't stop thinking about something e.g. a particular song (head)
4 when you think a friend is telling you something which isn't true as a joke (leg)
5 when you memorize something (heart)
6 when you have said something which you shouldn't have said because it is a secret or may cause embarrassment (foot)

d **4.19** Listen and mime the action.

4 PRONUNCIATION silent letters

a Cross out the 'silent consonant' in these words.

calf   wrist   palms   wrinkles   comb   kneel   thumb

b **4.20** Listen and check.

c Look at some more common words with silent consonants. In pairs, decide which they are and cross them out. Use the phonetics to help you.

asthma /ˈæsmə/   castle /ˈkɑːsl/   cupboard /ˈkʌbəd/   sign /saɪn/
doubt /daʊt/   half /hɑːf/   honest /ˈɒnɪst/   island /ˈaɪlənd/   knock /nɒk/
psychologist /saɪˈkɒlədʒɪst/   receipt /rɪˈsiːt/   whole /həʊl/

d **4.21** Listen and check.

e **4.22** **Dictation.** Listen and write down six sentences.

5 READING

a What do you understand by the phrase 'body language'?

b In pairs, look at the drawings and try to match the body language with the feelings.

A saying something important ☐
B feeling attracted ☐
C feeling defensive ☐
D feeling nervous ☐

E feeling superior ☐
F being honest ☐
G lying ☐
H thinking hard ☐

c Read *Let your body do the talking* and check your answers.

Let your body do the talking

One of the areas of our body which conveys most about how we feel is our hands and arms. Hand and arm gestures are sometimes deliberate, but most often they occur unconsciously and naturally.

Saying something important Open hands and arms, especially extended, and with palms up in front of the body at chest height, indicate that what you're saying is important, and, especially when people are speaking in public, a pointing finger or a hand waving above the shoulders emphasizes an individual point. However, research shows that people often find speakers who point their fingers a lot rather annoying.

Openness or honesty When people want to be open or honest they will often hold one or both of their palms out to the other person. Footballers who have just committed a foul often use this gesture to try to convince the referee that they didn't do it.

Nervousness If a person puts his hand to his mouth, this either indicates that he is hiding something, or that he is nervous. Fidgeting with your hands, for example tapping the table with your fingers also shows nervousness, and so does holding a bag or briefcase very tightly in front of the body.

Superiority People who feel superior to you often appear relaxed, with their hands clasped behind their heads. The chin and head is often held high. This gesture is typical of lawyers, accountants, and other professionals who feel they know more than you do. Another gesture of superiority is to put your hands in your pockets with the thumbs protruding.

Feeling defensive Arms folded tightly over the chest is a classic gesture of defensiveness and indicates that you are protecting yourself. It is often seen among strangers in queues or in lifts or anywhere where people feel a bit insecure. People also sometimes use this gesture when they are listening to someone, to show that they disagree with what is being said. However, this gesture can simply mean that the person is cold!

Thinking hard A hand-to-cheek gesture, where someone brings a hand to his face and extends his index finger along his cheek, with the remaining fingers positioned below the mouth, often shows that someone is thinking deeply. When someone strokes his chin, he is probably thinking about something important, or making a decision.

Attraction If men are attracted to someone, they sometimes play with one of their ear lobes, whereas women will play with a lock of hair or continually tuck their hair behind their ears.

Lying There are many gestures that indicate that someone is lying and in order to be sure you would expect a person to show more than one. Gestures include putting your hand in front of your mouth, touching your nose, rubbing your eyes, touching your ear, scratching your neck, pulling at your collar, or putting your finger or fingers in your mouth.

---

d Focus on the highlighted words which describe more parts of the body or gestures and, in pairs, try to work out what they mean.

e In pairs, read the article again paragraph by paragraph and try to do each of the gestures described. Do you use any of these gestures a lot?

6 SPEAKING

> **GET IT RIGHT** describing pictures
>
> When you are describing the pictures, use these expressions to explain precisely what / who you are referring to.
>
> *The woman…on the right / left / in the centre of the picture;…in the background / foreground…*
>
> Remember you can also use *might be / may be / could be* for speculating, as well as *looks*, *looks as if*, etc.

Cape Cod Morning (1950) Edward Hopper

a In pairs, look at the painting. Talk about where the woman is, how she is feeling, and what is happening or has happened. Use her body language to help you.

b ⬧ **Communication** *Two paintings A p.118 B p.120.* Describe your painting for your partner to visualize.

⬧ **p.157** *Phrasal verbs in context File 4.*

THE INTERVIEW

a You are going to listen to an interview with Trevor White, a Canadian actor. Before you listen, read the glossary and look at how the words are pronounced to help you understand what he says.

Glossary

voice-over /ˈvɔɪs əʊvə/ information or comments in a film or TV programme given by a person who you do not see on the screen

fringe theatre /frɪndʒ θɪətə/ plays, often by new writers, that are unusual and question the way people think

props /prɒps/ objects used by actors during the performance of a play or film

rehearsal /rɪˈhɜːsəl/ time that is spent practising a play or piece of music

Dictaphone /ˈdɪktəfəʊn/ a small machine used to record people speaking

oftentimes /ˈɒfəntaɪmz/ (North American English) often

Royal Shakespeare Company A British drama company which specializes in Shakespeare's plays

Coriolanus /kɒrɪəˈleɪnəs/ one of Shakespeare's lesser known plays set in Roman times

feature film /ˈfiːtʃə fɪlm/ a full-length film with a story, i.e. not a documentary

sword /sɔːd/ a weapon with a long metal blade

axe /æks/ a weapon with a wooden handle and a heavy metal blade, also a tool for chopping wood

parry /ˈpæri/ to defend yourself by stopping sb hitting you, e.g. with your arm or with a weapon

b (**4.23**) Listen to part 1. Answer the questions with a partner.

1 What kinds of acting does he do?
2 How did he become an actor?
3 What does he find most difficult about preparing for a part?
4 How does he learn his lines?
5 What kind of lines are difficult to memorize?

c (**4.24**) Listen to part 2. Answer the questions with a partner.

What does he say about…?

1 Coriolanus
2 a sword and axe fight
3 the difference between theatre acting and film acting
4 the good and bad side about TV and film work
5 being on a red carpet

d (**4.25**) Listen and complete the phrases. What do you think they mean?

COMMON PHRASES

1 There isn't much I don't do, I guess, _____ _____ as acting goes .
2 You just _____ _____ and you're expected to know all your lines. (**pv**, informal)
3 You do it a few times and _____ _____ .
4 It's amazing the _____ _____ _____ when the writing is good.
5 I gave the other guy three stitches on his fingers _____ _____ point when he parried in the wrong place.
6 You get to do it _____ and _____ again. (idiom)

e Listen to the interview again with the tapescript on page 126. Does he make acting sound like an attractive job to do?

IN THE STREET

a (**4.26**) You're going to listen to five people talking about acting. Write the number of the speaker next to what they appeared in. How many of them mention feeling nervous?

Ben   **Louise**   **Mike**   **Cherry**   **Ray**

a musical   a music video   a play   a school play   a show

b Listen again. Who…?

1 names the plays they have appeared in
2 hopes to become a professional actor
3 hasn't acted for a very long time
4 also helps other actors with their appearance
5 often appears on stage but not as an actor

c (**4.27**) Listen and complete the phrases. What do you think they mean?

COMMON PHRASES

1 I was in a music video once, and that's about as _____ as I've gone.
2 The _____ of it, being able to be someone else in front of people. (informal)
3 And you can just _____ of get taken away into this other world. (informal)
4 A _____ of plays I've been in.
5 It is nerve-wracking just as you're _____ to go on.

d Listen to the interviews again with the tapescript on page 12 Then answer the same questions with a partner.

Study Link MultiROM

Make your home a safer place!

You probably think that your home is the one place where you are safe. That's what I thought until last week. Now I know our flat is full of accidents waiting to happen. / Next month we're looking after my niece and nephew while their parents go away for a short break. We asked them to come and make sure everything was OK. We got a few surprises. We started in the spare bedroom, where the children will sleep. Everybody knows you shouldn't put children's beds under a window in case a child tries to climb out. Everybody except us! Next was the bathroom. We keep our medicines on a shelf above the washbasin. A terrible idea, as my sister explained. Never leave medicines somewhere children can find them. They might think they are sweets. Finally, the kitchen. This is the most dangerous room in the house. Knives should be kept in drawers which children can't reach, and all cleaning liquids in high cupboards. So we have three weeks to make our house safe. It's not difficult…once you know how.

a Look at the three pictures. What do you think the child's parents should / shouldn't have done? Read the article and check.

b This article was originally written in six short paragraphs. Mark (/) where each new paragraph should begin.

c You're going to write an article for a school magazine about how to be safe if you go walking in the country or the mountains. Look at the **Useful language** expressions and make sure you know how to use them.

Useful language

Giving advice
Don't forget to…Remember to…
Make sure you ….
You should…
Never…

Reasons
…in case
…so (that)
…because it might…

PLAN the content in pairs or small groups.

1 Think of a good title, and one or two introductory sentences.

2 Write down a few tips, e.g what to take with you (see picture below for ideas). Then divide the tips into two or three groups and put them into a logical order.

WRITE 120–180 words. Use a neutral or informal style.

CHECK your article for mistakes (grammar , punctuation , and spelling).

4 What do you remember?

GRAMMAR

a Complete the second sentence so that it means the same as the first.

1 They escaped from the jungle because they found the river.
   They wouldn't have escaped from the jungle if they _____ _____ the river.

2 I'm sure you left your glasses in the restaurant.
   You _____ _____ left your glasses in the restaurant.

3 Why didn't you tell me it was your birthday?
   You _____ _____ _____ me it was your birthday!

4 I don't have much time so I can't go to dance classes.
   I would be able to go to dance classes if I
   _____ _____ _____.

5 I'm sure the backpackers haven't got lost. They know the area well.
   The backpackers _____ _____ _____ lost. They know the area well.

b Choose a, b, or c.

1 The sky's very dark. It _____ there's going to be a storm.
   a looks
   b looks like if
   c looks as if

2 What _____ do tonight, eat out or stay in?
   a would you rather
   b had you rather
   c do you rather

3 If I hadn't really liked the jacket, I _____ it.
   a wouldn't buy
   b hadn't bought
   c wouldn't have bought

4 What lovely material! It _____ silk.
   a feels
   b feels like
   c feels as if

5 Mark's very late. Do you think he _____ forgotten about the dinner?
   a can't have
   b could
   c might have

VOCABULARY

a Word groups. Underline the word that is different. Say why.

1	upset	disappointed	relieved	offended
2	amazed	astonished	surprised	anxious
3	palm	calf	wrist	nail
4	kidney	heart	liver	hip
5	nod	wave	clap	point

b Circle the right verb.

1 Please *remind / remember* the children to do their homework.
2 **A** I'm terribly sorry.
   B Don't worry. It doesn't *mind / matter*.
3 The robbers *stole / robbed* €50,000 from the bank.
4 If you know the answer, *raise / rise* your hand, don't shout.
5 Don't *argue / discuss* with your father about it! He doesn't listen.

c Complete with one word.

1 I was ___ the moon when I heard I'd passed the exam!
2 You look fed ___. Have you been waiting for a long time?
3 I really put my foot ___ it when I mentioned the war.
4 We set ___ on our journey just after dawn.
5 My car broke ___ on the motorway.

d Write the verbs for the definitions.

1 **ch**_____ to bite food into small pieces in your mouth
2 **y**_____ to open your mouth wide, when you are tired or bored
3 **sc**_____ to rub your skin with your nails
4 **f**_____ to make a serious, angry, or worried expression
5 **st**_____ to look at something / somebody for a long time

PRONUNCIATION

a Underline the word with a different sound.

1	miserable	realize	notice	rise
2	devastated	delighted	terrified	desperate
3	blow	homesick	frown	lonely
4	tongue	lungs	discuss	comb
5	anxious	shrug	chew	brush

b Underline the stressed syllable.

exhausted   prevent   expect   kidney   elbow

CAN YOU UNDERSTAND THIS TEXT?

a Complete the article with a sentence A–F. There is one sentence you don't need.

A The photographs are then put in a drawer and forgotten.

B At the flick of a switch, the manufacturers claim, a woman can lose as much as a dress size.

C 'But it did just enough to hide some of the evidence of a few too many good restaurant meals.'

D The only victim will be the truth.

E They don't seem to notice that the lost weight seems to have mysteriously returned since the holiday.

F 'It worked better than a four-week diet of raw vegetables.'

b Look at the highlighted words and phrases. Can you guess what they mean?

CAN YOU UNDERSTAND THESE PEOPLE?

a **4.28** Listen and circle the correct answer, a, b, or c.

1 What does the speaker think is the most important piece of advice to avoid being bitten by a snake?
  a What you wear.
  b Where you camp.
  c Where you walk.

2 What is the main reason why the pilot is talking?
  a To introduce himself.
  b To explain the safety procedures.
  c To talk about what will happen during the flight.

3 What does the man think has happened to John?
  a He might have had an accident.
  b He's forgotten.
  c He'll arrive later.

4 What *doesn't* the man want the woman to do?
  a Spend a lot of money on a dress.
  b Spend more time shopping.
  c Go shopping again the next day.

5 Who are the people in the painting?
  a A beautiful girl with a sick old man.
  b An ugly child with his grandfather.
  c A young boy with an old man.

b **4.29** You will hear an interview with two young people. Write C next to what Caroline says, B next to what Ben says, and N next to what neither of them says.

1 I didn't think people's English would be so good. ☐
2 I had my credit card stolen. ☐
3 I enjoyed the freedom of choosing my route. ☐
4 My friends and I didn't always agree about what to do. ☐
5 I slept in a tent. ☐

Slimline 'snaps' that help holidaymakers to stretch the truth

A British chain store, Comet, is selling a new digital camera which will take pictures of you – and make you look thinner. The HP Photosmart R727 contains a 'slimcam' function which 'squeezes' the object at the centre of the frame without distorting the background. ¹☐ And a man can develop, if not a flat stomach, then at least a more respectably proportioned figure for the holiday photograph album.

Comet believes that the photography of self-delusion will become hugely popular in the future. In a culture obsessed with unrealistic ideas of the perfect body, the answer seems to be to show your friends holiday photographs in which you look healthily slim. ²☐

'Like many women in Britain, I am a size 16 and sometimes my holiday photos are not as flattering as I would like,' said Sally Cranham, 24, a professional singer from Reigate, who tried out the camera. 'The slimming button certainly trimmed off a bit where it counts,' she said. ³☐

People nowadays are very used to the doctored images of celebrity magazines, and some users of the camera might worry that the truth of their 'slimcam' photography would emerge when friends flicked through the holiday snaps. But Ms Cranham is convinced that her friends won't realize. 'If the camera had made me look like a size 8, then no one would believe it,' she said. ⁴☐

A spokeswoman for Comet said that it brought technology that usually favoured only the rich and famous within the grasp of ordinary people. ⁵☐

From The Times

CAN YOU SAY THIS IN ENGLISH?

Can you…?

☐ talk about what you would do and what you would have done in certain situations

☐ speculate about someone's past actions using *may / must / can't have*, and criticize how someone acted in the past using *should have*

☐ talk about why body language is important and explain what certain gestures indicate

5 A

G gerunds and infinitives
V music
P ch and y

The psychology of music

1 LISTENING & SPEAKING

a **5.1** Listen to some short pieces of music. How do they make you feel? Would you like to carry on listening?

> **Taking notes**
>
> We often need to take notes when we are listening, for example, to somebody giving a lecture. If you need to take notes when you are listening to someone speaking in English, try to write down key words or phrases because you won't have time to write complete sentences. After the lecture you may want to expand your notes into full sentences.

b **5.2** Listen to John Sloboda, a music psychologist, talking about why we listen to music. Try to complete the notes below by writing key words or phrases. Then with a partner try to remember as much as you can of what he said.

Why do we listen to music?

1 to make us...

e.g.

2 to help us...

e.g.

3 to intensify...

e.g.

c **5.3** Now listen to John explaining how music can affect the way we feel. Complete the notes below. Then compare with a partner and try to remember what he said.

How does music affect our emotions?

Three important human emotions

1 happiness

2

3

How we feel affects the way we speak, e.g.

1 happy – speak faster / higher

2

3

Music copies this, e.g.

1 fast / high music sounds happy

2

3

Examples

Music that sounds

1 happy, e.g.

2 angry, e.g.

3 sad, e.g.

This is especially exploited in...

e.g.

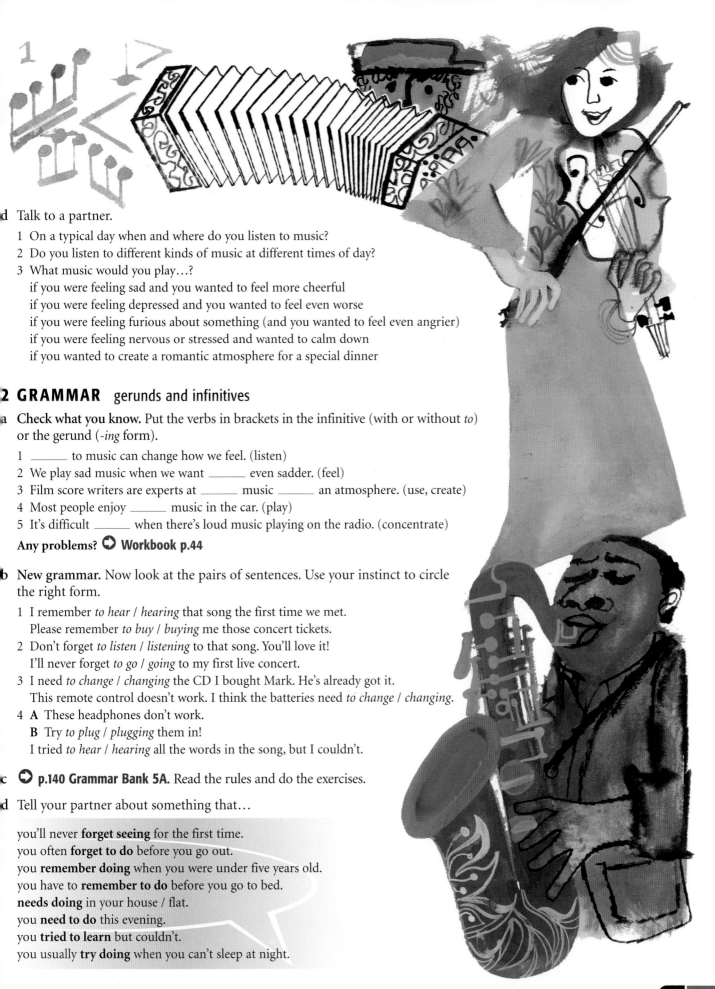

d Talk to a partner.

1 On a typical day when and where do you listen to music?
2 Do you listen to different kinds of music at different times of day?
3 What music would you play…?

if you were feeling sad and you wanted to feel more cheerful
if you were feeling depressed and you wanted to feel even worse
if you were feeling furious about something (and you wanted to feel even angrier)
if you were feeling nervous or stressed and wanted to calm down
if you wanted to create a romantic atmosphere for a special dinner

2 GRAMMAR gerunds and infinitives

a Check what you know. Put the verbs in brackets in the infinitive (with or without *to*) or the gerund (*-ing* form).

1 _____ to music can change how we feel. (listen)
2 We play sad music when we want _____ even sadder. (feel)
3 Film score writers are experts at _____ music _____ an atmosphere. (use, create)
4 Most people enjoy _____ music in the car. (play)
5 It's difficult _____ when there's loud music playing on the radio. (concentrate)

Any problems? ⊙ **Workbook p.44**

b New grammar. Now look at the pairs of sentences. Use your instinct to circle the right form.

1 I remember *to hear* / *hearing* that song the first time we met.
  Please remember *to buy* / *buying* me those concert tickets.
2 Don't forget *to listen* / *listening* to that song. You'll love it!
  I'll never forget *to go* / *going* to my first live concert.
3 I need *to change* / *changing* the CD I bought Mark. He's already got it.
  This remote control doesn't work. I think the batteries need *to change* / *changing*.
4 **A** These headphones don't work.
  B Try *to plug* / *plugging* them in!
  I tried *to hear* / *hearing* all the words in the song, but I couldn't.

c ⊙ **p.140 Grammar Bank 5A.** Read the rules and do the exercises.

d Tell your partner about something that…

you'll never **forget seeing** for the first time.
you often **forget to do** before you go out.
you **remember doing** when you were under five years old.
you have to **remember to do** before you go to bed.
needs doing in your house / flat.
you **need to do** this evening.
you **tried to learn** but couldn't.
you usually **try doing** when you can't sleep at night.

3 VOCABULARY music

a **5.4** Listen and say what instruments you can hear.

b ➡ **p.153 Vocabulary Bank** *Music.*

c **5.5** Listen and say what you can hear, e.g. *a choir singing.*

d With a partner, think of…

- a song with a catchy chorus.
- a singer with a monotonous voice.
- a classical composer.
- a kind of music which has a very strong beat.
- a song or piece of music you find very moving.
- a famous singer-songwriter.
- the lead singer of a well-known band.
- a world-famous tenor.
- a song which has incomprehensible lyrics.

4 PRONUNCIATION *ch* and *y*

a Use your instinct to put these words in the right columns:
character, *chef*, *research.*

🕯	🔑 k	∫

b Read the rules below and check your answers.

The letters *ch*
- are usually pronounced /tʃ/, e.g. *church.*
- are sometimes pronounced /k/, especially in words of Greek origin, e.g. *chemistry, Christmas.*
- are very occasionally pronounced /ʃ/, especially in words of French origin, e.g. *chauffeur, chef.*

c Use the rules to put some more words in each column.

change cheerful choir choose chorus
machine moustache orchestra psychologist

d **5.6** Listen and check.

e Now read the rules for the letter *y*. Then use them to put the words in the right columns.

The letter *y*
1 in the middle of a word…
- is usually pronounced /ɪ/ when it is between consonants, e.g. *symptoms, physics.*
- is pronounced /aɪ/ when *y* is followed by a consonant + *e*, e.g. *byte*, or in the prefix *psych-*, e.g. *psychoanalyst.*
2 at the end of a word…
- is pronounced /aɪ/ in words ending *-ify*, e.g. *terrify*, and words where the stress is on the last syllable, e.g. *deny*, and in one-syllable words, e.g. *fly.*
- is pronounced /i/, (a sound between /ɪ/ and /iː/)in all other words ending in *y*, e.g. *melody, windy*, etc.

apply country heavy lifestyle lyrics physical psychiatrist
qualify rhythm shy symphony try type typical

🚲	🐟	/i/

f **5.7** Listen and check.

5 SPEAKING

GET IT RIGHT *the*

Don't use *the* when you are talking in general about kinds of music, e.g. *I love classical music* NOT ~~the classical music~~.
Use *the* when you are talking about instruments, e.g. *I play the violin, the guitar*, etc.

Answer the questions with a partner.

What kind of music do you like?

Do you have a favourite…?
band solo artist
song (or album track) composer piece of music
(symphony, sonata, etc.) soloist conductor

Do you play a musical instrument?

YES
- Have you had lessons?
- Can you read music?
- Have you ever played in a band / orchestra?

NO
- Have you ever tried to learn to play an instrument?
- Is there an instrument you would like to learn to play?

What do you think of…?
alternative music classical music
country music dance music folk music funk
gangsta rap hip hop jazz opera
heavy metal pop music rock music
soul music

Have you ever…?
- sung in a choir
- been in a talent contest
- performed in front of a lot of people

What's the best live concert you've ever been to?

6 READING

a Do you think *What kind of music do you like?* is a good question when you are getting to know somebody? Why?

b Read the introduction to the article. Do you agree with the psychologists?

c Read the rest of the article. Which category(ies) do you fit into best?

What's your soundtrack?

Your taste in music can reveal a lot about you...

The question 'What kind of music do you like?' is very revealing. It is the number one topic of conversation among young adults who are getting to know each other, according to psychologists from the universities of Cambridge and Texas. Their research has shown that knowing another person's musical tastes can provide remarkably accurate personality predictions. For most people, music is a very important part of their lives and psychologists believe that their preferences reveal information about their character and their lifestyle. They think that personality clues are conveyed in the music's tempo, rhythm, and lyrics.

A Upbeat and simple music

Fans of 'Top 40' pop, country, and soundtrack music tend to be more conventional and conservative compared with fans of other genres; family and discipline are important life values. They are also typically cheerful, outgoing, and sociable kinds of people who enjoy helping people. In their free time they often enjoy doing or watching sport. They also enjoy watching major Hollywood films, especially comedies. According to the psychologists, 'People who like country and pop try to avoid making their lives unnecessarily complex.'

B Energetic and rhythmic music

Hip hop, funk, rap, soul, dance, and electronic music attracts people who are talkative, extrovert, and romantic and who tend to express their thoughts impulsively. They are the kind of people who love going to parties and for whom friendship and social recognition is very important. They tend to see themselves as physically attractive. When they go to the cinema, they typically enjoy watching action films, science fiction, gangster films, or comedies.

C Complex and reflective music

Fans of classical, jazz, and other 'complex' music typically have above-average intelligence. They tend to be creative and open to new experiences and lovers of classic or foreign films. Regarding lifestyle, fans of this kind of music tend to be politically liberal, are usually quite sophisticated, and often don't like sport. However, compared with other music fans, opera lovers are three times more likely to commit suicide, psychologists say. But don't blame *Madame Butterfly* – people with dramatic personalities, whose moods go up and down a lot, are attracted to opera, not influenced by it.

D Intense and rebellious music

Fans of alternative, heavy metal, rock music, and gangsta rap tend to be people who enjoy taking risks and having thrilling experiences. They are usually physically active. They are typically independent, curious about the world, and rebellious. They're the kind of people who are likely to enjoy watching action films, fantasy, war, and horror movies. Parents often worry that this kind of music promotes aggressive behaviour in teenagers, but research has found no direct link. In fact, younger fans of gangsta rap or heavy metal are often quieter and shyer than other young people.

d According to the article, what kind of music would these people like best? Write A, B, C, or D.

1 Someone who is quite vain. ☐
2 Somebody who enjoys doing dangerous sports. ☐
3 A person who speaks their mind without thinking. ☐
4 Someone who watches subtitled films. ☐
5 A person who does voluntary work in the community. ☐
6 Somebody who enjoys the simple things in life. ☐
7 A person who might have been quiet as a child. ☐
8 Someone who is intellectual. ☐

e Read the article again and <u>underline</u> five new words or phrases that you would like to learn, and compare with a partner.

f Think about people you know who like each kind of music. Do you agree with what the article says about their personalities?

5B
G used to, be used to, get used to
V sleep
P linking words

Counting sheep

Are you sleep deprived?

1 GRAMMAR   used to, be used to, get used to

a Take turns to interview each other with the questionnaire, *Are you sleep deprived?* Ask for and give as much information as you can. Circle the answer that best describes your partner.

b **◯ Communication** *Sleep p.118.* Read the results of the questionnaire. Are you sleep deprived?

c Match the sentence beginnings 1–4 with endings A–D.
1 *I usually* sleep 6 hours a night, ☐
2 *I used to* sleep 7 hours a night, ☐
3 *I'm not used to* only sleeping 4 or 5 hours a night, ☐
4 *I'm getting used to* only sleeping 4 or 5 hours a night, ☐

A but now I sleep less.
B so it's new and strange for me.
C so it's becoming less of a problem.
D or more if I can.

d **◯ p.140 Grammar Bank 5B.** Read the rules and do the exercises.

2 PRONUNCIATION   linking words

a **5.8** **Dictation.** Listen and write down six sentences. Try to separate the words in your head before you write.

b Practise saying the sentences quickly, trying to link the words.

c Ask and answer the questions with a partner.

When you were a child did you use to be frightened of the dark?
Did you use to share a room with a brother or sister?
Do you find it difficult to sleep when you're in a bed that you're not used to, for example, in a hotel?
Do you think you could get used to working at night and sleeping during the day?
What do you usually do as soon as you wake up in the morning?
What's the last thing you usually do before going to bed?

Answer these questions and find out.

1 **How long does it usually take you to fall asleep at night?**
a less than 5 minutes   b more than 5 minutes

2 **How many hours do you usually sleep?**
a fewer than 7   b 7–8   c more than 8

3 **Did you use to sleep…?**
a more than now   b the same amount   c less than now

4 **How do you feel about the amount you sleep?**
a I'm quite happy with it.
b I probably don't sleep enough, but I'm used to it. It's not a problem.
c I definitely need to sleep more. I usually feel tired.

5 **If you don't sleep enough at night during the week, what do you do**
a I take short naps during the day.
b I sleep late at the weekend.
c I don't do anything. You get used to not sleeping enough.
d I just get more and more tired.

6 **How do you usually feel during the morning?**
a Wide awake and energetic.
b Awake and able to concentrate, but not at my best.
c Half asleep and unable to concentrate well.

7 **How often do you have a nap on a weekday?**
a Never. I don't need one.
b Always. It's the only way I can get through the day.
c When I need one. I always wake up refreshed.
d I'd love to, but I never get the chance.

8 **Do you ever find it difficult to keep awake…?**
(Circle all the ones which apply to you.)
a at work or in class
b on the sofa in the evening
c in the cinema
d when you are driving

Tiredness can kill Take a break AA

3 READING & SPEAKING

a Read the first paragraph of the article. What exactly is the test and what does it show? What does the last sentence mean?

b Work in pairs. A read *So much to do, so little time* and *Going against nature*. B read *Sleepy people* and *SLEEP TIPS*. Then tick (✔) the questions which are answered in your paragraphs.

1 How did the invention of electric light change our sleep habits? ☐

2 Why is it probably better to have an operation during the day than at night? ☐

3 Are naps really useful? ☐

4 How much does the average person sleep? Does it vary according to profession? ☐

5 Why should politicians sleep more? ☐

6 What is our 'sleep debt'? ☐

7 What is the world's most popular drug? ☐

8 What's the difference between driving when you are drunk and when you are very tired? ☐

9 Do people sleep more or less than they used to? Why? ☐

10 What should your bedroom *not* be if you want to sleep well? ☐

11 How did lack of sleep cause the Chernobyl nuclear disaster? ☐

12 How much sleep does the average person need? ☐

c Read your two paragraphs again so you can answer the questions in **b**.

d In pairs, explain your answers giving as much information as you can.

e Now read the parts of the article that you didn't read, to see if your partner left anything out.

f In pairs, or small groups, discuss these questions.

1 Do you agree with Paul Martin that we live in a sleep deprived society?

2 Do you think it's wrong that doctors who are on 'night call' sleep so little?

3 Do you think it should be illegal to drive when you are too tired?

4 What do you think are the best three SLEEP TIPS?

Sleepy people – the dangers of sleep deprivation

Do this test tonight when you go to bed. Put a plate on the floor next to your bed. Lie down with one hand hanging over the bed holding a spoon above the plate. When you fall asleep, the spoon will fall on the plate and should wake you up. If you don't wake up until the next day, it probably means you are 'sleep deprived'.

We live in a world of tired, sleep deprived people. This is the theory of behavioural biologist, Paul Martin. In his book *Counting Sheep*, he describes a society which is just too busy to sleep and which does not give sleeping the importance it deserves. We all know the importance of having a healthy diet and doing exercise, but we don't worry enough about sleeping the hours we need. Paul Martin says: 'We might live longer and happier lives if we took our beds as seriously as our running shoes.'

So much to do, so little time

Modern society has invented reasons not to sleep. We are now a 24 / 7 society where shops and services must be available all hours. We spend longer at work than we used to, and more time getting to work. Mobile phones and email allow us to stay in touch round the clock and late-night TV and the Internet tempt us away from our beds. When we need more time for work or pleasure, the easy solution is to sleep less. The average adult sleeps only 6.2 hours a night during the week, whereas research shows that most people need eight or even eight and a half hours' sleep to feel at their best. Nowadays many people have got used to sleeping less than they need and they live in an almost permanent state of 'sleep debt', owing their bodies perhaps 25–30 hours of sleep.

Hours slept a night	
Lawyers	7.8
Architects	7.5
Social workers	6.9
Teachers	6
Politicians	5.2
Hospital doctors (on call)	4.5

UK Sleep Council survey

Going against nature

Until the invention of electric light in 1879 our daily cycle of sleep used to depend on the hours of daylight. People would get up with the sun and go to bed at nightfall. But nowadays our hours of sleep are mainly determined by our working hours (or our social life) and most people are woken up artificially by an alarm clock. During the day caffeine, the world's most popular drug, helps to keep us awake. 75% of the world's population habitually consume caffeine which, up to a point, masks the symptoms of sleep deprivation.

Sleepy people

What does a chronic lack of sleep do to us? As well as making us irritable and unhappy as people it also reduces our motivation and ability to work. This has serious implications for society in general. Doctors, for example, are often chronically sleep deprived, especially when they are on 'night call' and may get less than three hours' sleep. Lack of sleep can seriously impair their mood, judgement, and ability to take decisions. Our politicians are often 'jet-lagged' after crossing time zones. World summit meetings called to deal with a crisis often result in decisions being taken after marathon sessions when everyone is severely sleep deprived. Human error caused by tiredness contributed to the worst nuclear accident in history at Chernobyl in 1986. Tired engineers, in the early hours of the morning, made a series of mistakes with catastrophic results. On our roads and motorways lack of sleep kills thousands of people every year. Tests show that a tired driver can be just as dangerous as a drunk driver. However, driving when drunk is against the law but driving when exhausted isn't. As Paul Martin says, it is very ironic that we admire people who function on very little sleep instead of criticizing them for being irresponsible. Our world would be a much safer, happier place if everyone, whatever their job, slept eight hours a night.

SLEEP TIPS

1 Give sleep a high priority in your life.
2 Listen to your body. If you feel tired, you probably need more sleep.
3 Pay off your 'sleep debt' by going to bed half an hour earlier for a few weeks.
4 Have a regular routine – try to go to bed at roughly the same time every day.
5 Take a nap during the day (ideally after lunch). Research has shown that short naps are very effective in restoring our energy levels and mood.
6 Make sure your bedroom isn't too hot.
7 Don't use your bedroom as an office or for watching TV.

5B 73

4 VOCABULARY sleep

alarm blankets dreams duvet fall keep you awake insomnia jet-lagged log nap nightmares oversleep pillow set sheets siesta sleeping tablets sleepy snore yawn

a **Vocabulary race.** In pairs, write the correct word in the column on the right.

1   Most people start feeling _____ around 11.00 at night.   _sleepy_
2   They often open their mouth and _____.   _____
3   They go to bed and _____ their _____ clock.   _____, _____
4   They get into bed and put their head on the _____.   _____
5   They cover themselves up with a _____, or with _____ and _____.   _____, _____, _____
6   Soon they _____ asleep.   _____
7   Some people make a loud noise when they breathe. They _____.   _____
8   During the night people have _____ or _____.   _____, _____
9   If you don't hear your alarm in the morning, you might _____.   _____
10 If you drink coffee in the evening, it might _____.   _____ _____ _____
11 Some people can't sleep because they suffer from _____.   _____
12 These people often have to take _____ _____.   _____
13 Some people have a _____ or _____ after lunch.   _____, _____
14 A person who sleeps well 'sleeps like a _____'.   _____.
15 Someone who is tired after flying to another time zone is _____-_____.   _____-_____

b **5.9** Listen to the sentences and check.

c Cover the column of words and test yourself.

5 SPEAKING

Answer the questions in pairs.
Ask for more information.

Do you sometimes have problems getting to sleep? What do you do?

Have you ever overslept and missed something important?

Have you ever stayed up all night?

Is there any food or drink that keeps you awake, or that stops you from sleeping well?

Are you a light sleeper or do you sleep like a log?

Do you take or have you ever taken sleeping pills? Did they work?

Have you ever been jet-lagged? Where were you going? How long did it take you to recover?

Have you ever fallen asleep at an embarrassing moment, for example during a class?

Have you ever sleepwalked or do you know anyone who sleepwalks?

Do you often have nightmares or recurring dreams?

Do you sleep with a duvet or blankets? How many pillows do you like to have?

Do you remember a time or place where you slept very badly? Why?

Do you snore? Have you ever had to share a room with someone who snores? Was this a problem?

6 LISTENING

a Look at the photo and the headline. Why do you think the girl was asleep on the crane? How did she get there?

b **5.10** Listen to the first part of a radio news programme and check your answers. What happened next?

c Read a newspaper article about the same incident. The article got eight details wrong. Listen to the news programme again and correct the mistakes.

15-year-old girl found asleep on crane

Yesterday a 15-year-old girl was discovered lying on top of a 30-metre-high crane. A passer-by saw her when he was walking past a building site in Dulwich, south-west London, and immediately called the fire brigade. The police and fire brigade arrived at 1.30 in the morning. At first they thought the girl was suicidal but when a fireman climbed up the crane he realized she was drunk. The fireman crawled along the arm of the crane and carefully put a safety harness on the girl. Then the girl used her mobile phone to call her parents, who came quickly to the building site. The rescue took two hours and the girl was brought safely down from the crane on a ladder.

After talking to her parents, the police discovered that the girl had been sleepwalking. She had left her house during the night, and had been able to get into the building site because the security guard was asleep. Her parents said that it wasn't the first time that she had sleepwalked, and that she had left the house on several other occasions.

d You are going to listen to the second half of the programme. Before you listen, work with a partner and discuss if you think the information in sentences 1–10 is T (true) or F (false).

1 A sleepwalker can drive a car while he is asleep. ☐
2 It is easy to know if someone is sleepwalking or not. ☐
3 Sleepwalking is quite uncommon. ☐
4 Sleepwalking is most common among young boys. ☐
5 Stress can cause people to sleepwalk. ☐
6 You should never wake up a sleepwalker. ☐
7 A sleepwalker cannot hurt himself. ☐
8 People usually sleepwalk for a short time. ☐
9 Sleepwalkers don't remember anything afterwards. ☐
10 Sleepwalking is no excuse if you have committed a crime. ☐

e **5.11** Listen once to check your answers. Then listen again and correct the false statements.

7 **5.12** SONG ♫ *I don't want to miss a thing*

5C

G reporting verbs; *as*
V the media
P word stress

Breaking news

1 GRAMMAR reporting verbs

a Read the headline of this news story. What do you think it's about? Then read the story. What do you think of Mr Ivanov?

Man leaves wife at petrol station

A Macedonian man drove six hours across Italy at the start of his holiday before he noticed that he had forgotten something – his wife. Ljubomir Ivanov left her at a petrol station when he stopped to fill up with petrol, and didn't realize his mistake until he got a call from the police on his mobile phone.

'Are you Ljubomir Ivanov?' they asked.

'Yes, I am,' he said. 'What's the matter?'

'Where are you?'

'I'm in Germany.'

'Well your wife is waiting for you at a petrol station near Pesaro in central Italy.'

'I was very tired and not thinking,' Ivanov told reporters later. 'She usually sits in the back seat so I didn't notice that she wasn't there.'

Mr Ivanov immediately drove back to Pesaro to pick up his wife so that they could continue their holiday.

'I'll have to apologize a lot when I see her,' he said.

b **Check what you know.** Re-read the conversation between the policeman and Ivanov. Then complete the sentences in reported speech.

1 The police asked the man __*if*__ _____ _____ Ljubomir Ivanov and he said that _____ _____
2 Then they asked him _____ _____ _____ and he told _____ that _____ _____ in Germany.
3 He later told police that he _____ _____ that his wife wasn't there because she usually sat in the back seat.
4 He said that he _____ _____ to apologize a lot when he saw her.

Any problems? ➡ Workbook p.50

c **New grammar.** Read four more news stories. Three of them are true but one has been invented. Which do think is the invented one?

No, you can't have your ball back!

A football team <u>have threatened to sue a neighbour</u> because he refused to give back their balls. Appledore FC have kicked 18 balls over Paul Vose's garden wall, and they are now all locked inside his shed. Gary Ford, the coach of the team, says: 'His garden is eight metres from the back of the goal. Some balls are bound to go over the wall.' But Vose says, 'They should learn to shoot better.'

sue take somebody to court, usually to get money from them
shed a small building in a garden where people keep e.g. tools
bound to certain to, very likely to
shoot kick a ball towards the goal

Locked out of her life

When Andy Barker from Huddersfield forgot his wife's birthday for the third year running she decided she had had enough and locked him out of the house. Sue Barker had reminded her husband several times to book a table for a romantic meal, and she was hoping for a nice present too. Andy promised not to forget, but when the day came, it went right out of his mind. He was working late and when he got home the door was locked and a suitcase with his things in it was on the doorstep. Since then Andy has been living in a tent in the garden. He says, 'I'm hoping that if I stay here for a few days, she will forgive me.'

Back to school for red-faced council

Local council officials have apologized for misspelling the word 'grammar' on a new road sign outside a school in Stockton in north-east England. Council workers had to come back to take down the sign, which should have said 'Grammar School Road.' Children at the school (aged between four and eleven) immediately noticed that the sign said 'Grammer School' and told their teacher. A spokesman for Stockton council blamed the manufacturers for making the mistake. 'Our order for the sign was correct, but the manufacturers got it wrong. They have offered to make us a new sign free of charge.' Teacher, Mrs Taylor said: 'If they want someone to check the spelling, I'm sure the children can help!'

Builder mistaken for jumper

A German builder is expecting a big bill after emergency services mistook him for a potential suicide jumper. When police saw the man on the roof of a five-floor building, they closed off a busy main road and called the fire brigade. They then asked negotiators to talk to Dieter Holmblutter. The negotiators tried to convince him not to jump by shouting to him. But the builder was so busy talking on the phone to his girlfriend that he didn't realize what was happening below, until she asked him what the sirens were for. A police spokesman said that Dieter would be given a bill for wasting police time.

> **sirens** the noise made by a police car, fire engine, etc.

---

d Read the stories again and match sentences A–I with the people who said them. Then <u>underline</u> the words in the text where these ideas are reported.

1 The football team $\boxed{G}$
2 The angry neighbour   ☐
3 Sue Barker   ☐
4 Andy Barker   ☐
5 Stockton council officials   ☐
6 A spokesman for Stockton council   ☐
7 The sign manufacturers   ☐
8 The police   ☐
9 The negotiators   ☐

A 'Don't jump! It's not worth it.'
B 'I'm not going to give them back.'
C 'Please talk to this man.'
D 'It was their fault.'
E 'We'll make you a new one for free.'
F 'Don't forget to phone the restaurant.'
G 'We're going to take you to court!'
H 'We're terribly sorry. We spelt it wrong.'
I 'I'll remember this time. I really will.'

e ● **p.140 Grammar Bank 5C.** Read the rules and do the exercises.

2 PRONUNCIATION word stress

a Look at all the two-syllable reporting verbs in the list. All except three are stressed on the second syllable. Circle the three exceptions.

accuse	admit	advise	agree	convince	deny	insist	invite
offer	persuade	promise	refuse	regret	remind	suggest	threaten

b **5.13** Listen and check.

> If a two-syllable verb ends in consonant–vowel–consonant, and is stressed on the **second** syllable, the final consonant is doubled before an -ed ending, e.g. regret > regretted, admit > admitted.

c Complete the sentences below with the right reporting verb in the past simple. Practise saying the reported sentences.

1 'You sit down. I'll do it.'   He _offered_ to do it.
2 'No, I won't do it.'   He _____ to do it.
3 'OK, I'll do it.'   He _____ to do it.
4 'I'll do it, believe me.'   He _____ to do it.
5 'Don't forget to do it!'   He _____ me to do it.
6 'I think you should do it.'   He _____ me to do it.
7 'Would you like to do it?'   He _____ me to do it.
8 'I didn't do it!'   He _____ doing it.
9 'Yes, it was me. I did it.'   He _____ doing it.
10 'I wish I hadn't done it.'   He _____ doing it.
11 'Let's do it.'   He _____ doing it.
12 'You did it!'   He _____ him of doing it.

d **5.14** Now listen to the sentences in a different order. Respond with the reported sentence.

3 VOCABULARY the media

> **news** *noun* [u].
> 1 new information about anything, information previously unknown
> 2 reports of recent happenings, especially those broadcast, printed in the newspaper, etc.
> 3 **the news** a regular television or radio broadcast of the latest news

a Look at the dictionary extract for the word *news*. Then correct the mistakes in sentences 1–3.
  1 The news on TV are always depressing.
  2 I have a really exciting news for you!
  3 It's 9.00. Let's watch news.

b ○ p.154 Vocabulary Bank *The media.*

c Talk in small groups.

The media and you

What kind of news stories do you find most / least interesting? Write 1–6 (1 = most interesting).
  • celebrity gossip ☐
  • politics ☐
  • sport ☐
  • science /technology ☐
  • business ☐
  • health ☐

What stories are in the news at the moment?

How do you normally find out…?
  • what the weather's going to be like
  • the sports results
  • what's on at the cinema
  • the news headlines

Do you ever…? Where?
  • read your horoscope
  • do crosswords, sudoku, or other games
  • look at cartoons
  • read advertisements, e.g. jobs, flats

Do you have a favourite…?
  • newsreader
  • film critic
  • journalist
  • sports writer or broadcaster

Which newspapers / TV channels / radio stations in your country do you think are…?
  • biased
  • reliable
  • sensational

4 READING & LISTENING

a With a partner discuss what you think would be the good side and bad side of being a theatre critic and a sports writer.

b Now read the articles by two journalists who write for *The Times* newspaper and see if your ideas are there.

Irving Wardle, theatre critic

The positive side of the job is [1]_____ getting to see a lot of plays and shows which I love. But the really great thing about being a theatre critic is that, as theatre is an ongoing thing, something that's going to be repeated night after night for some time, there's also the feeling that you may have a [2]_____ impact on the work. If the producer or the actors read what you've written and agree with you, they might actually change something and improve the performance. That's not something that film or book critics can do. Some critics also like making friends with the stars and all that – but personally I don't.

For me the worst part of the job is all the travelling. Getting there on time, parking, getting back to the office to write for a nightly deadline. That all gets really stressful. Another awful thing is that editors [3]_____ bits from your review without you knowing. You learn as a critic that if you've got anything [4]_____, say it straight away because it might not get printed. I once wrote a review of a play by Julian Mitchell called *Another Country*. I didn't like it much, but there was a new young actor who I thought was great, called Kenneth Branagh. That was in the last paragraph and it got cut, so it looked as if I'd never [5]_____ this great new talent.

c Read the two articles again. Choose the best option a, b, or c.

	a	b	c
1	apparently	gradually	obviously
2	positive	harmful	negative
3	change	add	cut
4	to complain about	that isn't important	worth saying
5	noticed	spoken to	criticized
6	permission	opportunity	wish
7	more exciting	harder	easier
8	holidays	routine	unpredictability
9	drop	throw	lose
10	monotonous	exciting	frightening

Pat Gibson, sports journalist

The plus sides – I must have seen some of the most spectacular moments in cricket and football over the past forty years. I've also had the ⁶_____ to travel to places I wouldn't have seen otherwise, like India, Australia, New Zealand, the Caribbean, South Africa and Fiji. There are much ⁷_____ ways to make a living and it's great to get away from Britain as much as you can during the winter.

One of the main downsides is the ⁸_____. You don't work regular hours – you can spend a couple of days not working, but you never relax because you're waiting for the phone to ring. And then, when a story breaks – it might be on your day off, it might be in the middle of the night – you just have to ⁹_____ everything and go. And you never know what time you're going to be home. Another thing is the constant travelling. It's been fantastic visiting the Taj Mahal or spending Christmas Day on the beach in Australia, but it does get lonely and it can also be very ¹⁰_____. I've spent a large proportion of the last forty years driving up and down the motorways of Britain, which I can assure you isn't much fun.

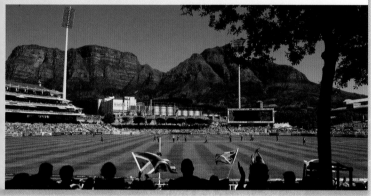

d You're going to listen to Alice, a freelance restaurant critic, and Tim, a war reporter, talking about the good and bad sides of their jobs. Before you listen, predict some of the things they might say.

e ⟨5.15⟩ ⟨5.16⟩ Listen and check. Then listen again and mark the sentences T (true) or F (false). Correct the false sentences.

The restaurant critic
1 She sometimes reviews restaurants in other countries.
2 She never orders the most expensive things on the menu.
3 She often misses having company when she's eating out.
4 She used to be slimmer than she is now.
5 She goes back to restaurants she has criticized.
6 She never feels like eating out at weekends.

The war reporter
1 Most war reporters would prefer regular hours.
2 They choose the job partly because it's dangerous.
3 The job can be quite lonely.
4 He has problems getting used to normal life when he comes home.
5 Being a war reporter is more dangerous than it used to be.
6 One of his best friends was kidnapped last year.

f From what you've read and heard, which person's job would you most like to have? Which one would you least like to have?

5 SPEAKING

a You are going to debate the following topic in small groups.

> Celebrities have to accept that the media publishes stories about their private lives. That is the price they pay for being rich and famous.

- Divide into groups of four, two As and two Bs.
- The As are going to defend the right of newspapers to publish stories about famous people's private lives.
- The Bs are going to defend the celebrities' right to keep their private lives private.
- Prepare at least four arguments, and give examples.

b Hold the debate. The As begin, each making two of their points. The Bs take notes. Then the Bs speak and the As take notes.

c Now, each side try to argue against the points made by the other side.

MINI GRAMMAR *as*

It's great to get away from Britain as much as you can during the winter.

I work as part of a team.

We can use *as* in many different ways:

1 to give a reason: *As it was raining, we didn't go out.* (*as* = because)
2 to compare people or things: *She's as tall as me.*
3 to describe somebody or something's job or function: *She works as a nurse. We had to use a handkerchief as a bandage.*
4 to say that something happened while something else was happening: *As they were leaving the postman arrived.* (*as* = when)

Decide how *as* is used in each sentence and write 1–4 in the box.

A The review in *The Times* wasn't as good as the one in *The Guardian*. ☐
B You can use that glass as a vase for the flowers. ☐
C I got to the airport really quickly as there was hardly any traffic. ☐
D As he was driving home it started to rain. ☐
E My son's hair got darker as he got older. ☐
F He got a job with the BBC as a programme researcher. ☐

↪ *Phrasal verbs in context p.157.*

THE INTERVIEW

a You are going to listen to an interview with Sir Nicholas Kenyon, who was the director of a festival of concerts called the Proms for twelve years. Before you listen, read the glossary and look at how the words are pronounced to help you understand what he says.

Glossary

impresario /ˌɪmprəˈsɑːriəʊ/ a person who arranges plays or concerts

the Queen's Hall /kwiːnz hɔːl/ a concert hall in London where the Proms were first held. It was bombed during the war so they moved to the Royal Albert Hall.

season tickets /ˈsiːzən ˈtɪkɪts/ tickets that are for many concerts and are cheaper than buying individual tickets

Faure a famous French composer 1845–1924

requiem /ˈrekwiem/ a piece of music composed for a person who has recently died

Sir Georg Solti A famous Hungarian conductor 1912–1997

Verdi a famous Italian composer 1813–1901

fanfare a short loud piece of music played to celebrate something important

The Rite of Spring a famous piece by the Russian composer Stravinsky

a bassoon /bəˈsuːn/ a wind instrument

Simon Rattle a famous British conductor currently musical director of the Berlin Philharmonic orchestra

the stalls /stɔlz/ the seats in a theatre on the ground floor

Radio 4 one of the BBC radio channels

b **5.17** Listen to part 1. Answer the questions with a partner.

1 What did an impresario want to do in 1895?
2 What was his brilliant idea?
3 Why are the concerts called the Proms?
4 How long do the Proms last?
5 What do people have to do to get the best places in the floor of the hall?
6 What is special about the Proms' audiences?

c **5.18** Listen to part 2. Answer the questions with a partner.

What does he say about…?

1 Princess Diana's funeral
2 Sir Georg Solti and the Verdi Requiem
3 Colin Davies
4 *Short ride in a fast machine*
5 Simon Rattle and *The Rite of Spring*
6 a Radio 4 interview

d **5.19** Listen and complete the phrases. What do you think they mean?

COMMON PHRASES

1 The Promenade Concerts started _____ _____ in 1895. (informal)
2 …it basically means that people are able to _____ _____ and stand during the music.
3 Very few people attend actually all of them, _____ _____.
4 _____ _____ , we had programmed two or three requiems in that last two weeks of the season.
5 As it _____ _____ , he died just a week later. **pv**
6 Unfortunately, _____ _____ it could have been called absolutely anything….

e Listen to the interview again with the tapescript on page 128. Would you like to go to the Proms? Do you have any similar concerts in your country?

IN THE STREET

a **5.20** You're going to listen to five people talking about music festivals. Write the speaker's number next to the festival(s) they have been to.

Anne

Jordan

Mike

Ray

Harley

Bath blues festival ☐   Isle of Wight festival ☐
The Big Chill ☐   Reading music festival ☐
Glastonbury ☐   Rock festival in Ohio ☐

b Listen again. Which speaker…?

1 went to a festival with members of their family
2 doesn't know the name of the festival they went to
3 has very clear memories of the experience
4 went to a festival where there were a lot of people
5 didn't sleep at all

c **5.21** Listen and complete the phrases. What do you think they mean?

COMMON PHRASES

1 There were thousands and thousands of people just chilling _____ . (inform
2 You can just go and hang_____ and listen to some music. (informal)
3 I didn't _____ any sleep at all.
4 In the 1970s, early 80s I went to _____ a few .
5 … and had no _____ whose tent we were in the next morning.

d Listen to the interviews again with the tapescript on page 128. Then answer the same questions with a partner.

Study Link MultiROM

14 Hampden Crescent
Cheltenham
Gloucestershire
GL50 10VB

Head Office
Café Royale
7 Charlton Road
Milton Keynes
MK1 5GB

Dear Sir / Madam,

[1] *I am writing* to complain about a meal my family and I had in the Café Royale restaurant in Market Square last Saturday night.

We have eaten in this restaurant [2]_____ and the background music has always been very low and [3]_____. However, [4]_____ the music was terribly loud, almost deafening. When the waiter took our order, I asked him politely if he could turn the music down, which he did.

However, while we were eating our main course, the music was turned up again and we could hardly hear ourselves speak. This time I asked to see the manager. She spoke to us in [5]_____ and unfriendly manner. She told us that we were the only customers who had ever complained about the music and [6]_____ turn it down. We were so angry we decided to leave without having dessert or coffee.

I have eaten in other branches of Café Royale all over the country, but I [7]_____ unless I receive an explanation and apology for the [8]_____ we received.

[9]_____,

Joseph Clements

Joseph Clements

a Read the letter and answer the questions.
1 Who is the letter to?
2 Why is Joseph writing?
3 What does he hope to achieve?

b Complete the letter with the more formal of the two phrases.
1 I'm writing / I am writing
2 lots of times / on many occasions
3 pleasant / nice
4 on this particular evening / when we were there this time
5 a really rude / an extremely rude
6 said she wouldn't / refused to
7 will not do so again / won't go there again
8 unacceptable treatment / awful treatment
9 Best wishes / Yours faithfully

c Last week you had a bad experience in an expensive hotel. When you get home you decide to write a letter or email to complain. Look at the **Useful language** expressions and make sure you know how to use them.

> **Useful language**
> **Typical openings**
> Dear Sir / Madam,
> Dear Mr Waters,
> I am writing to complain about…
> I am writing to express my dissatisfaction with…
>
> **Typical endings**
> I look forward to hearing from you.
> Yours faithfully (when you begin Dear Sir / Madam)
> Yours sincerely (when you begin Dear Mr Waters)

PLAN the content.
1 Decide where you were staying and imagine what problems there might have been. What kind of problem would make you complain?
2 Decide what you would like the hotel to do.

WRITE 120–180 words, organized in three or four paragraphs (reason for writing, details of the problems, conclusion / request for action). Use a formal style (no contractions or colloquial expressions). Use the phrases in **b** and in **Useful language**.

CHECK your letter for mistakes (grammar , punctuation , and spelling).

GRAMMAR

a Complete the second sentence so that it means the same as the first.

1 After being in London for a year, I still find driving on the left difficult.
   After being in London for a year, I still can't get _____ _____ _____ on the left.

2 My hair was very long when I was a teenager.
   When I was a teenager I used _____ _____ long hair.
3 'I think you should talk to a lawyer,' he said to Sarah.
   He advised _____ _____ _____ to a lawyer.
4 'I didn't kill my husband' she said.
   She denied _____ _____ _____.
5 'I'm sorry I'm late,' James said.
   James _____ _____ _____ late.
6 My brother is a waiter in a French restaurant.
   My brother works _____ _____ _____ in a French restaurant.

b Put the **bold** verb in the gerund or infinitive.

1 I don't remember _____ you before.   **meet**
2 The car needs _____. Shall I take it to the car wash?   **clean**
3 He managed _____ to the airport on time.   **get**
4 You must try not _____ late again.   **be**

VOCABULARY

a Make nouns for people from the following words. Under<u>line</u> the stressed syllable.

1 conduct _____
2 violin _____
3 drums _____
4 edit _____
5 compose _____
6 journal _____
7 solo _____
8 report _____
9 present _____
10 commentate _____

b Complete the missing words.

1 Did you hear the **w**_____ **f**_____? It's going to rain.
2 Let's not see that film. It had an awful **r**_____ in the paper.
3 This paper always supports the government. It's very **b**_____.
4 His latest song is really **c**_____. Everybody's singing it.
5 I can remember the lyrics, but I can't remember the **t**_____.
6 The report was **c**_____. He wasn't allowed to say what he wanted to say.
7 Could I have an extra **p**_____ for my bed, please?
8 My husband says I **s**_____ really loudly when I'm asleep.
9 I didn't get much sleep last night so I'm going to have a **n**_____ after lunch.
10 He has terrible **i**_____. It takes him ages to get to sleep.

PRONUNCIATION

a <u>Underline</u> the word with a different sound.

1	whisper	whistle	whole	awake
2	choir	keyboard	click	convince
3	crossword	reporter	snore	yawn
4	accurate	advise	admit	agree
5 /juː/	refuse	review	news	cartoon

b <u>Underline</u> the stressed syllable.

guitarist   orchestra   biased   sensational   critic

CAN YOU UNDERSTAND THIS TEXT?

Read the article and choose a, b, or c.

1 a night	b dawn	c mid-day
2 a nothing	b medicine	c injections
3 a asleep	b ill	c well
4 a Because of	b According to	c Thanks to
5 a cooking	b buying	c taking care of
6 a so that	b however	c because
7 a appetite	b sleep	c sleeping tablets
8 a so	b even	c although

CAN YOU UNDERSTAND THESE PEOPLE?

a **5.22** You will hear five extracts from a news broadcast. Match each extract with what it is about (A–G). There are two topics you don't need.

A business ☐   E sport ☐
B crime ☐   F travel ☐
C show business ☐   G weather ☐
D health ☐

b **5.23** Listen to a music expert talking and answer a, b, or c.

1 Music can sound like noise to you if _____.
  a it is the first time you hear it
  b it is sung in a foreign language
  c you don't understand the rules

2 Modern classical music _____.
  a does not have rules
  b can sound like noise
  c is only experimental

3 A lot of young people _____.
  a have negative feelings about some kinds of music
  b only like noisy music
  c never go to classical concerts

4 They changed the music in the shopping mall because _____.
  a the young people complained
  b they knew teenagers wouldn't like it
  c they wanted to attract more customers

5 A lot of older people _____.
  a never listen to pop music
  b associate pop music with crime
  c don't like music with a beat

CAN YOU SAY THIS IN ENGLISH?

Can you…?

☐ describe the kind of music you listen to and how it makes you feel
☐ describe your sleep habits and any problems with sleeping you have
☐ talk about things you used to do and things you have got used to doing
☐ talk about where you get your news from and compare the different kinds of newspapers in your country

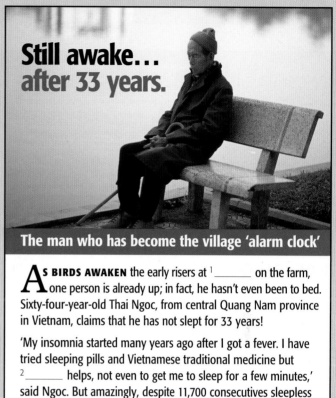

Still awake… after 33 years.

The man who has become the village 'alarm clock'

As BIRDS AWAKEN the early risers at [1] _____ on the farm, one person is already up; in fact, he hasn't even been to bed. Sixty-four-year-old Thai Ngoc, from central Quang Nam province in Vietnam, claims that he has not slept for 33 years!

'My insomnia started many years ago after I got a fever. I have tried sleeping pills and Vietnamese traditional medicine but [2] _____ helps, not even to get me to sleep for a few minutes,' said Ngoc. But amazingly, despite 11,700 consecutives sleepless nights since then, he has never once been [3] _____. 'Fortunately, the insomnia doesn't seem to have had a negative impact on my health. I still feel healthy and can farm normally like other men. I even carry two 50kg bags of fertilizer for 4km every day.' [4] _____ his wife, when Ngoc went for a medical check-up recently, his doctor said he was in perfect health except for a minor decline in liver function.

Ngoc lives with his six children on his farm at the foot of a mountain. He spends the day farming and [5] _____ his pigs and chickens, and at night he often does extra farm work or guards his farm to prevent theft. His neighbour Vu said that Ngoc volunteered to help beat a drum during the night and guard the house for the relatives of the dead during funeral ceremonies [6] _____ they could take a nap. Vu also said that when the villagers were planting sugar cane, several people asked Ngoc to be their 'alarm clock' and to wake them up early in the morning to go to work as he was up anyway.

Phan Ngoc Ha, director of the Hoa Khanh Mental Hospital in Danang, said that a chronic lack of [7] _____ often causes anorexia, lethargy, and irritability. But, in special cases, some extreme insomniacs can still live and work normally, [8] _____ this is a very small minority. Thai Ngoc is obviously one of them.

6 A

G articles
V collocation: word pairs
P sentence stress

Speaking to the world

One small word, one big difference in meaning

1 READING

a What do you know about the first moon landing? Answer the questions with a partner.

1 Who was the first man to set foot on the moon?
   a Yuri Gagarin   b Buzz Aldrin   c Neil Armstrong
2 When did he land on the moon?
   a In 1959.   b In 1969.   c In 1979.
3 What was the first thing he said when he landed?
   a 'Wow! It's so big!'
   b 'I'm floating in a most peculiar way.'
   c 'That's one small step for man, one giant leap for mankind.'

b Read the article and check. What controversy has there been since then about what Neil Armstrong actually said? Why is the missing 'a' so important?

c Read the article again. Then, in pairs, say why the following names and numbers are mentioned.

20th July 1969	*First Man*
6 hours and 40 minutes	James Hansen
500 million	Peter Shann Ford
Buzz Aldrin	

d Cover the article and try to complete the sentences making words from the words in **bold**. What do they mean?

1 Armstrong made the first human _footprint_ on the lunar surface. **foot**
2 His first words were 'That's one small step for man, one giant leap for _____.' **man**
3 It was the perfect quote for such a _____ occasion. **moment**
4 'One small step for *a* man' would have made it a more _____ sentence. **mean**
5 They were possibly the most _____ words in history. **memory**
6 Armstrong said the 'a' so quickly that it was _____ on the recording. **audio**

e **6.1** Listen to the original recording of Armstrong speaking. Can *you* hear the 'a'?

AS NEIL ARMSTRONG became the first man to walk on the Moon, a global audience of 500 million people were watching and listen 'That's one small step for man, one giant leap for mankind,' they he him say as he dropped from the ladder of his spacecraft to make th first human footprint on the lunar surface. It was the perfect quote f such a momentous occasion. But from the moment he said it, peopl have argued about whether the NASA astronaut got his lines wrong

Armstrong and Buzz Aldrin, who stepped outside a few seconds after hi landed the Apollo 11 spacecraft on the Moon on 20th July 1969. In the tense six hours and forty minutes between landing on the moon and stepping out of the capsule, Armstrong wrote what he knew would become some of the most memorable words in history.

Armstrong has always insisted that he wrote 'one small step for *a* mar one giant leap for mankind,' which would have been a more meaning and grammatically correct sentence. Without the missing 'a', the intenc meaning of the sentence is lost. In effect, the line means, 'That's one small step for mankind (i.e. humanity), one giant leap for mankind.'

But did he really say the sentence incorrectly? Until now Armstrong himself had never been sure if he actually said what he wrote. In his biography *First Man* he told the author James Hansen, 'I must admi that it doesn't sound like the word "a" is there. On the other hand, certa the "a" was intended, because that's the only way it makes sense.'

But now, after almost four decades, the spaceman has been vindicat Using hi-tech sound analysis techniques, Peter Shann Ford, an Australian computer expert has discovered that the 'a' was spoken by Armstrong, but he said it so quickly that it was inaudible on the recording which was broadcast to the world.

Mr Ford's findings have been presented to a relieved Mr Armstrong. James Hansen said, 'Neil is a modest guy, but I think it means a lot to him to know that he didn't make a mistake.'

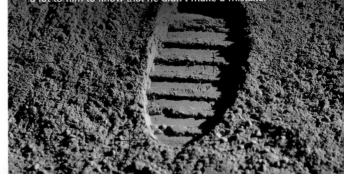

2 GRAMMAR articles

a Right (✔) or wrong (✘)? Correct the mistakes in the highlighted phrases.

1 Neil Armstrong was born in the USA.
2 He was a shy boy, who loved the books and the music.
3 He studied aeronautical engineering at the university.
4 He was the first man who set foot on a moon.
5 His famous words were heard by people all over the world.
6 Before becoming a astronaut, he worked for the US navy.
7 Since 1994 he has refused to give the autographs.
8 In 2005 he was involved in a lawsuit with an ex-barber, who tried to sell some of the Armstrong's hair.

b ⬤ **p.142 Grammar Bank 6A.** Read the rules and do the exercises.

c Read three extracts from some famous historical speeches. Use the glossary to help you. Complete the speeches with *a*, *an*, *the*, or (–).

Winston Churchill (1874–1965) was the British Prime Minister during the Second World War. In this extract from a speech given in 1946, the year after the war ended, Churchill first used the phrase 'iron curtain' to describe the boundary which ideologically and physically divided the East and the West. This speech marked the beginning of the 'Cold War'.

"From Stettin in ¹_____ Baltic to ²_____ Trieste in ³_____ Adriatic, ⁴___ iron curtain has descended across ⁵_____ continent. Behind that line lie all ⁶_____ capitals of ⁷_____ ancient states of ⁸_____ Central and Eastern Europe, Warsaw, Berlin, Prague, Vienna, Budapest, Belgrade, Bucharest, and Sofia. All these famous cities, and ⁹_____ populations around them, lie in what I must call ¹⁰_____ Soviet sphere."

descend come down	**ancient** very old
the continent Europe	**sphere** an area of influence or activity

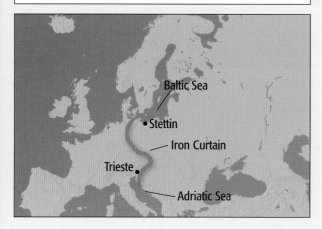

Baltic Sea
• Stettin
Iron Curtain
Trieste •
Adriatic Sea

Martin Luther King (1929–1968) was a leader of the American Civil Rights movement who was assassinated in Memphis in April 1968. In this extract from a speech made in 1963 King spoke of his 'dream' of a future when all people would be treated equally.

"I have ¹_____ dream. That ²_____ my four little children will one day live in ³_____ nation where they will not be judged by ⁴_____ color of their skin but by ⁵_____ content of their character."

King Edward VIII (1894–1972) was the only British king ever to abdicate. Edward had been king for only eleven months, when he announced his decision to give up the throne in order to marry an American divorcee, Wallis Simpson. The following is an extract from his abdication speech to the British nation, made in December 1936.

"At long last I am able to say ¹_____ few words of my own. I have never wanted to withhold anything, but until now it has not been constitutionally possible for me to speak. But you must believe me when I tell you that I have found it impossible to carry ²_____ heavy burden of ³_____ responsibility, and to discharge my duties as King as I would wish to do, without ⁴_____ help and support of ⁵_____ woman I love."

abdicate give up the position of being king or queen
at long last finally, in the end
withhold keep back, not say
burden sth which is carried with difficulty, an obligation
discharge a duty do what you have to do

d 🔊 **6.2** Now listen to the extracts spoken by the people themselves. Check your answers. Which of the three do you think was the best public speaker?

3 PRONUNCIATION sentence stress

a 🔊 **6.3** Dictation. Listen and write down six sentences.

b Listen again and underline the stressed words. What is the vowel sound in *a*, *an*, and *the* in 1–5? Why is *the* pronounced differently in number 6?

c Practise saying the sentences from **a**. Try to pronounce the weak forms correctly.

4 🔊 6.4 SONG ♫ *Space oddity*

5 LISTENING

a Have you ever had to make a speech or give a talk or presentation in front of a lot of people? When? Where? How did you feel? Was it a success?

b Read part of an article about presentation disasters. Which tip from *Ten top tips* below should the speaker have remembered?

PRESENTATION DISASTERS!

However **bad** you think your presentation has been, take some comfort from the fact that at least it probably wasn't as bad as these true stories...

A FEW YEARS AGO I had to give a presentation to the Belgian management team of an international IT company. Not wishing to be the typical 'Brit' presenting in English, I had carefully prepared my presentation in French. I intended it as a surprise so I didn't say anything beforehand. After speaking in French for 45 minutes I was halfway through my presentation and we had a break for coffee. At this point the manager of the company came up to me asked me if I would change to speaking in English. 'Is my French that bad?' I said. 'No,' he replied, 'it's just that we are all from the Dutch-speaking part of Belgium.'

Ten top tips for speaking in public
1   Don't make your presentation too long.
2   Don't have more than four or five main points.
3   Even if something distracting happens try not to lose your concentration.
4   Be careful about telling jokes – they may not be appropriate.
5   Always be punctual: start on time and try to finish on time.
6   Get to know as much as possible about your audience beforehand.
7   Try not to repeat yourself too much.
8   Be careful not to speak too fast.
9   Practise your presentation beforehand.
10 Make sure the equipment you need is working properly before you start.

c You're going to hear five other people talking about a disastrous presentation. Before you listen, look at pictures A–E. What do you think the problem was?

d **6.5** Listen and number the pictures in the correct order. Did you guess correctly?

e Listen again and write 1–5 in the boxes. Which speaker…?
A ☐ couldn't understand why nobody found his / her talk amusing
B ☐ felt very relaxed before his / her presentation
C ☐ did the last part of his / her talk very quickly
D ☐ made the problem he / she had worse
E ☐ didn't find out he / she had a problem until the end of the talk

f Talk to a partner.
1 Would any of the 'Ten top tips' have helped some of the speakers?
2 Which speaker do you think was the most embarrassed?
3 Have you ever been to a talk or presentation where something went badly wrong?

6 VOCABULARY   collocation: word pairs

> Some pairs of words in English which go together always come in a certain order, for example, we always say 'Ladies and Gentlemen' and 'right or wrong' NOT ~~gentlemen and ladies, wrong or right~~.

a Read the information in the box. How do you say 'Ladies and Gentlemen' and 'right or wrong' in your language? Is the order the same?

b Take one word from **A** and match it with another from **B**. Then decide which word comes first. They are all joined with *and*.

A
lemon
butter
thunder   knife
black
breakfast
backwards
quiet

B
fork
white
peace
bed
ice
forwards
bread
lightning

c Look at some common word pairs joined with *or*. What is the second word?

right or _____   now or _____   more or _____

sooner or _____   all or _____   once or _____

d (6.6) Listen and check your answers to **b** and **c**, and notice how the phrases are linked and how *and* and *or* are pronounced. Practise saying them.

e Match the word pair idioms with their meanings.

1 I'm sick and tired of hearing you complain. ☐
2 I didn't buy much, just a few bits and pieces. ☐
3 I've been having headaches now and again. ☐
4 He's unemployed and down and out. ☐
5 Every relationship needs a bit of give and take. ☐
6 We've had our ups and downs, but now we get on really well. ☐
7 The army were called in to restore law and order. ☐
8 Despite flying through a storm we arrived safe and sound. ☐

A problems
B a situation in which the law is obeyed
C fed up
D without problem or injury
E compromise
F occasionally
G small things
H without a home or money

f Complete the sentences with a word pair from **b**, **c**, or **e**.

1 He visits us _____, perhaps twice a year.
2 It's your last chance I'm afraid. It's _____.
3 After lots of adventures she arrived home_____.
4 Please stop making so much noise. I need a bit of _____.
5 _____ he'll realize that she's not the woman for him.
6 After the riots the government sent soldiers in to try to establish _____.
7 She's _____ of her husband. She wants to leave him.
8 It was an amazing storm. There was lots of _____.

7 SPEAKING

a (6.7) When people give a talk, they usually divide what they say into small chunks, with a brief pause between each chunk. Listen to the beginning of a talk and mark (/) the pauses.

> Good afternoon everyone / and thank you for coming. I'm going to talk to you today about one of my hobbies, collecting comics. Since I was a child I've been mad about comics and comic books. I started reading Tintin and Asterix when I was seven or eight. Later when I was a teenager some friends at school introduced me to Manga which are Japanese comics. I've been collecting them now for about five years and I'm also learning to draw them.

b Listen again and underline the stressed words. Practise reading the extract.

c You are going to give a short presentation to other students. You can choose what to talk about, for example:

- **a hobby you have or a sport you play**
- **something you really love doing**
- **an interesting person in your family**
- **a famous person you admire**
- **the good and bad side of your job**

Decide what you are going to talk about and make a plan of what you want to say.

> **GET IT RIGHT**   making a presentation
> Read through the tips in *Presentation disasters!* again to help you to prepare your presentation and to give it successfully. When you give your presentation, don't speak too quickly. Remember to pause and take a breath from time to time. This will help the audience to follow what you are saying.

d In groups, take turns to give your presentation. While they are listening, the other students should write down at least one question to ask the speaker after the presentation is over. Then have a short question and answer session.

6 B Bright lights, big city

G uncountable and plural nouns; *have something done*
V towns and cities
P word stress in multi-syllable words

1 READING & SPEAKING

a Look at the photos and read the quote. Do you know who the Amish are? What do you think happens in the programme?

b Read a preview of the series and find out. Discuss the questions with a partner.

1 What is Rumspringa? Do you think it is a good idea?

2 What do you think will be the biggest culture shock for the Amish when they go to Los Angeles?

3 What do you think the majority of the five young Amish will choose to do?

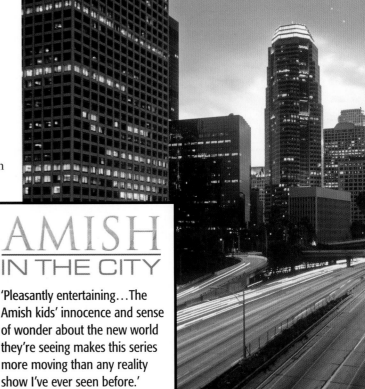

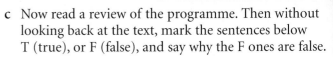

PREVIEW – Tonight's TV

AMISH
IN THE CITY

'Pleasantly entertaining…The Amish kids' innocence and sense of wonder about the new world they're seeing makes this series more moving than any reality show I've ever seen before.'

Los Angeles, home to many of the world's most famous movie stars, is known as the entertainment capital of the world – but it is completely unknown to one group of people – the Amish. For 300 years this fascinating community has lived in isolation, working together to grow their own food, make their own clothes, and build their own communities. They reject conveniences like electricity, telephones, and cars, and focus on hard work, Christian worship, and family.

However, once Amish people reach their late teens, they are allowed to explore modern society and are given the chance to experience the outside world for the first time. This period is known as Rumspringa, a time when Amish young people must decide whether to commit to the strict rules of their faith, or to leave behind the Amish lifestyle and their family forever. Amish teenagers can spend their Rumspringa anywhere, but most of them choose to stay near their homes, venturing only a few miles from their small communities.

But now five of them have chosen to spend their Rumspringa in a way no one has before – living with six city kids in Los Angeles, who have no idea that they will be sharing a house with the Amish. For ten weeks they will explore everything the modern world has to offer, with one thing in mind. Will they return to the simple life they've always lived, or will they choose to remain 'Amish in the City'?

c Now read a review of the programme. Then without looking back at the text, mark the sentences below T (true), or F (false), and say why the F ones are false.

1 The Amish kids aren't used to seeing such tall building.

2 They thought the parking meters were rather funny.

3 The Amish are very good at painting.

4 Mose thinks that 'Reggae' is the name of a singer.

5 The reviewer thinks that the Amish learned a lot from the city kids.

6 Nick felt sorry for the beggar.

7 Most adolescents leave the Amish community after Rumspringa.

8 Mose is not quite sure what he's going to do next.

9 Miriam is planning to travel.

10 The reviewer thinks the programme didn't end in a very positive way.

d Answer the questions.

1 Do you think that this kind of television programme is a good idea? Why (not)?

2 Do you think Rumspringa really gives Amish teenagers freedom of choice? Why (not)?

3 Do you think that the fact that only one of the Amish went back is a happy ending or a sad ending?

In the first episode, the five young Amish, three boys (Mose, Jonas, and Randy) and two girls (Miriam and Ruth) are amazed by the height of the skyscrapers , the noise of the traffic in Los Angeles and the number of cars on the five-lane 'freeways'. They are amused by parking meters – a totally new concept for them – and they love riding in elevators . Even a trip to a grocery store is an adventure. Mose said, 'I'm a farmer, but there are so many vegetables here that I've never seen before.'

Ruth is entranced by a visit to an art gallery as she has never seen art before. 'I didn't know you could make something from boards with paint on them that would look so nice,' she explains. 'The Amish don't do art at school because they feel it isn't important.' Ruth is also as excited as a little child when, for the first time in her life, she sees the ocean.

The Amish are not allowed to use CD players or iPods, and the city kids introduce them to pop music. City girl Megan asks if any of the Amish have heard any reggae at all. 'Reggae?' replies Amish boy Mose, 'I've never heard of him.' As the city kids burst out laughing, he adds, 'But he sounds interesting.'

But as the programme progresses, slowly but surely you feel that the people who are really learning something are the city kids. One evening when they are eating at a pavement café in a rather run-down neighbourhood , a beggar approaches them and asks them for money. City boy Nick ignores him, but Amish girl Miriam offers him a piece of her chicken. 'The Amish wouldn't let anyone be homeless,' she says. 'It just wouldn't happen.'

Of course the big question is, what happens at the end – what do the young Amish decide to do? Normally after Rumspringa the vast majority of adolescents choose to stay in the Amish community. However, in the case of *Amish in the City,* the majority decide, at least temporarily, not to go back to the Amish. Mose decides that the big city life is not for him, but that he probably won't go back to the Amish either. Jonas and Randy both want to go to college and Miriam wants to see more of the world. Of the five of them, only Ruth decides to go back to the Amish lifestyle. A sad ending or a happy ending? It depends on your point of view.

2 VOCABULARY   towns and cities

a   Look at the highlighted words and phrases. Explain in your own words what they mean. Do you have them where you live?

b   ⊙ **p.155 Vocabulary Bank** *Towns and cities.*

c   Make nouns from the **bold** words to complete the sentences.

> Typical endings for making a noun from a verb are:
>   -**ment**, e.g. *government*, -**ion**, e.g. *congestion*, and -**ation** e.g. *information.*
> Typical endings for making a noun from an adjective are:
>   -**ity**, e.g. *reality*, -**ness**, e.g. *darkness*, and -**ence** / -**ance**, e.g. *convenience, entrance.*
> Some nouns from verbs / adjectives are irregular, e.g. *poor>poverty, lose>loss, choose>choice*

1   Los Angeles is well known for its variety of _____. **entertain**
2   _____ is a big problem in many large cities. **homeless**
3   Tourist _____ in London is often very expensive. **accommodate**
4   There is a large Italian _____ in Buenos Aires. **commune**
5   Vandalism and _____ are often problems in some inner city areas. **violent**
6   The best way to see the _____ of Edinburgh is from a double-decker bus. **see**
7   Nowadays many churches and cathedrals charge for _____. **admit**
8   The _____ of a typical skyscraper in New York is 150m or above. **high**
9   A world-famous violinist is giving a _____ tonight at the Royal Albert Hall. **perform**
10   When I was in London, I saw a wonderful _____ at the National Gallery. **exhibit**

3 PRONUNCIATION   word stress in multi-syllable words

a   Underline the stressed syllable in these multi-syllable words.

> accommodation cathedral community cosmopolitan entertainment exhibition gallery historic homelessness industrial neighbourhood overcrowding pedestrian performance pollution poverty provincial skyscraper synagogue violence

b   **6.8**   Listen and check. Then practise saying the words.

4 GRAMMAR   uncountable and plural nouns

a   Circle the correct form.

1   Amish men can't have *long hair / a long hair*.
2   During Rumspringa the Amish tolerate bad *behaviour / behaviours*.
3   There is often *terrible traffic / a terrible traffic* in Los Angeles.
4   A good guidebook will give you *advice / advices* about what to see.
5   We usually have *some bad weather / a bad weather* in April.
6   Walking round cities in the summer can be *hard work / a hard work*.
7   It's best not to take *too much luggage / too many luggages*.
8   I've just heard a very interesting *news / piece of news*.

b   ⊙ **p.142 Grammar Bank 6B.** Read the rules and do the exercises.

c   Play *Just a minute.* In small groups, try to talk for a minute about:

modern furniture	the most beautiful scenery you've seen
good advice you've been given	politics
what's in the news	chocolate
cheap accommodation in your country	the police in your country
the weather you like most	clothes you love wearing

5 LISTENING

a **6.9** You are going to hear to part of a radio programme where Sebastian Hope, a travel writer, talks about London. Listen and match the questions with the photos.

1 What advice would you give to someone visiting London for the first time?
2 What's the one thing you would say someone visiting London should do or see?
3 What's the best place to have your photo taken?
4 What's your favourite landmark?
5 What's the best place to watch the sunset?
6 What's the best place to be at dawn?
7 What would be a good thing to do on a scorching hot day?
8 What's a good thing to do which is absolutely free?
9 What do you think is the most romantic place in London?

b Listen again and answer the questions.

1 What does he mean when he says 'get to know the village you are staying in'?
2 What is his recommendation for an indoor activity that visitors to London should do?
3 What building should you have as a background for a photo?
4 What's special for him about St Paul's Cathedral?
5 Where else can you go to watch the sunset apart from the Trafalgar Hotel roof garden?
6 Why does he like London at dawn?
7 Why is the London Aquarium a good place to go on a very hot day?
8 Why does he enjoy walking in Hyde Park?
9 What is special about the bird called the nightingale? Where can you hear it sing?

c **6.10** Now listen again to five extracts from the interview. Try to write in the missing words.

1 When you see what the people of ancient times were capable of, it makes you feel _____ about the achievements of our own age.
2 It's so _____ that when you catch your first sight of it it's always a thrill.
3 But I'm _____ to say I have never been on it.
4 I love _____ on the pavement outside for a salmon and cream cheese bagel in the early morning.
5 I have memories of _____ the squirrels there.

d Which of the places he mentions would you most like to see? How would you answer the same questions about a city or town that you know well?

6 SPEAKING & WRITING

a Read the questions in *Help me, I'm a tourist!* and decide how you would answer them about your town if you were asked by a tourist.

b Work with another student. A is a tourist and B is a local person. A asks B the questions from sections 1–3. B tries to answer A's questions as fully as possible. A should ask for as much information as possible. Swap roles for sections 4–6.

Help me, I'm a tourist!

1 Safety
Is crime a problem in the city? What should I be careful of?
Are there any areas of the city I should avoid…
a during the day?
b at night?
Can I trust the police if I have a problem?

2 Getting around
What's the best way to get around the city?
Is it OK to take taxis? Are there many taxi ranks?
Can I hire a bicycle? Is it a good city for cycling?
Are there any landmarks that will help me to know where I am?

3 Sightseeing
If I'm short of time, what *three* sights should I see?
What two galleries or museums should I visit? Do they charge for admission?
Where should I go to get the real atmosphere of the city
a by day? or **b** by night?

4 Local customs
Are there any dress rules if I go into a place of worship?
Are there any topics of conversation I should avoid if I talk to local people?
How much should I tip…?
a waiters
b taxi drivers

5 Shopping
What would be a good souvenir to take back with me?
What's the best market to visit?
Is there anywhere where I should haggle?

6 Food and drink
Is the local tap water drinkable?
Is there any food or drink I *must* try?
Is there any food or drink I should avoid or be careful with?

c Now go through the questions again together. Was there anything your partner said that you disagree with?

d Imagine that your school is going to produce a new website giving information about your country for tourists. Write a short description of your city for the website. You could use some of the tips you talked about in **b**.

MINI GRAMMAR   *have something done*

Where's the best place to have your photo taken?

Use *have (something) done* when you ask or pay another person to do something for you.

Compare:
I took a photo *of Westminster Bridge* = I took the photo myself.
I had my photo taken *on Westminster Bridge* = I asked someone to take my photo.

Have is the main verb in these sentences so it changes according to the tense.
I'm going to have *my hair cut tomorrow.*
I had *my car repaired after the accident.*

⚠ You can also use *get* instead of *have*.
I'm going to get my hair cut tomorrow.

Complete the sentences with the right form of *have* and the past participle of a verb from the list.

build	clean	cut	paint	renew	repair	service

1 We _____ our flat _____ next month.
2 **A** Your hair looks fantastic!
   B Thanks. I _____ it _____ yesterday.
3 My coat is really dirty. I need to _____ it _____.
4 You should _____ your car _____ every 10,000 kilometres.
5 **A** Our fridge is broken.
   B Are you going to buy a new one or _____ it _____?
6 I'll need to _____ my passport _____ before my next holiday.
7 Our neighbour is _____ a new garage _____ at the moment.

6C

G quantifiers: *all* / *every*, etc.
V science
P changing stress in word families

Eureka!

1 LISTENING & SPEAKING

a Read the first paragraph of an article about creative thinking. Do the experiment with a partner.

Eureka! Thinking outside the bath...

Master magician Harry Houdini once amazed the world by making an elephant vanish. You are now going to do the same thing.

LOOK AT THE PICTURE of Houdini's head and an elephant. Now close your left eye and hold the book up at arm's length. Now slowly bring the book towards your face, but make sure that you keep looking at Houdini's head with your right eye. At some point, usually when the book is about 20 cm from your face, the elephant will suddenly disappear. This simple illusion works because each of our eyes has a 'blind spot', a small area inside the eye which cannot see.

According to Dr Richard Wiseman, professor of psychology at the University of Hertfordshire, most people have psychological 'blind spots' which cause us to miss seeing the obvious, simple solution to a problem. The few people who do *not* have these psychological blind spots are the people like the Greek mathematician Archimedes, who was having a bath when he suddenly realized that the volume of an object could be calculated by the amount of water it displaced and cried 'Eureka' ('I have found it'), or the English scientist Isaac Newton, who developed the notion of gravity after seeing an apple fall. Dr Wiseman has studied people who frequently experience this kind of 'eureka moment' and thinks that the difference between them and ordinary people is that they think in a different way, what he calls 'creative thinking'.

From *The Times*

b Now look at the title of the lesson. Who said it, and why? Read the second paragraph and check your answer. What kind of people have 'Eureka moments'? Why don't most people have them?

c **6.11** You are going to listen to a radio programme about creative thinking. First look at the photo. What do you think is happening? Then listen to the first part of the programme and answer the questions.

1 Why don't most people think creatively?
2 What was the gorilla experiment?
3 What happened when Dr Wiseman tried the experiment on a group of top scientists?

Figure provided by Daniel Simons

This photograph was first published in *Gorillas in our midst: Sustained inattentional blindness for dynamic events – Perception, 28* (1059–1074) Simons D.J. and Chabris C.F.

d **6.12** Before you listen to the rest of the programme, look at the photos below. In what way do you think these three ideas were innovative? Then listen and answer the questions.

1 What does the gorilla experiment demonstrate?
2 Why are the three things in the photos examples of creative thinking?
3 What did Dr Wiseman recommend to the journalists? Why?
4 What was Dr Wiseman's creative idea?

e Do the test below to find out if you

Are you a creative thinker?

1 Circle true or false.

a I don't consider myself an especially lucky person.
true **false**

b If I'm working on a problem and I'm not making progress, I usually stop for a bit and wait for a solution to present itself.
true **false**

c I like dealing with problems that have clear answers.
true **false**

d I don't like breaking rules.
true **false**

e The best part about working on a problem is solving it.
true **false**

2 Think of a number between 1 and 50 that contains two odd digits but not the same digits.

3 In three minutes, add lines to these boxes to make each one into a different object.

a wall

4 Look at this clock and fill in the missing numbers.

⊃ **p.118 Communication** *Are you a creative thinker?*
Check with the answers.

2 GRAMMAR quantifiers: *all / every*, etc.

a Read these scientific facts. Use your instinct to circle the right word or phrase.

1 Deciduous trees lose their leaves *every year / all years*.
2 *All living things / All the living things* have cells.
3 *Both / Both of* insects and spiders are invertebrates.
4 If something absorbs *all / every* the colours of the spectrum, it appears black.
5 *All / Everything* is made up of atoms.
6 Without oxygen, neither humans *or / nor* animals can survive.

b ⊃ **p.142 Grammar Bank 6C.** Read the rules and do the exercises.

c Do the science quiz with a partner.

How much do you know about science?
Do our quiz and find out.

1 How much of human DNA is the same as chimpanzee DNA?
a Hardly any.
b Some of it.
c Most of it.

2 The air we breathe contains…
a both nitrogen and carbon dioxide.
b neither nitrogen nor carbon dioxide.
c only carbon dioxide.

3 When we breathe out, how much of that air is oxygen?
a None of it.
b All of it.
c Some of it.

4 While you are asleep, you are in REM sleep (or dreaming sleep) for…
a all of the night.
b some of the night.
c most of the night.

5 When does a lemon tree produce fruit?
a Nearly all year.
b Nearly every year.
c Some years.

6 If blue-eyed parents have one son and one daughter, who will also have blue eyes?
a Both of them.
b Neither of them.
c One of them.

3 READING

a You are going to find out about how scientists throughout history have suffered to make their discoveries. Read the extracts and label the illustrations A–D. How many of the scientists actually died as a result of their research?

Suffering for science
Throughout history scientists have risked their health and their lives in their search for the truth…

1

2

3

4

A   Sir Isaac Newton, the seventeenth century scientist, was a genius, but that didn't stop him from doing some pretty stupid things. In his laboratory in Cambridge he often did the most bizarre experiments. Once, while investigating how lenses transmit light, he inserted a long needle into his eye, pushed it to the back, and then moved it around just to see what would happen. Miraculously, nothing long-lasting did. On another occasion he stared at the sun for as long as he could bear, to discover what effect this would have on his vision. Again he escaped suffering permanent damage, though he had to spend some days in a darkened room before his eyes recovered.

B   In the 1750s the Swedish chemist **Karl Scheele was the first person to find a way to manufacture phosphorus . He in fact discovered eight more elements including chlorine , though he didn't get the credit for any of them. He was a brilliant scientist, but his one failing was a curious insistence on tasting a little of every substance he worked with, including mercury and cyanide . This risky practice finally caught up with him, and in 1786 he was found dead in his laboratory surrounded by a large number of toxic chemicals, any of which might have been responsible for his death.

C   In the early 1900s when **Pierre and Marie Curie discovered radiation , nobody realized what a dangerous and deadly phenomenon it was – in fact most people thought that it was beneficial. There was even a hotel in New York which, in the 1920's, advertised 'the therapeutic effect of its radioactive waters'. Both Pierre and Marie Curie experienced radiation sickness and Marie Curie died of leukaemia in 1934. Even now, all her papers from the 1890s, even her cookbooks, are too dangerous to touch. Her laboratory books are kept in special lead boxes and people who want to see them have to wear protective clothing. Marie's husband Pierre, however, did not die from radiation – he was run over by a carriage while crossing the street in Paris.

D   Eugene Shoemaker was a respected geologist. He spent a large part of his life investigating craters on the moon, and how they were formed, and later did research into the comets of the planet Jupiter. In 1997 he and his wife were in the Australian desert where they went every year to search for places where comets might have hit the earth. While driving in the Tanami desert, normally one of the emptiest places in the world, another vehicle crashed into them and Shoemaker was killed instantly. Some of his ashes were sent to the moon aboard the Lunar Prospector spacecraft and scattered there – he is the only person who has had this honour.

From A short history of nearly everything by Bill Bryson

b Read the extracts again and answer the questions. Write A–D in the right box.

Which scientist…?
1 ☐ had a very dangerous way of working with chemicals
2 ☐ was injured twice while he / she was doing experiments
3 ☐ discovered something which slowly killed him / her
4 ☐ was very unlucky to die doing his / her job

5 ☐ needed some time to recover from an experiment
6 ☐ was granted a special honour after his / her death
7 ☐ wasn't as famous as he / she should have been
8 ☐ left something behind which is still dangerous today

c 6.13 Look at the highlighted words, which are all related to science. What do they mean? Are they similar in your language? How do you think they are pronounced? Listen and check.

4 VOCABULARY & PRONUNCIATION

science; changing stress in word families

a Match the different kinds of scientists with what they study.

| a biologist   a chemist   a geneticist   a geologist   a physicist |

1 _____ natural forces, e.g. light, sound, heat, etc.
2 _____ living things, e.g. animals and plants
3 _____ the structure of substances, what happens in different situations, and when they are mixed with each other
4 _____ the cells of living things (genes) that control what a person or plant is like
5 _____ rocks and how they are formed

b In pairs, complete the table.

person	adjective	subject
1 scientist	scientific	science
2 chemist		
3 biologist		
4 physicist		
5 geneticist		
6 geologist		

⚠ In some word 'families' the stressed syllable changes in the different parts of speech, e.g. *photograph*, *photographer*, *photographic*.

c 6.14 Look at the words in the chart in **b** above and under<u>line</u> the stressed syllable. Listen and check. In which groups does the stress change?

d Practise saying the word families.

e Complete the sentences with the correct form of a verb from the list. Under<u>line</u> the stress in the verbs and also in the **bold** words.

| develop   discover   do (x3)   invent   make   prove   volunteer |

1 Pierre and Marie Curie _____ **radiation** in 1900.
2 Scientists _____ **experiments** in a **laboratory**.
3 Archimedes _____ an important **discovery** in his bath.
4 Isaac Newton's experiments _____ his **theory** that gravity existed.
5 The telephone was _____ in the 1870s.
6 **Pharmaceutical** companies try to _____ new drugs to cure illnesses and diseases.
7 Scientists have to _____ a lot of **research** into the possible side **effects** of new drugs.
8 Before a company can sell a new drug, they have to _____ tests and **trials** to make sure they are safe.
9 People can _____ to be **guinea pigs** in clinical trials.

f 6.15 Listen and check. Practise saying the sentences.

5 SPEAKING

Answer the questions with a partner.

Talk about science

Which scientific subjects do / did you study at school? Which did you enjoy the most / least?

Which ones do you think have actually taught you something useful?

Is there a scientist (living or dead) who you admire? Who?

What do you think is the most important scientific discovery of recent years?

Are there any scientific discoveries that you wish *hadn't* been made?

Would you ever agree to be a volunteer in a clinical trial of a new drug?

If you were ill, would you agree to be a guinea pig for a new kind of treatment?

What scientific stories are in the news at the moment?

Are you worried about any of the things scientists are currently experimenting with?

What would you most like scientists to discover in the near future?

➡ **p.157** *Phrasal verbs in context File 6.*

THE INTERVIEW

a You are going to listen to an interview with John Bigos, the managing director of London Duck Tours Limited. This company use 'Ducks', renovated World War II amphibious vehicles which can travel on land and water. Before you listen, read the glossary and look at how the words are pronounced to help you understand what he says.

Glossary

vessel /ˈvesəl/ a large ship or boat

anchor /ˈæŋkə/ a heavy metal object which is dropped over the side of a ship or boat to keep it in one place

Nelson's Column /ˈnelsənz cɒləm/ the statue of Admiral Nelson on a column in Trafalgar Square

the Thames /ðə temz/ the river which runs through London

MI6 the British Secret Intelligence Service, whose headquarters are on the banks of the River Thames

The Living Daylights and **The World is not Enough** two James Bond films

Emmeline Pankhurst /ˈeməliːn ˈpæŋkhɜːst/ the founder of the Suffragette movement which fought for women's right to vote in the early twentieth century.

Horse Guards (Parade) /hɔːs gɑːdz/ a place near Buckingham Palace where military ceremonies are held including the daily 'changing of the guard' by the Queen's cavalry.

mink /mɪŋk/ a small mammal whose fur is used to make very expensive coats

b **6.16** Listen to part 1. Answer the questions with a partner.

1 What are the advantages of Duck tours compared with other tours?
2 What happens if a Duck boat breaks down?
3 Who do they sometimes have to rescue?
4 What was the problem with the lady in a mink coat? What happened in the end?

c **6.17** Listen to part 2. Answer the questions with a partner.

What does he say about…?
1 Nelson Mandela's statue
2 Trafalgar Square
3 MI6
4 the Houses of Parliament
5 1928
6 200 different cultures
7 standards of service
8 travel and congestion

d **6.18** Listen and complete the phrases. What do you think they mean?

COMMON PHRASES

1 What makes Duck Tours more interesting in terms of the tour, as _____ _____ other tours…
2 …but that, fortunately, is _____ _____ rare thing
3 And that's the first statue that I'm _____ of that has been erected whilst someone is still alive…
4 Additionally, we have _____ _____ of heroes in our country…

e Listen to the interview again with the tapescript on page 129. Would you choose a Duck tour instead of a normal tour of London? Why (not)?

IN THE STREET

a **6.19** You're going to hear five people talking about their favourite cities and a city they would like to visit. Write the number of each speaker next to the two cities they mention. Who only mentions one city?

Theresa   Anne   Agne   Matandra   Harley

Barcelona ☐   Delhi ☐   Rome ☐
Cape Town ☐   London ☐   Stockholm ☐
Casablanca ☐   New York ☐   Sydney ☐

b Listen again.

1 Who especially likes the contrasts between their favourite city and the UK?
2 Who is only interested in cities for one reason?
3 Who has recently changed their mind about their favourite city?
4 Who talks about how the city makes them feel?
5 Whose favourite city is in fact their home town?

c **6.20** Listen and complete the phrases. What do you think they mean?

COMMON PHRASES

1 I would _____ like to visit Barcelona.
2 I like the hustle and _____. (idiom)
3 It's the right compromise between a laid-back _____ and, you know, the positive aspects of living in a metropolis. (informal)
4 _____ hot, _____ with shops.

d Listen to the interviews again with the tapescript on page 130. Then answer the same questions with a partner.

Study Link MultiROM

Eating out in London

a Read the report on restaurants and think of a suitable heading for paragraphs 1, 3, and 4.

b Find synonyms in the report for the expressions in **Useful language**.

Useful language
Talking in general

Most / _____ (*cinemas in my town…*) (paragraph 1)
(Cinemas) are usually / _____ to be (*quite cheap.*) (2)
In general / _____ (2)
Almost always / _____ (3)

c You have been asked to write a report on either entertainment or sports facilities in your town for an English language magazine. With a partner, decide what kind of information would be most useful for visitors to your town.

PLAN the content.
1 Decide which report you are going to write.
2 Decide what headings you can use to divide up your report.
3 Decide what information to include under each heading.

WRITE 120–180 words, organized in three or four paragraphs with a heading. Use a neutral style (no contractions or colloquial expressions).

CHECK your report for mistakes (grammar , punctuation , and spelling).

This report describes various options for students who want to eat out while staying in London.

1 _____

Fast food – The majority of fast food restaurants are clean and the service is fast, but they are often noisy and crowded, and of course the food is the same all over the world.

World food – London has restaurants offering food from many parts of the world, for example India, Thailand, and China. These are often relatively inexpensive and have good – quality food and a nice atmosphere.

2 *When you don't mind spending a bit more*

Gastropubs – These are pubs which serve high-quality food and tend to be slightly cheaper than the majority of mid-range restaurants. Generally speaking, the food is well cooked and some have very imaginative menus.

Italian restaurants – You can normally get a good pasta dish or a pizza and a salad in most Italian restaurants without spending too much.

3 _____

There are many options if you want to try somewhere special, but be aware that this nearly always means spending a lot of money. French restaurants are often quite expensive, and so are those run by celebrity chefs.

4 _____

• Even if you have a limited budget, take advantage of the different restaurants that London has to offer.

• Don't make your meal cost more by ordering expensive drinks.

• If you really want to go to a particular restaurant, make sure you book in advance, especially on a Friday or Saturday night.

• Be careful – many restaurants in London close early on Sunday evenings.

GRAMMAR

Choose a, b or c.

1 After the accident, I was in ___ hospital for three weeks.
   a the
   b –
   c a

2 I now live next door to ___ school I used to go to.
   a the
   b –
   c a

3 I think ___ Lake Constance is the biggest lake in Switzerland.
   a the
   b –
   c a

4 He's looking for ___ cheap accommodation in London.
   a a piece of
   b some
   c a

5 Let me give you ___ – don't marry him!
   a some advice
   b an advice
   c some advices

6 I need to buy a new ___.
   a trouser
   b trousers
   c pair of trousers

7 I'm going to the optician's. I need to ___.
   a have tested my eyes
   b test my eyes
   c have my eyes tested

8 There's ___ milk. I'll have to buy some.
   a no
   b any
   c none

9 I didn't buy my jeans in that shop because ___ were so expensive.
   a everything
   b all
   c all of them

10 They shouldn't go in the boat alone because ___ of them can swim.
   a both
   b either
   c neither

VOCABULARY

a Complete the sentences with the right form of the **bold** word.

1 Tonbridge is a small ___ town in south-east England.   **provin**
2 One of the biggest problems in big cities is ___.   **poor**
3 The ___ must do more to protect the environment.   **goverr**
4 A lot of research is being done into human ___.   **genes**
5 Many important ___ discoveries were made in the 19th century. **science**

b Complete the phrases.

1 Please turn the TV down. I need some peace and **q**___.
2 He arrived back from his adventure safe and **s**___.
3 The dancers moved backwards and **f**___ across the floor.
4 I don't know him very well. I've only met him once or **t**___.
5 We've moved almost everything to the new office. There are just a few bits and **p**___ left.

c Circle the right verb.

1 Scientists *do / make* experiments in a laboratory.
2 Archimedes *did / made* an important discovery in his bath.
3 Drugs companies have to *make / do* a lot of research into possible side effects.
4 These tablets are *made / done* in Germany.
5 Before a company can sell a new medicine it has to *make / do* tests and trials using volunteers.

d Word groups. Underline the word that is different. Say why.

1	cathedral	synagogue	harbour	mosque
2	taxi rank	cable car	bus station	airport
3	suburb	district	landmark	neighbourhood
4	square	skyscraper	town hall	law court
5	chemist	scientist	physicist	genetics

PRONUNCIATION

a Underline the word with a different sound.

1	neither	vibrant	science	neighbourhood
2	government	prove	slums	discovery
3	volunteer	theory	research	idea
4	clothes	both	neither	the
5	geologist	synagogue	genes	biology

b Underline the stressed syllable.

| biological | physicist | cosmopolitan | outskirts | industrial |

CAN YOU UNDERSTAND THIS TEXT?

a Complete the article with a sentence A–F.

A For most of us the idea of having the weaknesses of our speech exposed is scary.

B I talk for two minutes on four topics: a happy memory, a sad memory, something that makes me angry, and a neutral work-related topic.

C The idea is that when you are tempted to say 'um' you simply remain quiet.

D Mr Grant receives a report on the results and, armed with that information, he and his colleagues coach me to use my voice more effectively.

E On the other hand I do not vary my pitch much, which means I have a monotonous voice.

F Voice coaching, once only for actors, is now commonly used by politicians and business people.

b Look at the highlighted words and phrases. Can you guess what they mean?

CAN YOU UNDERSTAND THESE PEOPLE?

a **6.21** Listen and circle the correct answer, a, b, or c.

1 What does the woman offer to do?
  a Get a technician.
  b Fix the projector.
  c Make the room darker.

2 Which of these problems *doesn't* the man mention?
  a Too many people.
  b A lot of crime.
  c Too much traffic.

3 What does the tour guide recommend the tourists do?
  a Visit the Roman room.
  b Plan their own tour of the museum.
  c Buy postcards in the shop.

4 What is the teacher going to show the children?
  a How to use a microscope.
  b How to look at something closely without a microscope.
  c How to know which tree a leaf comes from.

5 Which of the following is true about Newton?
  a He was not a very healthy baby.
  b He was brought up by his father's mother.
  c His father was a poor farmer.

b **6.22** You will hear an interview with a woman who moved from the city to the country. Mark the sentences T (true) or F (false).

1 Her friends thought she would miss her job.
2 She sees friends more often than before.
3 She gets on well with the people in the village.
4 She often gets a takeaway for dinner.
5 There's a good bus service.

Loud and clear: the message sent by your voice

I am sitting in an office in Covent Garden having my voice recorded. [1] ☐ The reason? I am about to have my voice analysed, and expressing these feelings provides a balanced view of the voice's emotional content.

[2] ☐ A badly delivered speech can have a devastating impact on the public image of a politician, and for chief executives too an unconvincing speech can damage the company's standing with employees, customers, or investors.

When I have finished, the man who has been listening to me, Alastair Grant of presentation analysts Grant Pearson Brown, sends the recording to Branka Zei, a Swiss psychologist who specializes in linguistics. Using software, Ms Zei measures the recording against an 'ideal' voice, whose pitch, articulation, and fluency, among other things, are derived by analysing the voices of hundreds of good speakers. [3] ☐

So, what does my analysis show? The good news is that my median pitch is 158.25Hz compared with the standard reference for a woman of 200Hz – another way of saying that my voice is quite deep. 'Deeper voices carry more authority than high-pitched voices,' says Mr Grant. My loudness level and range are perfect. [4] ☐ Also my articulation is not clear enough, because I sometimes have difficulty pronouncing the letter 'r'. Lastly, I use 'disfluencies', which means that I overuse terms such as 'um' and 'er'. The best news, however, is that my 'vocal indicators' point to a balanced personality, with no clear tendency towards introversion or extroversion.

If Mr Grant were to work with me further, he would get me to read from a script and pause after each phrase. [5] ☐ 'If people are comfortable with silence, then they don't have to put in those filler words.' To counteract my problem of sounding monotonous he would ask me to imagine myself telling a story to a child, as this very naturally makes people vary their pitch.

[6] ☐ But for those brave enough to try it, voice analysis offers the chance of really improving the way we speak in normal life and when we are on the podium.

From *The Financial Times*

CAN YOU SAY THIS IN ENGLISH?

Can you…?

☐ give a short presentation on a subject you know about
☐ give advice about how to speak in public successfully
☐ describe a big city you know well and its attractions or problems
☐ talk about famous scientists and their discoveries

**7
A**

G structures after *wish*
V *-ed* / *-ing* adjectives and related verbs; expressions with *go*
P sentence rhythm

I wish you wouldn't...!

1 SPEAKING

> **GET IT RIGHT** **expressing annoyance**
>
> When you talk about things that annoy you, you can use these expressions:
>
> | | |
> |---|---|
> | *It really annoys me when…* | |
> | *It drives me mad when…* | *people shout on* |
> | *It drives me up the wall when…* | *mobile phones.* |
> | *It really gets on my nerves when…* | |
> | *People who shout on mobile phones…* | *really annoy me*, etc. |

a Read through the list of annoying things in the magazine article. With a partner, say which of these things annoy you too. Choose your top three pet hates.

b Think of three other things which annoy you. Then compare your three with other students.

2 GRAMMAR *wish* + past simple and *would*

a **7.1** Listen to four conversations. Which of the irritating things in the magazine article do they refer to?

   1 _____
   2 _____
   3 _____
   4 _____

b Listen again and complete the sentences.

   1 I wish ___ ___ ___ that!
   2 I wish ___ ___ a pound for every time I've picked the *one* broken one.
   3 I wish ___ ___, but it depends on the traffic.
   4 I wish ___ ___ ___ in the road.

c Which speakers would like *somebody else* to change their behaviour?

d ➡ **p.144 Grammar Bank 7A.** Read the rules for *wish* + past simple and *wish* + *would*. Do exercise **a**.

e Complete the sentences so that they are true for you. Compare with a partner.

   About me
   I wish I could _____. (ability)
   I wish I was more _____. (adjective of personality)
   I wish I wasn't so _____. (adjective of personality)
   I wish I had _____. (personal possession)
   I wish _____.

   Things people do that annoy me
   I wish my _____ wouldn't _____. (brother, sister, friend)
   I wish _____ would / wouldn't _____. (drivers / cyclists)
   I wish young people today would / wouldn't _____.
   I wish there was a law against people who _____.

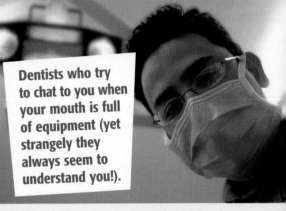

Things that really annoy us
– we asked people around the world..

Dentists who try to chat to you when your mouth is full of equipment (yet strangely they always seem to understand you!).

People who criticize politicians and the govern▶ but then don't vote in the elections.

I get into the shower and then either the wat▶ goes cold or there's no shower gel left.

Cyclists who ride on the pavement and nearly knock you over.

When I'm travelling on a plane or train and a child sitting behind me keeps kicking my seat.

People reading over your shoulder on a bus or train.

...V or radio news programmes with a male and female ...esenter, who each speak only a couple of lines at a time.

When I'm queuing for a train ticket and the person in front of me at the desk can't make up their mind what kind of ticket they want.

When you want to buy something in a shop and you have to wait for the shop assistant to finish a telephone conversation with a friend.

When you get a trolley in a supermarket and one of the wheels is broken.

When you get a taxi and the driver asks <u>you</u> the best way to go.

I'm talking on the phone and I need a pen quickly and I can't find one which works.

Drivers who double park in a busy street and then put their hazard lights on (as if this makes it OK!).

People who wear sunglasses indoors.

From the British press

Companies that call you during the evening, trying to sell you something.

3 VOCABULARY -ed / -ing adjectives and related verbs

> We often talk about feelings in three different ways, either by using a verb (e.g. *annoy*) or by using the *-ed* or *-ing* adjective (e.g. *annoying, annoyed*).
>
> *It really annoys me.* (verb)
>
> *That noise is really annoying / Jane is so annoying.* (*-ing* adjectives describe the thing or person that produces a feeling)
>
> *I'm really annoyed about last night.* (*-ed* adjectives describe how a person feels)

a Complete the sentences with the correct form of the word in **bold**.

1 I get very _____ when I speak French and people don't understand me. **frustrate**

2 It's very _____ when you can't remember someone's name. **embarrass**

3 It really _____ me when people are late. **irritate**

4 I wish the sun would come out. I find these grey days so _____. **depress**

5 We were _____ when the plane suddenly began to lose height. **terrify**

6 The journey had been very _____, so he decided to go to bed early. **tire**

7 I wish he'd come home! It _____ me when he's out late at night. **worry**

8 Jack wasn't very _____ when we laughed at his new tie. **amuse**

9 The end of the film really _____ me. It was totally unbelievable. **disappoint**

10 It was a _____ match! England won 3-2 with a goal in the last minute. **thrill**

11 He really _____ his parents when he told them he was getting divorced. **shock**

12 What an _____ day! I need to relax and put my feet up. **exhaust**

b A few 'feeling' verbs have an *-ed* adjective, but not the *-ing* form. Complete the adjective in the sentences below.

1 I was delight**ed** to meet her. She was a <u>*delightful*</u> person.

2 I was scar**ed** during the film. The film was very _____.

3 We were extremely impress**ed** by your CV. Your CV was extremely _____.

4 I'm very stress**ed** by my job. My job is very _____.

5 I was really offend**ed** by what you said. What you said was really _____.

c In pairs, talk about some of these:

• something in the news recently that shocked you
• a film you found really disappointing
• something that frustrates you about learning English
• the kind of weather that makes you feel depressed
• an embarrassing mistake you once made
• an area of your town / city which is scary at night

4 READING

a Look at the photos of the actress Paula Wilcox as she is today, and in the TV series which made her famous, *Man about the house*. How old do you think she is in each photo? How has she changed?

b Read a magazine article where Paula talks about things she regrets. In which paragraph does she talk about…?

- A ☐ a time when she misjudged other people
- B ☐ a time when she didn't want to seem different from other people
- C ☐ her insecurity about her appearance
- D ☐ how she regrets not taking more risks
- E ☐ situations when she shouldn't have talked so much
- F ☐ something she could have been better at

c Read the article again carefully. Find words or phrases which mean:

1 _____ it makes me remember (1)
2 _____ very beautiful (1)
3 _____ a missed opportunity (1)
4 _____ a lot of (2)
5 _____ amusing in a clever way (3)
6 _____ the most amusing and interesting person (3)
7 _____ kind, soft (4)
8 _____ something that is new or difficult, but stimulating (6)

d Use your own words to summarize the advice she gives in each paragraph to younger people. What do you think of her advice?

5 GRAMMAR *wish + past perfect*

a Underline the seven sentences in the article with *wish*. What tense is the verb after *wish*? Are they wishes about the present, the past, or the future?

b ⬭ **p.144 Grammar Bank 7A.** Read the rules for *wish* + past perfect. Do exercise **b**.

c What regrets might these people have? Make sentences with *I wish…* + past perfect.

1 John has always been extravagant and never has much money in the bank. Now he really wants to buy an expensive car, but he can't afford it.
2 Annie has just been to the hairdresser's. She isn't very happy with her new look.
3 Rafael was offered a job in San Francisco but didn't take it, because he didn't think his English was good enough.
4 Mark got really angry with his girlfriend last night. They had an argument and she left him.

> I wish I'd saved some of my salary. I wish I hadn't spent so much money on that holiday…

Regrets, I've had a few.

Actress Paula Wilcox, now in her fifties, was best known for her role in the TV series *Man about the house*, which she starred in when she was only 19. Here she talks about things she wishes she had known then…

1 Now when I look in the mirror and think, 'Oh dear, I'm getting older,' it reminds me that I used to do the same thing when I was 19 and 20. I used to look at myself and think I looked awful. I wish I'd known what I was going to look like thirty years later, because then I might have realized how gorgeous I was then. I looked great but I didn't appreciate it – what a waste!

2 I now understand that it's OK to be successful. When I was 19 I was starring on TV and making loads of money, but most of my friends were university students. I felt embarrassed, and used to walk around with my hands in front of my face so as not to be recognized. I wish I'd known that it's possible to enjoy the good things about fame, and that you can keep your friendships in spite of it.

3 I wish I had learned sooner how to listen to people properly. I used to think I had to be intelligent and witty in social situations. If I'd known how much people appreciate being listened to, I wouldn't have tried so hard to be the life and soul of the party.

4 Life has taught me that sometimes when people behave badly to you it is because of some unhappiness that they are carrying around with them, a problem that has nothing to do with you. I wish I had been more gentle with people in that situation and not reacted so angrily. Once you find out what's really going on, the whole relationship can change.

5 My dad always used to say, 'learn what you can while you are young and at school, because when you are older you either won't have enough time or won't have enough money to pay for lessons.' That was good advice, and I wish I'd spent more time on my piano lessons.

6 Finally, I wish I had always said yes to challenges. I'd say to young people today, if you are offered the opportunity to do something you have never done before, go for it. You might feel a little nervous, but say yes anyway.

6 PRONUNCIATION   sentence rhythm

a   **7.2**   **Dictation.** Listen and write down six sentences with *wish*.

b   Listen again and <u>underline</u> the stressed words.

c   Match each sentence with a sentence below. In pairs, practise the dialogues.
   A ☐ Do you want me to phone and make an excuse?
   B ☐ I thought you said we were in a hurry!
   C ☐ So do I. I didn't bring an umbrella today.
   D ☐ Well, it's not *my* fault. You've got no self-control!
   E ☐ Why don't you go back to the shop and see if they still have it?
   F ☐ Sorry, but it is. And I'm getting hungry.

7 LISTENING & SPEAKING

a   **7.3**   Listen to five people and match the speakers with the regrets.
   Who…?
   A wasted time when he / she could have been doing something else ☐
   B wishes he / she had said something to someone ☐
   C missed an opportunity because he / she wasn't independent ☐
   D wasn't old enough to take advantage of a situation ☐
   E regretted trying to change his / her appearance ☐

b   Listen again. Why do the speakers mention or say the following?
   1 'Mercedes and Bosch.'   'It would have opened doors for me.'
   2 'The top and skirt I wore were really skimpy.'
   3 'The Russian Revolution.'   'Old letters.'
   4 'I really fancied him.'   'Now it's too late.'
   5 'I just did the bare minimum.'   'This was a unique opportunity.'

c   Read about the website below. Do you identify with any of the regrets?

Psychologists at Cambridge University have been researching things that people regret about their lives. These were some of the things people wrote:

8 VOCABULARY   expressions with *go*

> Once you find out what's really going on, the whole relationship can change.
>
> If you are offered the opportunity to do something you have never done before, go for it.

a   Look at the highlighted phrasal verbs with *go* from the article about Paula Wilcox. What do you think they mean?

b   Complete the questions with the correct word.

| back on   far   for   off   on   sleep |
| through   with   without   wrong |

   1 Do you usually **go** _____ your notes after class?
   2 What do you usually do when something **goes** _____ with your computer?
   3 Have you ever promised someone something important and then **gone** _____ it?
   4 Do you think you could **go** _____ food for 24 hours?
   5 Do you normally choose shoes that **go** _____ the clothes you're wearing?
   6 How long does it usually take you to **go to** _____ at night?
   7 Do you think that speaking English will help you to **go** _____ professionally?
   8 Is there any singer or band you used to like but who you've **gone** _____ ?
   9 If you were offered a job abroad, would you **go** _____ it ?
   10 What's **going** _____ at the moment in the celebrity world in your country?

c   Now ask and answer the questions in pairs.

9   **7.4**   SONG ♫ *If I could turn back time*

Family
- I regret arguing with my parents yesterday.
- I wish I'd listened to my sister when she had problems.
- I regret not visiting my grandfather more when he was in hospital.

Lifestyle
- I wish I hadn't eaten so much last night.
- I wish I hadn't had my hair cut short last month.
- I regret not buying some really cheap shoes in the sales when I first saw them – when I came back an hour later they had gone.
- I wish I had been brave enough to go up to the top floor of the Eiffel Tower when I was in Paris.

Education, work, etc.
- I wish I'd studied more for my exams last year.
- I wish I'd saved more money when I was earning a good salary.
- I regret not learning the guitar when I was younger.

d   Think of three regrets (big or small) that you would add to the lists. Compare with a partner and ask for more information.

7
B

G clauses of contrast and purpose; *whatever, whenever,* etc.
V business and advertising
P changing stress in nouns and verbs

A test of honesty

1 READING & LISTENING

a Look at the title of the article and the photos. Try to guess what the article is about.

b Read *Honest workers or thieves?* and check. Then in pairs, cover the article and say what you can remember about…
1 Paul Feldman's original job.
2 the incident that made him decide to change his job.
3 how the 'bagel habit' started, and what it consisted of.
4 why he started asking for money, and the proportion of people who paid.
5 his friends' and family's reaction to his change of job.
6 how his business progressed.
7 the economic experiment he had (unintentionally) designed.

c You are going to hear an American economist talking about Paul Feldman's experiment. Before you listen, in pairs, predict the answers to the questions.
1 What do you think the average payment rate was?
   a 70–80%   b 80–90%   c 90–100%
2 Were smaller offices more or less honest than big ones?
3 How often has the cash box been stolen?
4 Did people 'cheat' more during good or bad weather?
5 Did people 'cheat' more or less before Christmas? Why?
6 Who 'cheated' more, executives or lower status employees?

d **7.5** Listen and check your answers to c.

e Listen again and choose a, b, or c.
1 More people paid in Feldman's own office…
   a after he had caught somebody stealing.
   b because he asked them personally for the money.
   c because the workers were his colleagues.
2 Feldman eventually stopped selling bagels to…
   a a company where less than 80% paid for their bagels.
   b a company where the money box got stolen.
   c a company where less than 90% paid for their bagels.
3 People are more honest in smaller companies because…
   a they are more likely to get caught.
   b they would be more embarrassed about being caught.
   c there is more control from the management.
4 People 'cheat' more…
   a after a day off.
   b before all public holidays.
   c before some public holidays.
5 Which of these people is most likely to pay?
   a An employee who doesn't like his boss.
   b An executive who is very popular with his staff.
   c An employee who likes the company where he works.

Honest workers or thieves? Take the bagel test.

Once upon a time, Paul Feldman dreamed big dreams. Trained as an agricultural economist, he wanted to tackle world hunger. Instead, he took a job in Washington, analysing weapons expenditures for the US Navy. He held senior-level jobs and earned good money, but he wasn't fully engaged in his work. At the office Christmas party, colleagues would introduce him to their wives not as 'the head of the public research group' (which he was) but as 'the guy who brings in the bagels'.

The bagels had begun as a casual gesture: a boss treating his employees whenever they won a research contract. Then he made it a habit. Every Friday, he would bring in some bagels, a serrated knife, and cream cheese. When employees from neighbouring floors heard about the bagels, they wanted some too. Eventually he was bringing in 15 dozen bagels a week. In order to recoup his costs, he set out a cash basket and a sign with the suggested price. His collection rate was about 95 per cent; he attributed the underpayment to oversight, not fraud.

In 1984, when his research institute fell under new management, Feldman decided to quit his job and sell bagels. His economist friends thought he had lost his mind, but his wife supported him.

Driving around the office parks that encircle Washington, he solicited customers with a simple pitch: early in the morning, he would deliver some bagels and a cash basket to a company's snack room; he would return before lunch to pick up the money and the leftovers. Within a few years, Feldman was delivering 8,400 bagels a week to 140 companies and earning as much as he had made as a research analyst.

He had also, quite without meaning to, designed a beautiful economic experiment. By measuring the money collected against the bagels taken, he found it possible to tell, down to the penny, just how honest his customers were. Did they steal from him? If so, what were the characteristics of a company that stole versus a company that did not? In what circumstances did people tend to steal more, or less?

f If Feldman left a basket of bagels in your school, what proportion do you think would pay?

How do you feel about people…?
- downloading music and films from the Internet without paying
- buying pirate DVDs / CDs
- photocopying a book
- taking home pens, paper, etc. from the office or school
- keeping a library book
- buying designer goods which they know are fakes
- not saying anything when a shop assistant gives back too much change

2 VOCABULARY business and advertising

a Look at the *Honest workers or thieves?* article again and find words which mean…

1 _____ the person who is in charge of a group or department in a company (paragraph 1)
2 _____ a person who works in the same company as you (paragraph 1)
3 _____ an employer (paragraph 2)
4 _____ people who work for somebody (paragraph 2)
5 _____ people who buy a product from a shop or company (paragraph 5)

b ⊙ **p.156 Vocabulary Bank** *Business and advertising.*

c Do the business quiz with a partner.

What's the difference between…?
1 an employer / an employee
2 a customer / a client
3 the boss / the staff
4 set up a company / take over a company
5 sack somebody / make somebody redundant
6 export a product / import a product

Name a business or company in your town / city which…
1 is part of a well-known chain.
2 is a multinational.
3 started as a small family business and then became much bigger.
4 was taken over by another company.
5 spends a lot of money on advertising.

3 PRONUNCIATION changing stress in nouns and verbs

> Some words change their stress depending on whether they are verbs or nouns. The nouns are usually stressed on the first syllable, e.g. *an export*, *a record* and the verbs on the second syllable, e.g. *to export*, *to record*. Words like this include: *increase, decrease, import, permit, produce, progress, record, refund, transport.*

a Read the information in the box and practise saying each word both ways, as a verb and as a noun.

b Under<u>line</u> the stressed syllable on the highlighted word.
1 We're making good progress with the report.
2 The new building is progressing well.
3 We export to customers all over the world.
4 One of our main exports is wine.
5 **A** Can you refund me the cost of my ticket?
   B Sorry, we don't give refunds.
6 Sales have increased by 10% this month, so there has been an increase in profits.
7 The demand for organic produce has grown enormously.
8 Most toys nowadays are produced in China.
9 They are planning to transport the goods by sea.
10 There has been a rise in the number of people using public transport.

c (7.6) Listen and check. Practise saying the sentences.

MINI GRAMMAR
whatever, whenever, etc.

The bagels had begun as a 'thank you' to his employees whenever they won a research project.

We use *whenever* to mean 'at any time' or 'it doesn't matter when', e.g. *Come and see me **whenever** you like.*

We can also use:

whatever (= any thing), *whichever* (= any thing, from a limited number), *whoever* (= any person), *however* (= it doesn't matter how), *wherever* (= any place). They also have the meaning *it doesn't matter what / which / who / how / where*, etc.

Complete the sentences with *whatever, whichever, whoever, whenever, however,* or *wherever.*

1 Please sit _____ you like.
2 There is a prize for _____ can answer the question first.
3 _____ she opens her mouth she says something stupid.
4 I'm going to buy it _____ expensive it is!
5 _____ I give her, it's always the wrong thing.
6 I'll go by bus or train, _____ is cheaper.

4 GRAMMAR   clauses of contrast and purpose

a Read the advert below. Would you try *Pumavite*? Why (not)?

PUMAVITE

Recommended by doctors

'I slept my way to fitness'

No exercise – but now Simon has muscles to die for!

Simon Sloth had never been a great one for exercise. With three children and a busy job there was very little time for the gym.

But then Simon discovered PUMAVITE tablets, an exclusive product marketed by Cure Everything Pharmaceuticals. A three-month course of the tablets has transformed him!

'You take it at night,' explains Simon, 'and its special secret ingredient gets to work immediately.' PUMAVITE contains plant extracts from the Andes and complex vitamins. Together these produce exactly the same effect as a two-hour workout at the gym or swimming pool.

**'Pumavite is absolutely fantastic and a miracle cure for people like me. It is guaranteed to work and is the best investment I have ever made,' says Simon.
'I slept my way to fitness!'**

Only £500
for a three-month supply
Limited stocks – offer closes on March 31st!

From *The Office of Fair Trading*

b Read the magazine article. Tick the 'tricks' that the *Pumavite* advert uses.

How advertisers win our hearts and minds..
and get our money

There's no such thing as a free lunch
'Get a free camera when you subscribe to our magazine for two years.' There's something about the word 'free' that immediately attracts us – something for nothing – I want it! The idea makes us feel clever, as if we've got the better of the company. But that camera (which will probably break as soon as you get it out of the box) wasn't a gift at all. In spite of [1]_____, its price was really included in the magazine subscription.

Buy now while stocks last!
'There are only a few left! And after they've been sold, there won't be any more available.' What happens when we read or hear these words? Even though [2]_____, maybe don't even like them, we immediately want to be among the lucky few who have them. But no manufactured products are ever scarce. Do you really think the manufacturers of that 'limited edition' DVD couldn't produce a few more, if they thought they could sell them?

Just sign your name here – and give us your address
'Just fill in this form for [3]_____.' Do you think manufacturers really want to spend their money on sending you a free brochure? It costs them to produce it and to mail it. In fact, these kinds of adverts are really produced so as to [4]_____. From then on, they will bombard you with more direct advertising, probably passing on your name and address to other companies too.

c Read the article again with the glossary and complete it with the phrases below.
  A free information
  B the actress is holding the product in the photo
  C get us to believe it
  D get your personal details
  E we can't fail to get the message
  F demonstrate the amazing effects of their product
  G we don't really need the products
  H the advert saying it was free

d Look at the eight phrases again, and the highlighted word(s) immediately before them. Which ones express a contrast? Which ones express a purpose?

e ⭕ p.144 Grammar Bank 7B. Read the rules and do the exercise

Everybody's doing it

And everybody can't be wrong, so the product must be fantastic. In order to 5_____, they use expressions like, 'It's the new sensation sweeping the country', 'People just can't get enough of them', 'Record sales', 'Unbelievable response!' and combine this with a photograph of a large group of people, so that 6_____. But don't be fooled. Even if it everybody is doing it (and they may not be), everybody can be wrong.

The camera never lies, or does it?

Adverts frequently use 'real people' to 7_____ on your health or fitness. But of course the person in the advert or TV commercial is a gym-toned model!

Trust me I'm a doctor (or a celebrity)

If a celebrity is using the product, it must be fantastic. If a doctor recommends it, it must work. The bigger the authority, the more powerful the advertising message is. But be careful. Although 8_____, do you really think she colours her hair with it at home? Do the authorities mentioned really exist? 'My dog biscuits are recommended by the International Association of Dog Nutritionists' (an organization I started last week). 'A recent study found that my lemonade tastes better than any other brand' (my mother liked it better).

Glossary

subscribe pay money regularly in order to receive sth
get the better of to defeat sb / sth or gain an advantage
available able to be bought or found
be scarce there is not much of it
bombard 'attack' sb with e.g. too many questions, too much information
be fooled be tricked

Sentence race. Try to complete all the sentences in two minutes.

1 The customer took the shoes back to the store to…
2 Even though I was really late, my boss…
3 She applied for a job with a company in London so that…
4 He got promoted to branch manager despite…
5 Most of the staff don't like the new MD, although…
6 He left the company he used to work for in order to…
7 Although Jim was the hardest worker in the company, …
8 In spite of a huge marketing campaign, …
9 I went to our head office in New York for…
10 I think the advertising of cigarettes and alcohol should be banned, so as not to…

---

5 SPEAKING

Talk in small groups.

1 Are there any products that you have bought recently…
  a because of the adverts?
  b in spite of the adverts?
2 Have you bought something recently which wasn't as good as the advertisement made you think?
3 Are there any adverts which make you *not* want to ever buy the product? Why do they have this effect on you?
4 Do you think people should be allowed to advertise the following? Why (not)?
  - alcoholic drinks
  - expensive children's toys
  - junk food
  - political parties
5 How successful do you think the following forms of advertising are?
  - cold-calling
  - leaflets / brochures in your letter box
  - junk emails
  - website pop-ups
  - sports sponsorship
6 Think of adverts which use the following to sell a product:
  - a celebrity
  - an authority (e.g. a doctor)
  - a good song
  - something free
  - humour
  - a good slogan
  - a story
  - animals or nature
7 Which of the above marketing techniques might influence you to buy the product?

G relative clauses
V prefixes
P word stress

7C

Tingo

1 GRAMMAR relative clauses

a English has borrowed many words and phrases from other languages. In pairs, try to match the words with the languages they come from. Do you use any of these words (or very similar ones) in your language?

1	muesli /ˈmjuːzli/	☐	A Arabic
2	igloo /ˈɪgluː/	☐	B Czech
3	chauffeur /ˈʃəʊfə/	☐	C French
4	shampoo /ʃæmˈpuː/	☐	D German
5	algebra /ˈældʒɪbrə/	☐	E Hindi
6	robot /ˈrəʊbɒt/	☐	F Inuit
7	macho /ˈmætʃəʊ/	☐	G Italian
8	tycoon /taɪˈkuːn/	☐	H Japanese
9	graffiti /grəˈfiːti/	☐	I Spanish
10	yogurt /ˈjɒgət/	☐	J Turkish

b **Check what you know.** Complete definitions 1–6 with *which*, *who*, or *whose* and write the correct word from **a**.

1 ___robot___ a machine __which__ can perform a complicated series of tasks automatically

2 _____ a house _____ walls and ceilings are made of hard snow

3 _____ a mixture of grains, nuts and dried fruits _____ is usually eaten for breakfast

4 _____ a person _____ is successful in business or industry

5 _____ a person _____ job is to drive a car, especially for somebody rich or important

6 _____ writing or drawings _____ people do on a wall or building

c What word could you use instead of *who / which*?

d How would you define the other four words in **a**?

Any problems? ⟳ **Workbook p.70**

e **New grammar.** Read about the book **THE MEANING OF Tingo**. Do you have words for any of these concepts in your language?

f Now complete the definitions with *which* (x4), *who* (x5), *whose* (x2), *whom*, or *what* (x2).

g Look at the completed definitions in **f**. Answer the questions with a partner.

1 Which two sentences contain non-defining relative clauses (ones which add extra information to a sentence)?

2 In which sentences could you also use *that*?

3 In which sentences can you leave the relative pronoun out altogeth[...]

4 Look at the definitions for *Puntare* and *Rujuk*. How does the po[...] of the preposition affect the relative pronoun?

h ⟳ **p.144 Grammar Bank 7C.** Read the rules and do the exercises.

i ⟳ **Communication** *What's the word? A p.118 B p.120.* Define more foreign words that English has borrowed for your partner to guess.

2 SPEAKING

GET IT RIGHT **giving examples**

If you want to give examples when you are speaking English, you can use these phrases: *for example, for instance,* or *such as.*

English has borrowed many words from other languages, such as 'shampoo' and 'yogurt'.

Work in groups of three or four. Discuss the questions, giving as many examples as you can.

- Which *three* of the twelve words in **1e** would you choose to add to your language? Why?
- Think of *five* words or phrases that your language has borrowed from English?
  Have these words been borrowed because there wasn't an existing word for this concept in your language?
  If not, why do you think this word or phrase is being used in your language?
- How do you feel about these borrowed English words?
- Can you think of any words / phrases which have been borrowed from other languages?
- Can you think of *two* English words or phrases that don't have an exact translation in your language? Why do you think that is?
- Do you know any words in your language that don't have an exact translation in English?
- Do you have any favourite words in English? Why do you like them?

THE MEANING OF Tingo

In this book, Adam Jacot de Boinod, [1] _____ works as a researcher for BBC quiz programmes, has collected words from all over the world which do not exist in English, but which he thinks that perhaps English ought to incorporate into the language. The title of the book comes from one of his favourites. 'Tingo', [2] _____ is a word from the language spoken on Easter Island in the Pacific Ocean, means to borrow things from a neighbour's house one by one until there is nothing left!

Bakkushan (Japanese) A woman [3] _____ you think is pretty when you see her from behind, but is not when you see her from the front.

Drachenfutter (German) The presents [4] _____ guilty husbands give their wives (literally 'dragon's food').

Fucha (Polish) A job [5] _____ you do in your free time without paying any tax.

Lampadato (Italian) An adjective to describe a person [6] _____ skin has been tanned too much by a sun lamp.

Neko neko (Indonesian) To have a creative idea [7] _____ only makes things worse.

Puntare (Italian) To stare intensely at a person [8] _____ you are attracted to.

Rujuk (Indonesian) To remarry a woman to [9] _____ you had been married before.

Seigneur-terrasse (French) A person [10] _____ spends a lot of time but very little money in a café.

Sunasorpok (Inuit) To eat [11] _____ other people have left.

Termangu-mangu (Indonesian) Sad and not sure [12] _____ you should do.

Zechpreller (German) Someone [13] _____ leaves without paying the bill.

Zhengron (Chinese) A person [14] _____ looks have been improved by plastic surgery.

From *The meaning of Tingo*

3 READING & LISTENING

a Read about the origin of ten English words. Can you guess what any of them are? Use the pictures to help you.

The story behind the words

1 _____ Comes from two Old Norse words (the language spoken by the Vikings) which mean 'house' and 'owner'. The word originally had nothing to do with marital status, except for the fact that home ownership made these men extremely desirable marriage partners.

2 _____ From 'cabrioler', a French word which means 'jump like a goat'. The first carriages for public hire bounced up and down so much that they reminded people of goats jumping on a hillside.

3 _____ From the Italian 'To arms!', which was what soldiers shouted when they saw that the enemy was attacking.

4 _____ Genoa, called 'Gene' by sixteenth-century Europeans, was the first city to make denim cloth. The trousers were named after the city.

5 _____ In Latin, this means 'without your cape'. The ancient Romans would often avoid capture by throwing off their capes when fleeing so that they could run more quickly.

6 _____ It is believed that this term originated because of an Irishman called Patrick with this surname who, with his family, terrorized a section of London in the 1890s.

7 _____ Many banks in post-Renaissance Europe issued small, porcelain 'borrower's tiles' to their customers. Like credit cards, these tiles were imprinted with the owner's name, his credit limit, and the name of the bank. Each time the customer wanted to borrow money, he had to present the tile to the bank clerk, who would compare the imprinted credit limit with how much the customer had already borrowed. If the borrower was over the limit, the clerk broke the tile on the spot.

8 _____ From the Latin, originally meant 'placed on the knees'. In Ancient Rome, a father legally claimed his newborn child as being his by sitting in front of his family and placing the child on his knee.

9 _____ The popular explanation of the origin of this word is that it is an acronym meaning 'To Insure Promptness', that is to make sure the service in e.g. a restaurant is fast. This is incorrect. The word was underworld slang from the early 1600s meaning 'to pass on a small sum of money'.

10 _____ This was the Latin name for a slave given to Roman soldiers to reward them for performance in battle. Eventually, this term was applied to anyone who was a slave to anything, e.g. a drug.

b Now complete 1–10 with the words below. Did you guess any of them?

| addict   alarm   broke (adj = having no money)   cab (= taxi) |
| escape   genuine   jeans   hooligan   husband   tip |

c Read the article again carefully. Underline any words you don't know and try to guess their meaning from the context. Check with your teacher or a dictionary.

d Now cover the article and focus on the words in the list in **b**. In pairs, try to remember the origin of each word.

Glossary

bounce (paragraph 2) move up and down like a ball

cape (5) a piece of clothing with no sleeves worn around your shoulders

tile (7) flat bricks used to cover roofs or floors

acronym (9) a short word which is made using the first letters of a group of words e.g. **PIN** = personal identification number

promptness (9) quickness

slang (9) very informal words and expressions

e **7.7** You're going to listen to a dictionary expert talking on the radio about the origin of the words below.

• ketchup • orange • tennis

1 Which word's origin is related to a legend?
2 Which word changed its form because the original word was hard for the English to say?
3 Which word originated from the way the English pronounced a foreign word?

f Listen again and complete the summaries with one or more words.

Ketchup

The original sauce was invented by
¹_____. It was made from
²_____. British explorers first tried
it in the ³_____ century, and really
liked it. Later some colonists from
⁴_____ mixed ⁵_____ into
it, and it became the sauce it is today.

Orange

This word, and also the word for orange
in ⁶_____ and ⁷_____,
doesn't come from ⁸_____, it comes
from ancient Sanskrit. The Sanskrit word,
'narangah', may come from 'naga ranga' which
means ⁹_____. The story is that an
¹⁰_____ once ate so many that he
¹¹_____, and some orange trees grew
from his ¹²_____.

Tennis

The sport started in ¹³_____.
It was ¹⁴_____ called 'tenez' which
means ¹⁵_____. The sport
¹⁶_____ there and became popular
in ¹⁷_____. But the 'tenez' sounded
more like 'tennis' when it was said with an
¹⁸_____.

4 VOCABULARY & PRONUNCIATION
prefixes and word stress

> One way of making new words is by adding a prefix at the beginning of a word, e.g. *over-*, *under-*, *mis-*, etc. These prefixes change the meaning of a word. They are usually used without a hyphen, but sometimes need one.

a Look at the words in the list. Then match the **bold** prefixes with their meanings.

antisocial **auto**graph **ex**-husband **bi**annual **mis**spell **micro**scopic
monosyllable **multi**national **over**worked **post**graduate **pre**conceived
rewind **semi**-final **under**paid

1	after	_____	8 many	_____
2	again or back	_____	9 not enough	_____
3	against	_____	10 of or by oneself	_____
4	badly / wrongly	_____	11 one	_____
5	before	_____	12 small	_____
6	former	_____	13 too much	_____
7	half	_____	14 twice	_____

> ⚠ Unlike suffixes (which aren't stressed), prefixes are often stressed, so a word with a prefix may have two stressed syllables, the main stress on the base word and secondary stress on the prefix, e.g. *antisocial*).

b **7.8** Listen and under<u>line</u> two stressed syllables in the words in **a** (except *autograph* and *monosyllable*, which just have one).

c Which prefix(es) could you add to the words in the list to describe…?

circle   cook   Impressionists   pilot   sleep   understand

1 food that tastes a bit raw in places
2 when you wake up later than you had planned to
3 the instrument that controls a plane without the need of a person
4 the artists who came after Monet, Van Gogh, etc.
5 what happens if you don't understand something correctly
6 the shape of a half moon

d Ask and answer the questions with a partner. Ask for more information.
• Are there any professions which you think are **overpaid**?
• How often do you take **antibiotics**?
• Do you like reading **autobiographies**?
• Do you know any **ex-smokers**?
• Do you know any people who are **bilingual**?
• Are there any English words you sometimes **mispronounce**?
• Who do you think are better at **multitasking**, men or women?
• How often do you buy **pre-cooked** meals?
• When was the last time you **redecorated** your room or flat?

➲ **p.157** *Phrasal verbs in context File 7.*

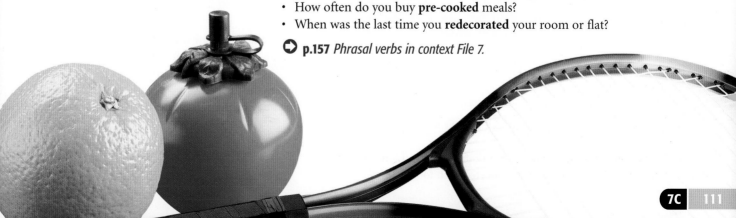

THE INTERVIEW

a You are going to listen to an interview with Susie Dent, who is a well-known English lexicographer and who also appears in the popular British TV Quiz *Countdown*. Before you listen, read the glossary and look at how the words are pronounced to help you understand what she says.

Glossary

bling /blɪŋ/ expensive shiny jewellery and bright clothes which people wear to attract attention

Baby Gangsta an American rapper, better known as BG

WAP /wæp/ Wireless Application Protocol, an application which allows mobile phones to access the internet

Charlie Parker a very influential American jazz musician

coin *v* (a word or phrase) /cɔɪn/ to invent (a new word or phrase)

hoover *n and v* /ˈhuːvə/ a vacuum cleaner, to clean a carpet or floor with a vacuum cleaner

marmalade /ˈmærməleɪd/ jam made from oranges which is very popular with toast for breakfast in the UK

muffin /ˈmʌfɪn/ a small cake in the shape of a cup often eaten for breakfast in the US

b **7.9** Listen to part 1. Answer the questions with a partner.

1 How many new words are 'born' every year?
2 How many go into the *Oxford English Dictionary* every year?
3 Why do dictionary makers usually wait five years before including a new word?
4 Where did the word 'bling' come from?

c **7.10** Listen to part 2. Answer the questions with a partner.

What does she say about...?

1 'chofa', 'waparazzi', and 'mandals'
2 'cool'
3 'wireless'
4 'sushi' and 'sashimi'
5 'Kleenex' and 'Hoover'
6 'a marmalade dropper' and 'a muffin choker'

d **7.11** Listen and complete the phrases. What do you think they mean?

COMMON PHRASES

1 Normally dictionary makers will wait about five years to see whether _____ _____ a word will survive.
2 And it went _____ _____ mainstream incredibly quick[
3 One of my favourites is 'chofas', which is a _____ _____ a chair and a sofa.
4 ...basically citizen journalists, if you like, going around _____ celebrities with their WAP-enabled phone.
5 So 'cool', for example, _____ _____ probably in the late nineteenth century.
6 They are still brand names, but we've _____ imported ther[

e Listen to the interview again with the tapescript on page 131. Can you think of any new words that have come into your language recently?

IN THE STREET

a **7.12** You are going to hear four speakers talking about English words used in their language. Who is most positive about using English words? Who is most negative?

Mateusz   **Victoria**   **Matandra**   **Volke**

b Listen again.

1 Who says that their own language is dominant in one particular field?
2 Who mentions a language which <u>doesn't</u> use English words for many modern inventions?
3 Who talks about an 'English word' that isn't really English?
4 Who mentions two words connected with food?

c **7.13** Listen and complete the phrases. What do you think they mean?

COMMON PHRASES

1 It's used, I think _____ .
2 ...which actually doesn't _____ sense in English.
3 ...everything to _____ with technology.... pv
4 Most people just _____ with *downloadare*. pv
5 And if there are new inventions or _____ like that, we don't invent new words (informal)

d Listen to the interviews again with the tapescript on page 13[
Then answer the same questions with a partner.

Which is better, working for someone else or being your own boss?

More and more people are choosing to give up their jobs and follow their dream of setting up their own company.

Being your own boss has many obvious advantages. [1]_____ is that you are in charge. You have the opportunity to do something you really believe in, [2]_____ offering a new product or providing a new service. [3]_____ is that you do not have a boss watching over you, which gives you more freedom to do things your way. Finally, the greatest advantage of all for some people, you could [4]_____ become extremely rich if your company becomes successful.

This all seems very tempting, but [5]_____, there are a number of disadvantages. You have to make a lot of big decisions, [6]_____ whether to expand, or whether to employ new staff. This is often very stressful. [7]_____ you are the boss and in theory can decide what time you finish work, you might find that instead of finishing early, you have to work all night [8]_____ an important deadline. Finally, there is an element of risk. If the company fails, you could lose not only your job, but also your home and your life savings.

[9]_____, owning a business has both advantages and disadvantages. Whether it would suit you or not depends on your skills, your personality and your family circumstances.

a Complete the composition with a linking expression from the list. Use capital letters where necessary.

also   although   another advantage   because of
for example   on the other hand   such as
the main advantage   to sum up

b Put the linking expressions in the correct spaces below.

Useful language

To list advantages / disadvantages
_____
_____

To add more points to the same argument
In addition, …
Furthermore, …
_____

To introduce an example
For instance, …
_____

To make contrasting points
However, …
In spite of (the fact that)…
_____

To give a reason
Because (+ clause)…
_____ (+ noun)…

To introduce the conclusion
In conclusion, …
_____

c You are going to write a composition titled *What are the advantages and disadvantages of being famous?*

PLAN the content.
1 Decide what you could say about how people today are interested in famous people or want to be famous themselves. This will give you material for the introduction.
2 List two or three advantages and disadvantages, and number them in order of importance.
3 Decide if you think on balance there are more advantages than disadvantages.

WRITE 120–180 words, organized in four paragraphs: introduction, advantages, disadvantages, (or disadvantages then advantages), and conclusion. Use a formal style (no contractions or colloquial expressions). Use the linking expressions in **Useful language**.

CHECK your report for mistakes (grammar , punctuation , and spelling).

GRAMMAR

a Complete the second sentence so that it means the same as the first.

1 I don't have a car, but I would like one.
I wish _____ _____ a car.

2 Please stop whistling. I'm trying to concentrate.
I wish _____ _____ stop whistling. I'm trying to concentrate.

3 I regret not speaking to her before she left.
I wish I _____ _____ to her before she left.

4 He got a good job although he didn't have the right qualifications.
He got a good job despite _____ _____ the right qualifications.

5 That's the man for whom I used to work.
That's the man I used _____ _____ _____.

b Choose a, b, or c.

1 I opened the door quietly _____ my father up.
   a to not wake
   b so that I don't wake
   c so as not to wake

2 He still works _____ he won a million pounds on the lottery last year.
   a in spite of
   b despite
   c even though

3 That's the house in _____ Shakespeare was born.
   a which
   b that
   c where

4 Do you realize _____ you've done?
   a that
   b what
   c which

5 That dog follows me _____ I go.
   a wherever
   b however
   c whatever

VOCABULARY

a Circle the right word.

1 That walk was *exhausted / exhausting*. I need a good rest now.
2 I was really *shocked / shocking* when I read the email.
3 This company has forty *employees / employers*.
4 Do you *do /make* business with many foreign companies?
5 That lawyer must be very successful – he's got so many *customers / clients*.

b Complete the missing words.

1 Will the company make a **p**_____ or loss this year?
2 The **s**_____ for their new advertising campaign is 'You'll never find a better one'.
3 My uncle was made **r**_____ and had to look for another job.
4 We are planning to **l**_____ our new product in September.
5 The bank has **br**_____ all over the country.

c Complete the sentences with one word.

1 He has set _____ a new company which makes software.
2 Our local shop has been taken _____ by a big supermarket chain.
3 They missed the last bus so I ended _____ having to drive them home.
4 There are many different kinds of pasta, such _____ *fettucine*.
5 Many English words come from French, _____ example *royal*.

d Complete the sentence using the **bold** word and a prefix.

1 This word is very difficult to say. I always _____ it. **pronounce**
2 When I finish my first degree I want to get a _____ qualification. **graduate**
3 The city centre was completely _____ after the war. **build**
4 We are really _____. We can hardly survive on our salary. **paid**
5 The actress wrote her _____ after she retired. **biography**

PRONUNCIATION

a Underline the word with a different sound.

1		amusing	business	whose	misunderstand
2		staff	branch	launch	market
3		colleague	logo	though	owner
4		client	biannual	irritate	tiring
5		company	shocked	money	worried

b Underline the stressed syllable.

disappointed   increase (verb)   export (noun)   employee   autograph

What can you do?

CAN YOU UNDERSTAND THIS TEXT?

a Read the article and choose a, b, or c.

1 Over the centuries the Pirahã tribe has _____.
  a not decreased in numbers
  b kept its customs
  c communicated without words

2 Their language is unusual because _____.
  a some concepts don't exist
  b men and women use different vocabulary
  c there is no grammar

3 When the Pirahã women speak together they _____.
  a can't be understood by men
  b usually whistle to each other
  c sound as if they are just making noises

4 When Everett tried to teach them arithmetic, _____.
  a he quickly gave up
  b he eventually realised it was impossible
  c they didn't want to learn

5 Chomsky's Theory of Universal Grammar maintains that _____.
  a children can learn a language quickly
  b all languages have some rules in common
  c all languages count in the same way

b Look at the highlighted words and phrases. Can you guess what they mean?

CAN YOU UNDERSTAND THESE PEOPLE?

a **7.14** Listen and circle the correct answer, a, b, or c.

1 What does the woman find irritating?
  a The man never does the washing-up.
  b The man leaves dirty dishes on the table.
  c The man eats so slowly.

2 Why does the man regret not going to university?
  a He would have been able to get a more interesting job.
  b He would be earning much more money.
  c He would have enjoyed the experience.

3 People who buy the fitness programme _____.
  a can work out with a personal trainer
  b get a free set of weights
  c can consult a trainer if necessary

4 What profit did the company make this year?
  a 132 billion pounds.
  b 43 million yen.
  c 550 million pounds.

5 What is the woman's new boss like?
  a She's rather arrogant.
  b She's quite friendly.
  c She makes people feel inferior.

A world without time or number

The Pirahã are an isolated Amazonian tribe of hunter-gatherers who live deep in the Brazilian rainforest. The tribe has survived, their culture intact, for centuries, although there are now only around 200 left. The Pirahã, who communicate mainly through hums and whistles, have fascinated ethnologists for years, mainly because they have almost no words for numbers. They use only three words to count: *one*, *two*, and *many*.

We know about the Pirahã thanks to an ex-hippy and former missionary, Dan Everett, now a Professor of Phonetics, who spent seven years with the tribe in the 70s and 80s. Everett discovered a world without numbers, without time, without words for colours, without subordinate clauses and without a past tense. Their language, he found, was not just simple grammatically; it was restricted in its range of sounds and differed between the sexes. For the men, it has just eight consonants and three vowels; for the women, who have the smallest number of speech sounds in the world, to seven consonants and three vowels. To the untutored ear , the language sounds more like humming than speech. The Pirahã can also whistle their language, which is how men communicate when hunting.

Their culture is similarly constrained . The Pirahã can't write, have little collective memory, and no concept of decorative art. In 1980 Everett tried to teach them to count: he explained basic arithmetic to an enthusiastic group keen to learn the skills needed to trade with other tribes. After eight months, not one could count to ten; even one plus one was beyond them . The experiment seemed to confirm Everett's theory: the tribe just couldn't conceive the concept of number.

The Pirahã's inability to count is important because it seems to disprove Noam Chomsky's influential Theory of Universal Grammar, which holds that the human mind has a natural capacity for language, and that all languages share a basic rule structure, which enables children to understand abstract concepts such as number. One of Chomsky's collaborators has recently gone on an expedition with Everett to study the tribe. We do not yet know if the Piraha have persuaded him to change his theory.

b **7.15** You will hear part of a radio programme about a book called *The Surgeon of Crowthorne*. Listen and answer the questions.

1 What is the book's subtitle?
2 Who was W.C. Minor?
3 What did he help to create?
4 What happened when Murray, the editor, went to meet him?
5 What crime had Minor committed?

CAN YOU SAY THIS IN ENGLISH?

Can you…?

☐ describe things that irritate you and that you would like people to stop doing using *I wish*

☐ talk about things you regret in life

☐ talk about advertisements you like or dislike and explain whether they make you want to buy the products

☐ talk about foreign words which are used in your language and how you feel about them

Communication

1B You're psychic, aren't you? **Student A**

a Imagine you're a psychic. Make guesses and complete the sentences below about **B**.

   1 Your favourite colour is _____, …?
   2 You really like _____, (a sport or hobby)…?
   3 You went to _____ last weekend, …?
   4 You haven't been to _____ (a country), …?
   5 You were born in _____ (place), …?
   6 You'd like to be able to _____, …?
   7 You can't _____ very well, …?
   8 You're very good at _____, …?

b Check if your guesses are true, by saying the sentences to **B** and checking with a question tag, e.g. *Your favourite colour is pink, isn't it?* Try to use a falling intonation.

c Now **B** will check his / her guesses about you. Respond with a short answer. If the guess is wrong, tell **B** the real answer.

d Count your correct guesses. Who was the better psychic?

1C You're the doc! **Students A + B**

Check your answers.

1	*c*	The correct treatment is to pinch the soft part of the nose. This will usually cure a nosebleed if you do it for five minutes. If not, repeat for 10 minutes, and if that still doesn't work, go to your nearest hospital.

2	*a*	The correct treatment is first to pour cold water on the burn for at least 10 minutes and then to cover it with a loose bandage. If you haven't got a bandage, you can use a clean plastic bag or kitchen film. Do not break blisters and don't put any cream on the burn.

2A Clothes quiz **Student A**

a Ask **B** the questions (the answers are in *italics*).

   1 What's the opposite of…?
     • These trousers are too tight. (*These trousers are too loose.*)
     • trendy clothes (*old-fashioned clothes*)
     • get dressed (*get undressed*)
   2 What material are the following usually made of?
     • a sweater (*wool*)
     • cycling shorts (*Lycra™*)
     • a tie (*silk*)
   3 What does it mean if you say 'These shoes don't fit me'? (*They're too big or too small.*)
   4 When do people normally…?
     • try clothes on (*in a shop before they buy them*)
     • dress up (*for a party, a wedding, etc.*)
   5 What does it mean if you say 'Paula's dressed to kill tonight'? (*People will admire her because of her clothes.*)

b Answer **B**'s questions.

2B Flight stories **Student A**

a You're going to read a newspaper article and then tell your partner about it. Read the article and write down 10 words that will help you remember the story.

Lovesick violinist grounds plane

Nuala Ni Chanainn, an Irish violinist, had been travelling round San Francisco as part of a theatre group. When the tour was over, she went to the airport and boarded the plane that would take her back home to Ireland. She was in her seat, waiting for the plane to take off, when she suddenly decided not to go after all. She rushed off the plane at the last minute, leaving TWA airline officials thinking that she perhaps had planted a bomb on the plane and escaped. The plane and all the luggage were thoroughly searched by a bomb-sniffing dog. Meanwhile, the airport authorities stopped Nuala and took her away to be questioned. However, after extensive questioning, she managed to convince them that she hadn't planted a bomb: she simply couldn't bear to leave her new boyfriend! The plane was allowed to depart nearly four hours later, minus the love-struck violinist, who then spent another two weeks in the States with the boyfriend.

b Close your book and tell **B** your story in your own words, e.g. *There was a woman called Nuala who was a violinist from Ireland…*

c Now listen to **B**'s story, and ask your partner to clarify or rephrase if there's anything you don't understand

2C Reading habits **Students A + B**

a Answer the questions in the reading questionnaire with a partner.

b How similar are your reading habits?

The press
national newspapers
local papers
sports papers
magazines
comics
academic journals

Books
novels
classics
short stories
non-fiction, e.g.
biographies, history
textbooks
manuals

Online
web pages
blogs
chats and forums
academic / work-
related texts
news websites
song lyrics

The reading questionnaire

General reading
Which of the above do you read? How often?
Do you ever read any of them in English?
Do you read anything specifically to improve your English?
Do you enjoy reading on screen?
Do you read more or less than you used to?

If you read books...
What was the last book you read?
Why did you choose to read it?
What are you reading at the moment?
Do you have a favourite author or authors?
What's the best book you've read recently?

If you don't read books...
Why don't you read books?
If you had more time, would you read more?
Did you use to read books when you were younger?
What's your favourite way to relax?

3A There's only one place burglars won't look... **Students A + B**

Read and check your answers.

> **50 professional burglars described their working methods to researchers who visited them in jail. Their research revealed:**

1 **b** An experienced burglar searches a house in 20 minutes, and usually takes £1,500 worth of goods.

2 **a** Favourite items to steal are expensive goods which are fairly easy to transport including digital cameras and flat screen TVs.

3 **a** The criminals unanimously considered a noisy dog more of a deterrent than a burglar alarm.

4 **a, b, d** However, ten of the fifty burglars said they actually preferred homes to be occupied, as there was less risk of being disturbed by returning residents.

5 **b** The burglar's favourite method was dismantling windows or patio doors.

6 **1** the main bedroom, **2** the living room, **3** the dining room, **4** the study, **5** the kitchen, **6** a child's bedroom.

> **So if you want a tip from the professionals, hide your jewellery in the children's bedroom and leave the dog at home when you go out!**

4B Argument! **Student A**

Read the situations and roleplay the arguments.

1 It's your birthday today. Your husband (B) had promised to come home early. You have prepared a great dinner. You have been dropping hints for the past month that what you really want for your birthday is some jewellery as your partner is usually very unimaginative about choosing presents. Last Christmas he bought you some DVDs which you didn't particularly like. He arrives home late, and produces a box of chocolates (you're on a diet, and he knows this) which looks as if it was bought at a petrol station.

You start. **B** has just given you the chocolates.

2 You're in your first year of university, studying medicine. You haven't enjoyed it at all, and have just failed all your first year exams. In fact, you never really wanted to study medicine, but your parents are both doctors and you feel they pushed you into it. You would like to change courses and study journalism, which you think would suit you better. You want to try to convince your mother / father, although you know they're not very pleased with your exam results.

B will start

Communication

4C Two paintings Student A

The Hotel Lobby (1943) Edward Hopper

a Look carefully at your painting. Then describe it in detail to **B**, focusing especially on the people and their body language. Say who you think they are and what you think they're doing.

b Show your picture to **B** and see if he / she agrees with you.

c Listen to **B** describe another painting. Try to visualize it.

d **B** will now show you the picture to see if you agree with his / her description and interpretation.

5B Sleep Students A + B

Read the results of the questionnaire and calculate your score. The higher your score the more sleep deprived you are. The maximum is 14.

```
1  a 0      b 1
2  a 1      b 0      c 0
3  a 1      b 0      c 0
4  a 0      b 1      c 2
5  a 0      b 1      c 2      d 2
6  a 0      b 1      c 2
7  a 0      b 1      c 0      d 1
8  1 point for each one you circle
```

6C Are you a creative thinker? Students A + B

Check your answers to the test.

Are you a creative thinker?

1 The more times you have circled false, the more creative you are and the higher your 'eureka potential'.

2 The vast majority of people choose either 35 or 37. However, truly creative people usually come up with a different number, e.g. 17 or 31.

3 The more boxes you were able to fill, the more creative you are. The following are some of the more creative ideas that people have come up with:

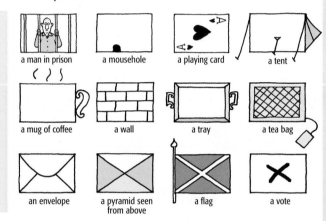

a man in prison   a mousehole   a playing card   a tent

a mug of coffee   a wall   a tray   a tea bag

an envelope   a pyramid seen from above   a flag   a vote

4 The important question concerns how you represented the number 4. In Roman numerals the number 4 is always represented as 'IV'. However, on almost all clocks and watches except for Big Ben in London, the number is represented as 'IIII'. If you filled it in as 'IV', that means that although you have probably seen clocks and watches with Roman numerals hundreds of times, you have not really seen or remembered what is right in front of your eyes.

7C What's the word? Student A

a Check that you know what your list of words below mean. Then define them to **B**, saying which language they come from.

1 **caravan** /ˈkærəvæn/ (Persian)
2 **blanket** /ˈblæŋkɪt/ (French)
3 **embarrassed** /ɪmˈbærəst/ (French)
4 **tsunami** /tsuːˈnɑːmi/ (Japanese)
5 **soprano** /səˈprɑːnəʊ/ (Italian)
6 **massage** /ˈmæsɑːʒ/ (Portuguese)
7 **mosquito** /mɒsˈkiːtəʊ/ (Spanish)
8 **fog** /fɒg/ (Danish)

b Listen to **B**'s definitions and say what the word is.

c Has your language 'borrowed' any of these words?

1B You're psychic, aren't you? **Student B**

a Imagine you're a psychic. Make guesses and complete the sentences below about **A**.

1 You're going to _____ tonight, …?
2 You don't like _____, (a kind of music)…?
3 You've seen _____ (a film), …?
4 You didn't _____ last night, …?
5 You were born in _____ (month), …?
6 You wouldn't like to be a / an _____ (a job), …?
7 Your favourite season is _____, …?
8 You can speak _____, …?

b **A** is going to make some guesses about you. Respond with a short answer. If the guess is wrong, tell **A** the real answer.

c Now check if your guesses about **A** are true, by saying the sentences and checking with a question tag, e.g. *You're going to see a film tonight, aren't you?* Try to use a falling intonation.

d Count your correct guesses. Who was the better psychic?

2A Clothes quiz **Student B**

a Answer **A**'s questions.

b Ask **B** the questions (the answers are in *italics*).

1 What's the opposite of…?
   • He looks smart. (*He looks scruffy.*)
   • a short-sleeved T-shirt (*a long-sleeved T-shirt*)
   • put your shoes on (*take your shoes off*)
2 What material are the following usually made of?
   • tights (*nylon*)
   • shoes (*leather*)
   • jeans (*denim*)
3 What does it mean if you say 'That shirt doesn't suit you'? (*It doesn't look good on you.*)
4 When do people normally…?
   • hang clothes up (*after they've ironed them or after they take them off, e.g. in the evening*)
   • get changed (*to go to the gym, when they get home from work*)
5 What does it mean if you say 'Mark needs to pull his socks up'? (*He needs to work harder.*)

2B Flight stories **Student B**

a You're going to read a newspaper article and then tell your partner about it. Read the article and write down 10 words that will help you remember the story.

Tourist stranded at airport for five months

When student Sheridan Gregorio arrived at Fortaleza airport in Brazil, he was planning to fly home to Holland. He had had a great holiday, but unfortunately he had spent all his money. All he had was his return air ticket to Amsterdam. But when he checked in, the airline staff at the airport told him that he would have to pay airport tax before he could leave the country. Sheridan explained that he was completely broke, but he wasn't allowed to fly and so he missed his flight home. His ticket was non-refundable, so now he needed to buy a new ticket *and* pay the airport tax.

As he had no money, Sheridan's only option was to sleep in the airport and clean restaurants in exchange for food and some money. After working for five months, he had saved enough for the airport tax and the Brazilian police persuaded the airline to let him use his old ticket to go home. Sheridan told a newspaper reporter from *Jornal da Globo*, 'The Brazilian people were really nice to me, they treated me very well.' Sheridan finally arrived home safe and sound last week.

b Listen to **A**'s story, and ask your partner to clarify or rephrase if there's anything you don't understand.

c Close your book and tell **A** your story in your own words, e.g. *There was a Dutch man who was on holiday in Brazil…*

Communication

4B Argument! **Student B**

Read the situations and roleplay the arguments.

A is your partner. He / She will start.

1 It's your partner's birthday today. You know that she wants some jewellery, but you have been very busy at work and haven't had time to go shopping. You had intended to finish work early and go shopping today, but you couldn't, so you stopped at a petrol station on the way home and bought some chocolates which you know she usually likes.

2 Your son / daughter is in his / her first year of university studying medicine. You yourself are a doctor and you really encouraged your child to follow in your footsteps. He / She was good at science at school, and you think he / she would make an excellent doctor. He / She was quite keen on studying journalism, but you think that this is a 'lazy option' and that it's very difficult to get a good job in journalism nowadays, so you were very relieved when he / she agreed to study medicine. Although he / she worked hard at school, this year at university he / she seems to be out with friends all the time and spends a lot less time studying than you did at the same age. You have just discovered that he / she has failed all the first-year exams.

You start.

4C Two paintings **Student B**

a Look carefully at your painting, which you're going to describe to **A**.

b Listen to **A** describe another painting. Try to visualize it. **A** will now show you the picture to see if you agree with his / her description and interpretation.

c Now describe your painting to **A**. Focus especially on the people and their body language. Say who you think they are and what you think they're doing.

d Show your picture to **A** and see if he / she agrees with you.

7C What's the word? **Student B**

a Check that you know what your list of words below mean. You're going to define them to **A**.
   1 **bungalow** /ˈbʌŋgələʊ/ (Hindi)
   2 **monsoon** /mɒnˈsuːn/ (Arabic)
   3 **lottery** /ˈlɒtəri/ (Dutch)
   4 **poodle** /ˈpuːdl/ (German)
   5 **bonsai** /ˈbɒnsaɪ/ (Japanese)
   6 **parasol** /ˈpærəsɒl/ (Italian)
   7 **kidnap** /ˈkɪdnæp/ (Norwegian)
   8 **iceberg** /ˈaɪsbɜːg/ (Dutch)

b Listen to **A**'s definitions and say what each word is.

c Now define your words to **A**, saying which language they come from

d Has your language 'borrowed' any of these words?

Listening

1.3 Interviewer … and with me I've got Emily and Alex. Emily, what kind of questions did you ask?

Emily Well, the organizers of the event suggested a list of topics, you know, sort of pre-prepared questions, but I thought that they were very er artificial, you know strange. So I asked quite normal questions like, 'Why did you come tonight?' or 'Have you been speed dating before?' or 'What do you like doing in your free time?' I found that the conversation ran more smoothly when I asked people these kinds of normal questions.

Interviewer How about you Alex?

Alex Yes, same as Emily, really. I also asked quite normal things like, 'What do you do? Have you done this before? Do you enjoy living in Oxford?' Things like that.

Interviewer Did other people ask *you* interesting questions?

Alex Yes, some were quite interesting. Ones I can remember are, 'If you were an animal, what would you be?' Or, 'If you had to choose a different career from your current one, what would it be?' One woman even said 'I've heard that you were in prison once – is that true?' I don't know where she got that from!

Interviewer And you, Emily. Were you asked anything unusual?

Emily Not really! The most common questions were 'Are you American?' or 'Where are you from?' The second most common was, 'Why do you live in England?' Although one person did ask me, 'If you could be invisible for a day, what would you do?'

Interviewer How did you answer that?

Emily I said I'd go to work and play tricks on my colleagues in the office like hiding things!

Interviewer How many matches did you get?

Emily I chose six men that I would be happy to see again, and of those six, four of them had chosen me too, so I got four matches.

Alex I got three.

Interviewer Did you go out with any of the people?

Emily Yes, I went on one date with a guy who teaches biochemistry at university. It was a bit of a disaster though, because earlier that morning I'd been to the dentist, and I'd had an injection, so by the time that we met for coffee I had terrible toothache and I was in agony. I had to go home after half an hour. We've exchanged a few emails since then, but we haven't managed to meet. We're both very busy. Also, to be honest, I don't think he's really my type. He seems to be really keen to get married and have children straight away and I'm not.

Interviewer What about the other three matches?

Emily The second man contacted me directly after the event and invited me to dinner. But then he sent me a text message the next day and cancelled. He said that he had met someone else. The other two have been in touch, but we haven't been able to meet yet. In fact, I've decided that for the moment, I'm actually happy being single so I don't think I'll be speed dating again any time soon.

Interviewer How about you Alex?

Alex I emailed one of the matches, a woman I quite liked and we met at a bar in Oxford. At the speed dating event she seemed really bubbly and good fun, but after spending a few minutes with her it was very clear that we had *nothing* in common. The atmosphere was awful and it was all very awkward and I think she felt the same so we just finished our drinks and left. We didn't contact each other again.

Then I arranged to meet another of my matches. We'd really got on well at the speed dating so I was quite excited about meeting her. Unfortunately, on that morning, I'd found out that I'd lost my job and I was really worried that I would not give the right impression because I was feeling so unhappy about my work situation. But actually, Susanna quickly made me forget everything and we had a great evening. We then met up the next day and went for a long walk. And well, to cut a long story short, six months later I took her to Paris and proposed, and two months ago we got married!

Emily Aaaah!

Interviewer So a real success story for you then?

Alex Absolutely!

1.6 Jane When I arrived I was shown into Sally's office – which was much more normal than I'd expected. Sally looks like a kind and sincere woman. She says that she inherited from her grandmother the ability to 'see' the past and future of other people. First she asked me a few basic questions – was I married, did I have children, and so on. However, her next questions rather surprised me …

Sally Who's Caroline?

Jane I'm afraid I don't know. I don't know anybody called Caroline.

Sally Well, somebody called Caroline is going to have a powerful and positive effect on your finances. Australia is very important in your life.

Jane Is it? I've never been to Australia.

Sally Well, you'll be going there very soon.

1.7 Sally Another place which is very important in your life is Ireland.

Jane Yes, that's true. Ireland *does* play a big role in my life. In fact, I grew up there.

Sally Ireland is a place where you will find answers to a lot of your problems. Look for the Irish connection. I'm very very optimistic that an Irish man is going to be 'the one for you'.

Jane Ah, very interesting! What does he look like?

Sally He's very tall.

Jane That's good – I'm 1 metre 90 myself.

Sally And he's highly intelligent; in fact it's his brain that will really attract you to him. He's a distinguished public figure – perhaps a professor?

Jane So when am I going to meet him?

Sally Actually, you already know him. It's just you don't think of him in that way.

Jane I immediately started thinking about all the people I know, but, to be honest, I couldn't think of anyone who fitted the description.

1.8 Jane I decided to ask Sally some questions myself.

Jane What about my health?

Sally Let's see, your mother suffers from headaches, doesn't she?

Jane Yes she does, actually. She gets bad headaches.

Sally Well, you'll need to watch out for headaches, and so will your mother, because hers are going to get worse. But in general, you're a healthy woman, and you'll have a long life without any major illnesses, but you must *never* be tempted to have plastic surgery – if you do, it will go horribly wrong.

Jane So far it had all been quite positive, but I wasn't really convinced. It was only when she started talking about my children that I really started listening.

Sally Your son Conor is very like you. He's good with language and he may end up working with words, maybe a poet or a songwriter.

Jane In fact he *does* like words and writing, and last week he won a poetry prize at school.

Sally But your daughter Clara is more like your ex-husband. She's not good with words at all.

Jane It's true! They're both dyslexic. This was beginning to make me wonder…

1.9 Jane I left Sally's office feeling very positive. She gave me a recording of our conversation on a CD, because she said I needed to listen to everything she had told me a few times. When I got home, I put on the CD. When I listened again, I realized that for every thing that Sally got right, she got several things wrong. I came to the conclusion then that Sally *doesn't* have any paranormal abilities. She is just very good at judging people's character and makes good guesses about their lives from the information she gets from you. But strangely enough, recently I've been seeing a lot more of an old friend of mine who is a professor. He's not Irish, but he has just invited me to join him on a lecture tour… of Australia.

1.15 When I saw the lady's face, I knew it was really serious. Her face was starting to turn blue. I put my arms around her waist and I pulled hard in and up three times and the piece of steak came out. Then I just put my arm round the lady and gave her a hug.

I knew exactly what to do because before I started to work as a television presenter, I used to be a flight attendant. We were taught a lot about first aid. The technique I used is called the Heimlich manoeuvre and it's what you should do when someone is choking. I must admit I was a bit embarrassed by all the attention I got in the restaurant and then the next day the story was in all the newspapers. But I'm very glad I was there to help. And maybe this story will make people think about learning first aid. I really think it's something which should be taught at school. It's so important!

1.16 I knew I was hurting Peter, but I carried on pushing my fingers down his throat. I managed to touch the tomato with two of my fingers and I was able to move it a little. That was enough – Peter started coughing and the tomato came out.

But I was very lucky. Afterwards, I found out that my ignorance of first aid had nearly killed my son. Hitting Peter on the back was OK, but putting my fingers down his throat was a big mistake. I could have pushed the tomato even further down his throat and he could have died. I'd made every mistake possible and I nearly killed him because of my ignorance. I should have called an ambulance immediately, because I don't know first aid, and the ambulance staff would have told me exactly what to do… and what not to do.

1.18 Interviewer Frank Clifford is an astrologer and palmist. What does an astrologer do?

Frank An astrologer will take your date, place, and time of birth, construct a map of the heavens, a horoscope, that will look at temperament, character, emotional needs and a number of other different factors.

Interviewer What does being a palmist mean?

Frank Well, as a palmist is quite different from being an astrologer, a palmist will look at your hands as they are now of course, or he may do a print and have a look at what is being shown in the hands now, but whereas astrology is a birth chart set up, a horoscope set up for somebody's birth moment, the hands are your living hands so they've developed and grown with you of course, so they reflect where you are today and what you do and palmists will read, again, character, perhaps past events, possible future events from the hand.

Interviewer So can astrologers and palmists predict people's future?

Frank A lot of astrologers and palmists would say that it's not really about reading somebody's future, it's about understanding where they are today and being able to understand who they are, where they are today, and future possibilities and I think people should come to a palmist or astrologer not to be told about an unalterable destiny or future, but to be told or given tools enough to make it themselves, and be very proactive in that area themselves. So it's our job really to encourage people to live their own lives and decide their own future, not feel as though it's written anywhere and that they have nothing to do or say about the outcome.

Interviewer If you saw on someone's hand that they were going to have a serious illness, would you tell them?

Frank I'm not a doctor so I wouldn't go there. I certainly wouldn't talk about anything medical. But if somebody comes and they've had cancer or they're in the process of being treated for an illness, that's something we might discuss, but it's certainly something I wouldn't predict, because I don't necessarily believe in making predictions.

1.19 **Interviewer** How should people choose which astrologer or which palm reader to see?

Frank Well, I would recommend going to somebody who has been recommended to you, there are a lot of people out there who, a lot of people doing a genuine job, but will talk about things that no palmist really should talk about, like health matters, as I've spoken about, death, other illnesses, things that take away somebody's ability or right to choose. The reason that I got into palmistry was at the age of seventeen, I was told by a palmist that I would be married at 21 and then my partner would die, which scared the life out of me at the time, and I felt I had this curse on my back, and so I thought I'd learn this subject and understand what on earth she was talking about and I realized that what she was looking at was a very big 'if', a very big possibility rather than a probability and it never happened.

Interviewer What kind of people come to see you?

Frank A lot of people would expect bored housewives and people with nothing better to do, or too much money, more money than sense, to come, but in fact the truth is you tend to get all sorts of people from every type or walk of life. I've had sportspeople, politicians, people in the media, in every type of profession you can think of, male, female. Usually it tends to be more women, you tend to get more men looking at palmistry because it's perhaps more physical and open and they feel that… some men tell me they believe more in the hand rather than a horoscope, because a horoscope is something that women read in their magazines or newspapers.

Interviewer Do you ever look at your own future?

Frank Well, rather than try to look at my own future or predict it I try and have it, I try and experience it. And I don't think most astrologers or palmists actually do predict or try to predict what's going on in their life. They just live it from day to day as anyone else would, but they try to live it with some understanding and some knowledge or at least some meaning of why we're here and what is happening at this time.

1.21 **Interviewer** What's your star sign?

Cherry Capricorn.

Interviewer Do you ever read your horoscope?

Cherry Occasionally, but not because I particularly believe in them, but just because they're there. And it's quite fun.

Interviewer Do you think someone's star sign has an influence on their personality?

Cherry Not particularly, no. I don't really think so.

Interviewer What's your star sign?

Miles Scorpio, I had to think about that one.

Interviewer Do you ever read your horoscope?

Miles No, never.

Interviewer Do you think someone's star sign has an influence on their personality?

Miles Well, possibly. I'm not a great believer I have to say, although perhaps the time of year someone is born may vaguely reflect on their characteristics. But I think it's pretty minimal the effect, to be perfectly honest.

Interviewer What's your star sign?

Mike Aries.

Interviewer Do you ever read your horoscope?

Mike Oh, I'm a big believer in horoscopes. Some people say it's quite sad, but I tend to live every day on a horoscope. See if it ever comes true. It doesn't really, but it's just nice to know.

Interviewer Do you think someone's star sign has an influence on their personality?

Mike Yes, I think it does. You can definitely tell with some star signs. You can definitely tell their, sort of, personality straightaway. It does play a big role, I think.

Interviewer What's your star sign?

Theresa I was born under the star sign of Capricorn, so I'm an old goat, basically.

Interviewer Do you ever read your horoscope?

Theresa I do occasionally, yes.

Interviewer Do you think someone's star sign has an influence on their personality?

Theresa Well, I think it has an influence on mine because Capricorn is the goat and goats are always climbing onwards and upwards and that really is very much me.

Interviewer What's your star sign?

Kurt Aries, Aries.

Interviewer Do you ever read your horoscope?

Kurt No.

Interviewer Do you think someone's star sign has an influence on their personality?

Kurt None, whatsoever, not unless they read it first and then change their personality to match.

2.1

1 I think above all we are strong individualists. We want as few rules as possible governing our lives. We are also very hard-working. People here live to work and don't work to live. We are also very optimistic, and we think that if we work hard, we can achieve anything. On the negative side, I think we are extremely materialistic. The measure of success for most people here is money. We are extremely concerned with 'things' – possessions and the bigger the better. Personally, I think I have inherited the typical optimism and drive, and I'm also an individualist, so I think I'm probably quite typical, but I hope I'm less materialistic than many of my countrymen seem to be.

2 Generally speaking, I think we're very sociable and easy-going, and we're great storytellers. People are also quite religious and family oriented, we're also very patriotic. Maybe this is because we're a small country and so many of us live abroad. Historically there has always been a lot of emigration. Weaknesses? I think we can be very melancholic and nostalgic, you only have to listen to our music to hear this – it's often quite sad and slow. It's probably because of our climate and our history. The stereotypical image is that one minute we're laughing and telling you a funny story and the next minute we're crying into our beer. Which reminds me that we also drink quite a lot. I think I'm quite typical in many respects, although I'm not particularly melancholic.

3 It's difficult to generalize about us as a people, especially as our big cities now have such a multi-ethnic population, but I would say that we're basically very tolerant and open-minded. We're not nearly as insular as we used to be. We defend the things that we believe in – when we have to – and we avoid taking extreme positions, which I think is another strength. One of our main weaknesses, though, is that we can be quite self-satisfied and arrogant towards foreigners. Just think of our inability, or our unwillingness, to learn foreign languages! I'd also say that that we can be lazy, and we're a bit careless about the way we dress, and also we drink too much. I don't think I'm very typical, though I do definitely have one of the weaknesses – but I'm not going to say which!

4 As a nation we're very proud of our identity and our cultural heritage. We're an inventive people, but we often feel marginalized and forgotten by our bigger neighbour, England that is. We're very sociable and like to have a good time. We're also great travellers and people often compliment us on the good behaviour of our sports fans abroad.

On the other hand, we do have a tendency to melancholy – maybe it's something to do with the weather, you know we tend to think that life is hard. There's also a negative attitude towards our neighbour – and this can range from humorous comments to actual violence. And although we are keen travellers, we can be quite negative towards foreigners. Some people would like to see the country kept only for us, without apparently understanding how negative that could be.

I don't think of myself as a typical example. I love the country, and think it has some of the most beautiful scenery in the world, but I feel that we tend to focus too much on the wrongs done to us in the distant past, rather than trying to move on.

2.6 **Interviewer** With me in the studio today I have two pilots, Richard and Steven, who are going to answer some of the most frequently asked questions about flying and air travel. Hello to both of you.

Pilots Hello.

Interviewer Right, the first question is what weather conditions are the most dangerous when flying a plane?

Steven Probably the most dangerous weather conditions are when the wind changes direction very suddenly. This tends to happen during thunderstorms and typhoons and it's especially dangerous during take-off and landing. But it's quite unusual – I've been flying for 37 years now and I've only experienced this three or four times.

Interviewer Is all turbulence dangerous?

Steven No, in fact it's not normally dangerous. Pilots know when to expect turbulence and we try to avoid it by changing routes or flight levels.

Interviewer Which is more dangerous, take-off or landing?

Richard Both take-off and landing can be dangerous. They're the most critical moments of a flight. Pilots talk about the 'critical eight minutes' – the three minutes after take-off and the five minutes before landing. Most accidents happen in this period.

Steven I would say take-off is probably slightly more dangerous than landing. There is a critical moment just before take off when the plane is accelerating, but it hasn't yet reached the speed to be able to fly. If the pilot has a problem with the plane at this point, he has very little time – maybe only a second – to abort the take off.

Interviewer Passengers often think that putting on seat belts in a plane is really a waste of time. Is that true?

Richard Not at all. When the plane is moving on the ground and the pilot suddenly puts the brakes on, passengers can be thrown out of their seats, just like in a car. But more importantly, during the flight if there is sudden and severe turbulence, you could be thrown all over the cabin if you aren't wearing your seat belt. That's why airlines usually recommend you wear your belt even when the seat belt light is off.

Interviewer Should we really listen to the safety information?

Steven It's definitely worth listening to the information about emergency exits. If there's a fire on a plane, it may be dark and the plane will be full of smoke and fumes. So listening to where the exits are and working out which one is the nearest exit to you might save your life. Most air crew can even tell you where the emergency exits are in the hotels where they stay.

Interviewer What about life jackets?

Richard Fortunately, planes very rarely have to land in the sea, but to be honest the chances of surviving if your plane did crash into the sea are not high.

Interviewer Are some airports more dangerous than others?

Steven Yes, some are – particularly airports with high mountains around them and airports in countries with older or more basic navigation equipment.

Richard For some difficult airports like, let's say Kathmandu, they only allow very experienced pilots to land there. And for some of these airports pilots have to practise on a simulator first before they are given permission to land a plane there.

Interviewer How important is it for pilots and controllers to have good clear English?

Steven It's the official language of the air, so obviously it's vital for pilots and controllers to have good English. To be honest, it doesn't always happen.

Richard And apart from people's English not being good, some countries don't respect the convention and don't force their pilots to speak in English. But most of them do, luckily.

2.7 Interviewer Have you ever had a problem with a famous person as a passenger?

Richard I've carried a lot of famous people and they are usually very well behaved. But I remember once I had the actor Steven Seagal as a passenger – and the cabin crew told me that he had just got on board and he was carrying an enormous samurai sword. Weapons aren't allowed on board, of course, so I had to go and speak to him. He looked very imposing standing in the cabin. He was nearly 2 metres tall, dressed completely in black, carrying a sword and he is – as you probably know – a martial arts expert. But in fact he was very happy to give us the sword, which was gold and which had been given to him as a present in Bali.

Interviewer What's your most frightening experience as a pilot?

Steven Crossing the road outside the airport terminal! That's certainly the most dangerous thing I do. Probably in connection with flying, my most frightening experience would have to be a near miss I had when I was flying a Boeing 747 at night. A small aeroplane passed in the opposite direction just 15 metres below my plane. Just after this happened, a flight attendant brought us some hot snacks and I distinctly remember how good they tasted!

Interviewer Have you ever been taken ill during a flight?

Richard Once I was flying from Hong Kong to London, that's a 13-hour flight, and I got food poisoning after six hours. I felt terrible – incapable of doing anything at all for the rest of the flight. Luckily though, the rest of the crew were fine, because on all flights the crew are given different meals, just in case. So as my co-pilots had eaten a different meal and felt fine, the flight was able to continue safely.

2.15 "No!" Peter shouted.

The windshield cracked and popped out as the fire engine hit the floor. Broken. Peter hadn't even played with it once, and his second best Christmas present was broken.

Later, when Mommy came into the living room, he didn't thank Peter for picking up all the wrapping paper. Instead, she scooped up Little Brother™ and turned him on again.

He trembled and screeched louder than ever.

"My God! How long has he been off?" Peter's mother demanded.

"I don't like him!"

"Peter, it scares him! Listen to him!"

"I hate him! Take him back!"

"You are not to turn him off again. Ever!"

"He's mine!" Peter shouted. "He's mine and I can do what I want with him! He broke my fire engine!"

"He's a baby!"

"He's stupid! I hate him! Take him back!"

"You are going to learn to be nice with him."

"I'll turn him off if you don't take him back. I'll turn him off and hide him someplace where you can't find him!"

"Peter!" Mommy said, and she was angry. She was angrier than he'd ever seen her before. She put Little Brother™ down and took a step toward Peter. She would punish him. Peter didn't care. He was angry, too.

"I'll do it!" he yelled. "I'll turn him off and hide him someplace dark!"

"You'll do no such thing!" Mommy said. She

grabbed his arm and spun him around. The spanking would come next.

But it didn't. Instead he felt her fingers searching for something at the back of his neck.

2.16 Interviewer Hayley Levine is a flight attendant for *First Choice Airways*. What made you want to be a flight attendant?

Hayley I never really wanted to be a flight attendant, I just kind of knew I always wanted to travel, always had this idea that I wanted to see the world, saw an advert in a newspaper, went for the interview, got the job and loved it. So …, and it's definitely for me, definitely.

Interviewer What kind of training did you have?

Hayley In order to become a flight attendant, you have your group interview first, you're singled out, you have a one-on-one interview, and then if you pass that stage, you go on to your training which is five weeks: first week's all about customer service, relations, things like that, and then you go on to all your safety training which is four weeks' intensive training, you know, how to deal with fires, evacuations, water landing, passengers and then you're also, you're quite well trained on immediate care, so you know, that's quite an important part of our job, if something happens up in the air, something medical, you know, you need to be trained to deal with it quickly, efficiently.

Interviewer What kind of person do you think the airlines are looking for? I mean what kind of person makes a good flight attendant?

Hayley I don't know exactly what they're looking for but I can only think they look for someone who's quite outgoing, someone who can work quite well in a team, you have to be a certain kind of character to do what we do, I mean you fly with different people every day, you know, you go into work, anything could happen, there's thousands and thousands of crew, you don't work with the same people, you need to be able to just get on with people that you've never met before, work under pressure sometimes, so I think they're looking for someone who is, you know, quite competent in what they do, quite confident, just someone who's a team player really.

Interviewer Tell me, what do you think are good and bad sides of the job?

Hayley Good sides, obviously I get to see the world pretty much for free. I mean it's amazing, you couldn't ask for anything more really.

Bad sides, probaby sick bags, probably, and obviously it's really gruelling on your social life, it's more like a way of living than a job. You know, you have to work around it. So…, but yeah, it's good. I wouldn't change it for the world.

Interviewer Are there any other downsides?

Hayley Probably the jet lag, that's quite bad. Definitely, you do suffer a lot, but you know, it's part of the job. You just sort of get on with it.

Interviewer Have you got any tips for dealing with jet lag?

Hayley Tips? I don't wear a watch, sometimes that helps. And if you're going sort of east, just try and stay up, just try and fight the jet lag, that's the best way. I definitely find it easier going east than I do west. I don't know why that is.

2.17 Interviewer You must come into contact with a lot of passengers who are afraid of flying. How do you deal with this?

Hayley A lot of passengers are afraid of flying. There's not really a lot you can do. Just try and sit and talk to them, calm them down. I think your confidence is sort of always a good booster as well, if they know that you're competent in what you do, I think that helps. Most of them are OK after take-off, it's just that initial getting into the air, and then they're all right.

Interviewer How can you tell if someone's scared?

Hayley If they're a scared flyer, they do usually let you know, or they walk on shaking so much that it's pretty obvious that they're scared of flying.

You do feel sorry for them. Everyone's scared of something. But, yeah, they usually make themselves known. Or come straight up and ask for vodka. That's when you usually know someone's scared of flying. I did have a guy once, though, just before take-off and he was really really scared of flying and I'd spent a good half an hour with him before the flight trying to calm him down and we just got towards take-off and he tried to open the emergency exit door. He was having a panic attack. So, yeah, that was probably the worst thing. He didn't want to fly, we got him off. Poor guy, I felt really sorry for him.

Interviewer Have you ever been in a dangerous situation, for example, have you had to evacuate a plane?

Hayley I've never had to evacuate an aircraft, never, and hopefully never will. But we're trained to do that, so, you know, really well trained to do that, but hopefully nothing like that will ever happen. Never even remotely come close to it. So, that's good.

Interviewer Have you ever felt nervous or frightened on a flight?

Hayley No, not really. Never, actually. I think the worst thing is probably a bit of turbulence, but to be honest, that's an excuse to sit down and have a cup of tea. So, you know, no, I've never really felt frightened in the air. I feel really safe up there, really safe, otherwise I wouldn't do it.

2.19 Interviewer How do you feel when you fly?

Anne I love it. I really love flying. I like going to different places, it doesn't matter how long it takes. I just love flying.

Interviewer What do you least like about flying?

Anne The meals on the plane, that's what I don't like about flying.

Interviewer Have you ever had a frustrating experience when you were flying?

Anne Yes, I did actually. Last year, but it wasn't actually on the plane, it was beforehand. I had too much luggage at Delhi airport and they wouldn't let me on the plane and they were trying to say that I had to pay a lot of money. But eventually I bribed somebody.

Interviewer How do you feel when you fly?

Jordan I love flying. I do.

Interviewer What do you least like about flying?

Jordan I don't like turbulence a lot because when it shakes it makes me a little nervous. But I like flying because you're isolated and you can't use your cell phone or anything. I like that.

Interviewer Have you ever had a frustrating experience when you were flying?

Jordan Yeah, one time they lost my baggage, so I had to spend my holiday without my luggage.

Interviewer How do you feel when you fly?

Jeff Predominantly comfortable, I think it's a state of mind.

Interviewer What do you least like about flying?

Jeff That I'm not in control of the situation that I'm in, that I'm putting my safety in somebody else's hands.

Interviewer Have you ever had a frustrating experience when you were flying?

Jeff Air travel, security-wise is very frustrating – not being able to take things on a plane and the huge queues at the airports

Interviewer How do you feel when you fly?

Ben Safe, I mean I have no problems with travelling at all. Security checks are a bit annoying, but it's a kind of necessary evil, I suppose.

Interviewer What do you least like about flying?

Ben Probably either the leg room or the food. They're probably the two worst.

Interviewer Have you ever had a frustrating experience when you were flying?

Ben A stopover in Chicago for quite a while, a few years ago but nothing major, no.

3.1 Interviewer How did you become the pickpocket consultant for *Oliver Twist*?

John Well, I'm the director of a company which supplies magicians for live events, and for TV and films. Roman Polanski, the director of the film, he was looking for someone to train the actors – the young boys – to teach them to be pickpockets. He wanted them to be able to pick pockets so fast and so skilfully that it would look like they'd been doing it for years, so that they would look like professional pickpockets. So anyway, the film company got in touch with my company, and then I flew to Prague where they were shooting the film, to meet Polanski.

Interviewer What happened when you met him?

John Well, he didn't give me a normal interview. He just asked me to steal his watch, without him noticing.

Interviewer And did you?

John Yes, I did. So he gave me the job!

Interviewer How long did it take the boys to learn to pick pockets?

John Not very long. They learned really quickly. To be a good pickpocket you need confidence and children have that confidence. In the end, they got so good that they were stealing from everybody on the film set, even from me. I started to feel a bit like Fagin myself.

Interviewer So what's the trick of being a pickpocket?

John The real trick is to make people notice some things but not others. Some magicians call it 'misdirection', but I call it 'direction' – you have to direct people *towards* what you *want* them to see, and of course *away* from what you *don't* want them to see. Let me show you. What do you have in your jeans pockets?

Interviewer Er just keys.

John Can you show me them?

Interviewer Wow! That's amazing! You've stolen my wallet … and my pen. I really didn't notice a thing…

John That's the trick you see. All I had to do was to direct your attention to your jeans pocket and your keys, and you forgot about your jacket pocket and your wallet.

Interviewer That's incredible. I mean I was prepared – I knew you were going to try to steal from me. And I still didn't see you. So if someone wasn't prepared, it would be even easier.

John That's right. If you know where people are looking, you also know where they're *not* looking. So for example if someone comes up to you in the street with a map and asks you where something is, they make you look at the map, and perhaps while you're doing that they're stealing your wallet or your phone from your back pocket.

Interviewer Tourists are especially at risk from pickpockets, aren't they?

John Yes, and that's because pickpockets know exactly what they're going to look at, which is usually a building or a monument. For example, take tourists in London. When they come out of Westminster tube station, the first thing people do is look up at Big Ben. And when they look up, it's easy for pickpockets to do their work. And of course, thieves *love* the posters in the tube that warn people to be careful with their belongings – you know the ones that say 'Watch out! Pickpockets about!' As soon as men read that, they immediately put their hand on the pocket that their wallet is in, to make sure it's still there. The pickpockets see that and so they know exactly where it is.

Interviewer Well, I'm sure that information will be very helpful to everyone and especially to tourists. John Freedman, thank you very much for talking to us this afternoon.

John You're welcome.

3.6 I was at work when I heard the news on TV. It had been pouring with rain for several days and I could see that the River Vltava was swollen. Now it appeared that there was a real danger that the river would overflow. All of us who lived or worked near the river were being advised to get out and move to a place of safety. My office is in the centre of Prague only a hundred metres from the river bank and I live in a flat in a small town just a few kilometres north of Prague, right on the banks of the River Vltava, so I was in danger both at work and at home.

My wife and baby were at my flat, so I did the sensible thing and went home immediately. I packed my wife and my child into the car and I drove them to her parents' house. They would be completely safe there. So far, so good! But then I stopped being sensible, and I jumped back into the car and went back to our flat. Why did I do that? I told myself that it was because I was afraid of looters breaking into our flat and stealing things, but the truth was that I sort of felt that I wanted to be in the middle of things, to be involved in what was happening.

I stayed up all night watching the TV bulletins. They were giving regular reports on how fast the water level was rising at various places throughout the Czech Republic. There was a journalist reporting from just down the road from where I was, north of Prague, so I could sit in my sitting room and watch the danger increase as the minutes passed, but I still didn't move. I suppose I had a kind of perverse desire to be the last person to leave our block of flats. I could hear cars starting up and setting off all evening, and from time to time I looked out at our car park and I could see that it was almost empty.

At about three in the morning, my car was the only one left in the car park and my nerves gave out – or maybe I just came to my senses, because I finally decided to get into the car and escape. The roads towards Prague were flooded, so I decided to try to get to a relative's house which was a few kilometres away in the opposite direction, away from the river. I tried various escape routes but even these roads were impassable now. I was about to give up – I thought I'd left it too late. On my last attempt, I drove until I met another car which was blocking the road. The road ahead was flooded, but the driver of the other car was wading into the water to see how deep it was. He said he thought he could make it, so I decided to follow him. The water was rising quickly now, but he drove really really slowly through the water and I felt a bit impatient. Anyway, he managed to get through the water safely. I followed him, but I went much more quickly. Water was coming into the car under the door, and the engine made a funny noise like a cough a couple of times, but I got through and finally arrived safely at my relative's house.

I was one of the lucky ones. My office escaped the flood and my flat wasn't damaged at all as it's on the third floor. But the poor people who lived on the ground floor – their flats were very badly damaged. They had been completely under water.

3.8 More and more of us are trying to do our bit for the environment. But would you go as far as Barbara Haddrill?

Six years ago, Barbara from Powys in Wales, decided to make big changes to her lifestyle because she was worried about climate change, especially about the amount of carbon dioxide emissions that she herself was producing. So she stopped driving, and she started buying organic food from local shops and using a wood fire to heat her home.

But then Barbara was invited to be a bridesmaid at her best friend's wedding in Australia. The flight to Australia takes 24 hours and produces a huge amount of carbon dioxide emissions. But she really wanted to go to the wedding. So now she had a terrible dilemma. To fly or not to fly?

Instead of flying, Barbara decided to travel to Australia overland! She travelled by train and bus through Russia, China, Vietnam, Thailand, then by boat to Singapore, and finally to Australia. The epic journey took her nearly two months. Fortunately, Barbara works part-time at the Centre for Alternative Technology and they were happy to give her such a long holiday.

3.9 But… how much has Barbara *really* done to help the planet? Let's compare the two journeys.

Barbara's trip cost her £2,000. She travelled 14,004 miles, and it took her 51 days. The total amount of CO_2 emissions her trip produced was 1.65 tonnes. If she'd travelled by plane, it would have cost her a quarter of the price, only £450. She would have travelled 10,273 miles, and it would have taken her just 25 hours. But the CO_2 emissions would have been 2.7 tonnes.

So yes, Barbara's overland journey did produce less carbon dioxide. On the other hand, of course, if she hadn't gone at all, she wouldn't have produced *any* emissions. So, what do you think of Barbara's trip? We would be very interested in hearing your comments. You can email us at newsday@radio24.co.uk.

3.10 We spend an awful long time in our cars. The average driver spends nearly an hour and a half a day in the car, so obviously the risks involved in driving are something we should take very seriously.

Driving gets a lot of bad publicity and there are a lot of myths about how dangerous it is – but the fact is that, kilometre for kilometre, it is riskier to be a pedestrian or a jogger than to drive a car, or ride a motorbike for that matter. We are also more likely to be injured at work or at home than we are driving a car.

But accidents *do* happen and the reason why a lot of them happen is because people break the rules. In fact 50% of all fatal accidents occur because someone has broken the law. The most frequent reason is breaking the speed limit and the second most frequent is drunk driving. The third cause of fatal accidents is when a driver falls asleep, a surprising 10 %.

When we drive is also a significant factor in assessing our risk of having an accident. Driving at night, for example, is four times as dangerous as during the day. This is mainly because visibility is so much worse at night. By day a driver's visibility is roughly 500 metres, but at night driving with headlights it is much worse, maybe as little as 120 metres.

What are the most dangerous times and days to be on the road? Well, between 2.00 and 3.00 a.m. on a Saturday morning is the most dangerous time of the week, when you are most likely to have a *fatal* accident. So if possible, try to stay off the road then.

The time of day when you are most likely to have a *non-fatal* accident is Friday afternoon between 4.00 and 6.00 p.m. This is when people are finishing work for the week and it is a time when drivers need to concentrate especially hard. Curiously, Tuesday is the safest day of the week to be on the road.

Which brings us onto *where* accidents happen. Most fatal accidents happen on country roads, so highways or freeways (what you call A-roads or motorways) are much safer. Also 70% of fatal accidents happen within 30 or 40 kilometres of where we live. Why should that be? The answer seems to be that we concentrate less when we are in familiar territory.

And finally let's look at *who* has accidents. Another myth about driving is that women are worse drivers than men. While it's true that kilometre for kilometre women have more *minor* accidents than men, a man is *twice* as likely to be killed in a car accident as a woman. Men take too many unnecessary risks when they're driving. Women are more careful and cautious drivers.

But the most important factor of all is age. A driver aged between 17 and 24 has double the risk of an older driver. Which is why a lot of people would like to see the age limit for having a driving licence raised to 21.

3.12 **Interviewer** And this afternoon on *Around Britain* we are visiting an unusual little nursery school in a village in southern England. What makes this school different is that whatever the weather's like, the 20 children spend most of their day not in a classroom, but playing outside. Sue Palmer is the head of the nursery. Hello Sue.

Sue Hello.

Interviewer Sue, do the children *really* spend all day outside?

Sue Yes, even in the winter, and even if it's raining. They only come inside for breaks, so they probably spend about 90% of their day outside. We think this is a much better way of teaching children than by shutting them up in classrooms all day.

Interviewer What kind of things do children learn from being outside?

Sue They can learn about the world by doing things. We have a large field next to the nursery so they are in the field all day – playing, exploring, experimenting. They learn about how plants and trees grow, they can learn about insects. They learn about the danger of fire by sitting around a real fire. They can climb trees and walk on logs…

Interviewer And don't you think that this is a bit dangerous for young children? They might easily fall over, have accidents.

Sue No, no, not at all. I think that today's children are totally overprotected, they don't have enough freedom. People have forgotten just how important it is to give our children some freedom. They need to be allowed to take risks during play. My children know which plants can hurt them. They know that fire is dangerous. But nowadays schools do all they can to avoid adventure and risk.

Interviewer Why do you think schools have become so obsessed with eliminating risk?

Sue I think it's because schools and teachers are so worried nowadays that if a child has an accident of any kind, however small, that the child's parents will sue the school for thousands of pounds, and maybe put them out of business.

Interviewer Have you ever had any problem with parents?

Sue On the contrary, they are very positive indeed about the school and our teaching methods and philosophy. I've heard parents say that children who come to our school are healthier and stronger than other children – and that's in spite of being out in the rain – or maybe it's because of that. I think, and the parents agree with me, that the way we are teaching is the way that childhood should be.

Interviewer Well, thanks very much Sue, that's all we've got time for. Coming up on the show next …

3.13 Interviewer EZ is a free runner who started the organization Urban Freeflow. Free runners use obstacles in a town or city to create movement, by running, jumping, and climbing.

Interviewer Can you do free running anywhere, I mean, for example, if you're on your way somewhere?

EZ Yeah, I mean if you wanted to, you could, you know do it anywhere, if you're on your way to work you could do it, but generally the people who practise would go to a particular spot and practise there and then move on elsewhere.

Interviewer Where do you most enjoy doing it?

EZ The most rewarding for me would be running in London, here, around the South Bank, and we'd do it in a team of maybe ten of us, and just like someone leading the way and the rest following, and just using basic obstacles, like lamp posts and walls and just moving.

Interviewer How did you first get into free running?

EZ My background is in boxing, which I did for about 20 years and I boxed at international level. And I got married and had a kid and had to just change my life around and become sensible all of a sudden. So I gave up the boxing and there was a huge void in my life, so I drifted into martial arts, which didn't really do it for me. And I was looking for the next thing to do and I saw this on TV one day, and I remember sitting in bed watching it and said 'That's what I'm looking for'.

Interviewer Tell us about the organization Urban Freeflow.

EZ Well, Urban Freeflow started out as a website, but then we devised a performance team, we have 20 athletes in the team now, eight who are very very high-profile now we're sponsored by Adidas now. We take care of all sorts of commercials and movies in that sense. We teach as well, we teach in schools, we've taught the army and police.

Interviewer What do you do with police?

EZ The police run these schemes for youth offenders, and they're trying to get them out of, you know, doing bad things. So it's seen as a very positive thing to do, it's seen as a very cool thing to do and for the youths it's very engaging, so that's what we do for them.

Interviewer What about in schools?

EZ In terms of schools, same again, there's a big problem in the UK with obesity and kids just aren't practising anything. They're not doing any PE, they're not doing any kind of sport, whereas what we do is perceived as being very cool, and unwittingly they're taking part and exercising so that seems to be a very positive thing.

3.14 Interviewer How dangerous is free running?

EZ On the face of it, what we do seems to be quite dangerous, but it doesn't touch on what we do. We're very very safety conscious, we work in movies and commercials where safety is paramount, I mean, everything we do is calculated, there's no risk-taking. If you see a big jump being done, we'd have practised that at ground level thousands of times, over and over and over. I think if anything, the key word for what we do is repetition.

Interviewer What attracted you especially about free running? Was it the risk element?

EZ To a degree, the risk element played a part, but it was more about the sense of freedom, the way to be able move within your environment with no limitations, you know, you don't need any equipment to take part, no skateboard, or no BMX, you can just, a pair of trainers and I'm ready to go, that was the real draw for me, just the freedom aspect.

Interviewer Have you had many accidents since you've been doing it?

EZ If you're practising this sport, you will pick up the odd scrapes here and there, you'll get blisters on your hands and calluses, which is normal. You might get the odd sprained ankle. Personally, I fell out of a tree once, and fell on my head, which wasn't very nice and I had to go to hospital here.

Interviewer Is free running really something that anyone can do?

EZ It helps if you have a background in some kind of sport, but it isn't essential, you can start from being a complete beginner. Gymnastics would help, but you could be just someone who plays football, or does a bit of running and pick it up straight away. As long as you start out very small-scale, take your time, there's no problem.

3.16 Interviewer Have you ever done any high-risk sports or activities?

Agne Yeah, I've done skiing.

Interviewer What was it like?

Agne It was pretty difficult because it's difficult to coordinate. So it was scary and it was funny, and it was just making a fool of myself.

Interviewer Have you ever done any high-risk sports or activities?

Anne Not really, no, except for potholing, but that was in my younger days.

Interviewer What was it like?

Anne I wouldn't say it was particularly high-risk, but it was a very enjoyable experience.

Interviewer Is there anything you'd like to try?

Anne I've always wanted to try skiing. I've never done it, but I think that would be really exciting – to go skiing and to go down the mountains free and what have you, but I think I'm a bit old now.

Interviewer Have you ever done any high-risk sports or activities?

Mark Yeah, I've jumped out of a plane.

Interviewer What was it like?

Mark Oh, it was awesome. You see the ground below you and the plane door opens and you're suddenly … the distance goes like from there to there as soon as the door opens you're suddenly, you know, you're hurtling towards the ground, you know, at a couple of hundred miles an hour or whatever. And your chute opens and you get sucked back up into the sky. It's kinda cool.

Interviewer Have you ever done any high-risk sports or activities?

Ray I've climbed, I've caved, I've white-water rafted down the Zambezi. Do they count?

4.3 Yossi and Kevin soon realized that going by river was a big mistake. The river got faster and faster, and soon they were in rapids.

The raft was swept down the river at an incredible speed until it hit a rock. Kevin managed to swim to land, but Yossi was swept away by the rapids.

But Yossi didn't drown. He came up to the surface several kilometres downriver. By an incredible piece of luck he found their backpack floating in the river. The backpack contained a little food, insect repellent, a lighter, and most important of all … the map. The two friends were now separated by a canyon and six or seven kilometres of jungle.

4.4 Kevin was feeling desperate. He didn't know if Yossi was alive or dead, but he started walking downriver to look for him. He felt responsible for what had happened to his friend. Yossi, however, was feeling very optimistic. He was sure that Kevin would look for him so he started walking upriver calling his friend's name. But nobody answered. At night Yossi tried to sleep but he felt terrified. The jungle was full of noises. Suddenly he woke up because he heard a branch breaking. He turned on his flash light. There was a jaguar staring at him…

Yossi was trembling with fear. But then he remembered something that he once saw in a film. He used the cigarette lighter to set fire to the insect repellent spray and he managed to scare the jaguar away.

4.5 After five days alone, Yossi was exhausted and starving. Suddenly, as he was walking, he saw a footprint on the trail – it was a hiking boot. It had to be Kevin's footprint! He followed the trail until he discovered another footprint. But then he realized, to his horror, that it was the same footprint and that it wasn't Kevin's. It was his own. He had been walking around in a circle. Suddenly Yossi realized that he would never find Kevin. He felt sure that Kevin must be dead. Yossi felt depressed and on the point of giving up.

4.6 But Kevin wasn't dead. He was still looking for Yossi. But after nearly a week he was weak and exhausted from lack of food and lack of sleep. He decided that it was time to forget Yossi and try to save himself. He had just enough strength left to hold onto a log and let himself float down the river.

Kevin was incredibly lucky – he was rescued by two Bolivian hunters in a canoe. The men only hunted in that part of the rainforest once a year, so if they had been there a short time earlier or later, they would never have seen Kevin. They took him back to the town of San José and he spent two days recovering.

4.7 As soon as Kevin felt well enough, he went to a Bolivian Army base and asked them to look for Yossi. The army were sure that Yossi must be dead, but in the end Kevin persuaded them to take him up in a plane and fly over the part of the rainforest where Yossi could be. It was a hopeless search. The plane had to fly too high and the forest was too dense. They couldn't see anything at all. Kevin felt terribly guilty. He was convinced that it was all his fault that Yossi was going to die in the jungle.

Kevin's last hope was to pay a local man with a boat to take him up the river to look for his friend.

4.8 By now, Yossi had been on his own in the jungle for nearly three weeks. He hadn't eaten for days. He was starving, exhausted and slowly losing his mind. It was evening. He lay down by the side of the river ready for another night alone in the jungle. Suddenly he heard the sound of a bee buzzing in his ear. He thought a bee had got inside his mosquito net. When he opened his eyes he saw that the buzzing noise wasn't a bee…

It was a boat. Yossi was too weak to shout, but Kevin had already seen him. It was a one-in-a-million chance, but Yossi was saved.

When Yossi had recovered, he and Kevin flew to the city of La Paz and they went directly to the hotel where they had agreed to meet Marcus and Karl. But Marcus and Karl were not there. The two men had never arrived back in the town of Apolo. The Bolivian army organized a search of the rainforest, but Marcus and Karl were never seen again.

4.14 In life we sometimes have disagreements with people. It could be with your partner, with your boss, with your parents, or with a friend. When this happens, the important thing is to try not to let a calm discussion turn into a heated argument. But of course this is easier said than done.

The first thing I would say is that the way you begin the conversation is very important.

Imagine you are a student and you share a flat with another student who you think isn't doing her share of the housework. If you say, 'Look, you never do your share of the housework. What are we going to do about it?', the discussion will very soon turn into an argument. It's much more constructive to say something like, 'I think we'd better have another look about how we divide up the housework. Maybe there's a better way of doing it.'

My second piece of advice is simple. If you're the person who is in the wrong, just admit it! This is the easiest and best way to avoid an argument. Just apologize to your flatmate, your parents, or your husband, and move on. The other person will have more much respect for you in the future if you do that.

The next tip is don't exaggerate. Try not to say things like 'You *always* come home late when my mother comes to dinner' when perhaps this has only happened twice, or 'You never remember to buy the toothpaste.' This will just make the other person think you're being unreasonable, and will probably make him or her stop listening to your arguments.

Sometimes we just can't avoid a discussion turning into an argument. But if you do start arguing with someone, it is important to keep things under control and there are ways to do this.

The most important thing is don't raise your voice. Raising your voice will just make the other person lose their temper too. If you find yourself raising your voice, stop for a moment and take a deep breath. Say 'I'm sorry I shouted, but this is very important to me', and continue calmly. If you can talk calmly and quietly, you'll find your partner will be more ready to think about what you are saying.

It is also very important to stick to the point. Try to keep to the topic you are talking about. Don't bring up old arguments, or try to bring in other issues. Just concentrate on solving the one problem you are having, and leave the other things for another time. So, for example, if you're arguing about the housework, don't start talking about mobile phone bills as well.

And my final tip is that if necessary call 'Time out', like in a sports match. If you think that an argument is getting out of control, then you can say to the other person, 'Listen, I'd rather talk about this tomorrow when we've both calmed down'. You can then continue the discussion the next day when perhaps both of you are feeling less tense and angry. That way there is much more chance that you will be able to reach an agreement. You'll also probably find that the problem is much easier to solve when you've both had a good night's sleep. Well, those are my tips.

But I want to say one last important thing. Some people think that arguing is always bad. This is not true. Conflict is a normal part of life, and dealing with conflict is an important part of any relationship, whether it's three people sharing a flat, a married couple, or just two good friends. If you don't learn to argue properly, then when a real problem comes along, you won't be prepared to face it together. Think of the smaller arguments as training sessions. Learn how to argue cleanly and fairly. It will help your relationship become stronger and last longer.

4.17 **Presenter** And welcome to tonight's edition of *Use your senses*. First with us we have Joanna and Steve from Stepney.
Joanna Hi.
Steve Hello.
Presenter Now, the blindfold's on – you can't see anything, can you?
Joanna and Steve No, nothing at all.
Presenter Right so first the mystery drink. Remember you can smell it but you can't taste it… starting… now!
Joanna It doesn't really smell of anything.
Steve It smells fruity to me, not very strong but definitely fruity.
Joanna Yeah, it smells a bit like orange juice but sweeter.
Steve It could be (beep) then.
Presenter OK so now the food. This you can taste, but you can't see of course… ready… now!
Joanna Well, it's meat, isn't it? It tastes a bit like chicken, but I don't think it is chicken.
Steve I don't think I've had it before – the texture isn't quite like chicken – it tastes quite light, I don't think it's duck…
Presenter You've got ten more seconds…
Joanna It must be (beep).
Steve OK.
Presenter Now the object.
Steve It feels like a coin.
Joanna Can I feel it? Yes, it definitely feels metallic, but it's completely smooth – it doesn't seem to have any markings – oh, it's got two tiny little holes in the middle. I know, it's a (beep).
Steve That's it.
Presenter So now we're going to take off the blindfolds – there we are.
Joanna and Steve Thanks / That's better.
Presenter And now to the sound effect. I'm going to play you a sound and you've got to decide what it is you're hearing. Remember you can hear it twice only. Ready? Now…
Steve It sounds like thunder to me.
Joanna Well, maybe, but it sounds very distant. Could it be a train?
Steve No, I think it's something natural, you know not a machine. Can we hear it again, please?
Presenter Of course.
Steve Yes, I think it's (beep). What do you think?
Joanna Could be. I'll go with that.
Presenter Right. Time's up. So now, the moment of truth. Did Steve and Joanna get it right? Remember you need all the answers right to win today's prize. Our assistant Vanessa will give us the answers, a round of applause for Vanessa.

4.23 **Interviewer** Trevor White is a Canadian actor. Can you tell us a bit about the kind of acting you do?
Trevor There isn't much I don't do, I guess, as far as acting goes. There's theatre, obviously, film work, television work, sometimes commercials and even voice-over work, which is for radio or for television or even sometimes animated shows where you lend your voice to those as well. So, I've rarely said 'no' to an acting job.
Interviewer Did you always want to be an actor?
Trevor Well, it's something that I always loved to do, act, as a kid in high school, in school plays, and in my spare time, just playing around with friends.

You know, acting and improvising and that kind of thing. But I don't think I ever believed that I could … or ever took it seriously to act as a profession for the rest of my life. So I went in to university and took economics as a more practical thing to do, but I didn't really enjoy it, I guess and ultimately, after university, I started taking some acting classes and really enjoyed that. And then started doing student films and fringe theatre and unpaid work just to get experience in acting and loved it and then started doing it more seriously and got an agent and started getting proper acting jobs and that was about 13 years ago.
Interviewer What's the most difficult thing about preparing for a new role?
Trevor It really depends. When you do a play for example, you have three, four, sometimes even six weeks to rehearse with the other people and the director and the props and everything, so you have a long time to learn your lines, to as it were find the character. The memorization is the most like real work, that can be difficult, you know, just memorizing lots of lines. In film and television you don't have the benefit of rehearsal. You just show up and you're expected to know all your lines and then you do it a few times and that's it. So you have to be very disciplined and get all that ready in advance.
Interviewer How do you learn your lines?
Trevor I have a Dictaphone actually, which I just record the other people's lines, obviously in my voice, I don't do strange character voices because that would be weird, and, you know I just say their line, I stop it, I say my line, I play the next lines, so you just basically record all the other lines in any given scene and play it back and just work through it slowly. It's amazing the difference it makes when the writing is good and it makes sense. It's much easier to memorize. But if sometimes you audition for a bad science fiction TV show or a horror movie or something, you often have a much harder time memorizing poorly written lines, because they're just bad. But of course it's your job so you do it.

4.24 **Interviewer** Is there any role you've particularly enjoyed?
Trevor There's a few roles that I've played or oftentimes when you do something it's the whole experience of a job, not necessarily just the part you have in it. Earlier this year, I got to work for the Royal Shakespeare Company for the first time and we did *Coriolanus*, one of Shakespeare's lesser performed plays, in Stratford, in Washington in America, also in Newcastle here in the United Kingdom and in Madrid in Spain for five months, which was amazing
Interviewer What's the most difficult role that you've ever had to play?
Trevor Well, I suppose, this last role that I played is one of the most difficult parts, Tullus Aufidius in Coriolanus, because there were lots of things that were very demanding about the part. We had to do a huge sword and axe fight in the middle of the play. Which … I'd done stage combat before, but never anything like this. We were using actual … I mean they were blunt swords and axes, but they were still very large pieces of metal. And we had a couple of small accidents, but no major ones luckily I gave the other guy three stitches on his fingers at one point when he parried in the wrong place – that's my opinion anyway.
Interviewer Do you prefer working in the theatre or in film and TV?
Trevor I think theatre is the most satisfying work in acting oftentimes, because you get to do it over and over again in front of a live audience, but it doesn't tend to pay as well as film and television, which is also fun, but not as glamorous as people might think it is, I guess.
Interviewer So being an actor isn't really glamorous?
Trevor No, I don't think acting is a glamorous life, particularly, well I guess in any way. In theatre it's

you know, you don't really earn that much money and you work hard. Yeah, and film and television work is, you know, can be a lot of fun, you can get to work with some famous people sometimes or some very talented people that you admire and that's a thrilling thing and you get to shoot guns or, you know, go on car chases and all those things are really fun, but most of the time, the 90% of the day, even when you're doing exciting things, you're just sitting and waiting around, you're always waiting around, they're always fixing lights, setting up new camera positions, trying to figure out who's going where when and it takes … To film a proper feature film takes months and maybe in all that time only two or three of those days all told is actually you doing anything. So yeah, I think a lot of people get into extra work and stuff because they think this will be really glamorous, but you end up reading a book about nine hours a day. And I've never been on a red carpet so I suppose I can't judge. That looks glamorous.

4.26 **Interviewer** Have you ever acted?
Ben I was in a music video once, and that's about as far as I've gone. But I mean, I'm a musician so I kind of appear on stage quite a lot.
Interviewer How does it make you feel?
Ben I suppose nervous at first but then you settle in and within a couple of minutes and before you know it you kind of lose any awareness of kind of any external factors or anything like that. And you're not aware of anything else outside of this kind of bubble that you've kind of managed to transport yourself into.
Interviewer Have you ever acted?
Louise Yes, I was in the Royal Shakespeare Company up in my area and did a few plays and a few musicals and I'm a specialist make-up artist, so I kind of work with actors, doing all their make-up, and zombies and that.
Interviewer What do you like about it?
Louise The buzz of it, being able to be someone else in front of people – just being someone else is good.
Interviewer Have you ever acted?
Mike Yes, I have. I'm studying acting now. I'm a student studying theatre and music. Er, I've been in a few things, when I was little, I've been in a few shows around London, things like that. But I plan to go further.
Interviewer How does it make you feel?
Mike I love it. I think it's really great. Because you don't have to be yourself for once. You're onstage and you can just be whoever your character is meant to be. And you can just sort of get taken away into this other world and you can get really into it. That's what I really like about acting.
Interviewer Have you ever acted?
Cherry Yeah, I'm in like a drama youth group so a couple of plays I've been in, like Bugsy Malone and the Wizard of Oz. A modernized one and stuff.
Interviewer How does it make you feel?
Cherry Yeah, it is nerve-wracking just as you're about to go on, but apart from that, yeah, once you're on it's fine.
Interviewer Have you ever acted?
Ray Possibly not since I was at school. No, I don't think so. Not since I was at school, no.
Interviewer How did it make you feel?
Ray Very nervous beforehand, very apprehensive beforehand and then quite excited when it all went well, yes.

5.2 I think it's very interesting that human beings are the only animals which listen to music for pleasure. A lot of research has been done to find out why we listen to music, and there seem to be three main reasons. Firstly, we listen to music to make us remember important moments in the past, for example when we met someone for the first time. Think of Humphrey Bogart in the film Casablanca saying 'Darling, they're playing our song'. When we hear a certain piece of music, we remember hearing it for the first time in some very special

circumstances. Obviously, this music varies from person to person.

Secondly, we listen to music to help us change activities. If we want to go from one activity to another, we often use music to help us make the change. For example, we might play a certain kind of music to prepare us to go out in the evening, or we might play another kind of music to relax us when we get home from work. That's mainly why people listen to music in cars, and they often listen to one kind of music when they're going to work and another kind when they're coming home. The same is true of people on buses and trains with their iPods. The third reason why we listen to music is to intensify the emotion that we're feeling. For example, if we're feeling sad, sometimes we want to get even sadder, so we play sad music. Or we're feeling angry and we want to intensify the anger then we play angry music. Or when we're planning a romantic dinner, we lay the table, we light candles, and then we think what music would make this even more romantic?

5.3 Let's take three important human emotions: happiness, sadness, and anger. When people are happy they speak faster, and their voice is higher. When they are sad they speak more slowly and their voice is lower, and when people are angry they raise their voices or shout. Babies can tell whether their mother is happy or not simply by the sound of her voice, not by her words. What music does is it copies this, and it produces the same emotions. So faster, higher-pitched music will sound happy. Slow music with lots of falling pitches will sound sad. Loud music with irregular rhythms will sound angry. It doesn't matter how good or bad the music is, if it has these characteristics it will make you experience this emotion.
Let me give you some examples. For happy, for example, the first movement of Beethoven's *Seventh Symphony*. For angry, say *Mars*, from *The Planets* by Holst. And for sad, something like Albinoni's *Adagio for strings*.
Of course the people who exploit this most are the people who write film soundtracks. They can take a scene which visually has no emotion and they can make the scene either scary or calm or happy just by the music they write to go with it. Think of the music in the shower scene in Hitchcock's film *Psycho*. All you can see is a woman having a shower, but the music makes it absolutely terrifying.

5.10 And finally on *News Today* the amazing story of a teenager who woke up this morning and discovered that she wasn't in bed – she was lying on top of a 40-metre-high crane!
In the early hours of this morning a man on his way to work was passing a building site in Dulwich, south-east London when he spotted the 15-year-old girl lying on the arm of the crane. He immediately called the police on his mobile phone. The police and fire brigade arrived on the scene at 1.30 and at first they were worried that the girl might be intending to commit suicide by throwing herself off the crane. But when a fireman climbed up the crane, he could see that the girl was asleep.
The fireman realized that it could be very dangerous if the girl woke up suddenly. So he crawled along the 21-metre arm of the crane and carefully wrapped the girl in a safety harness before waking her up gently. The girl had a mobile phone with her and the fireman was able to call her parents, who came to the building site straight away. Finally, the girl was brought down from the crane on a ladder. The whole rescue operation had taken two and a half hours. Her parents were waiting for her on the ground and obviously they were very relieved to see her safe and well. The question everyone wanted to know was 'why did the girl go to sleep on the top of a crane?' Well, the answer is that she had been sleepwalking! She had walked out of her house during the night without her parents noticing and sleepwalked to the building site. There was a security guard but he didn't see her climbing the crane because he was

watching TV. The girl's parents told the police that this wasn't the first time that she had sleepwalked but that she had never left the house before.

5.11 **Presenter** Now I imagine some of you are finding this story a bit difficult to believe, so I've invited into the studio Professor Miller, who is an expert in sleepwalking. Professor Miller, does this story surprise you?
Professor Not at all. I have treated people who have driven cars, ridden horses and I had one man who even tried to fly a helicopter while he was asleep.
Presenter But how did this girl manage to climb a 40-metre crane?
Professor It would have been no problem for her. She would climb the crane just as easily as if she were awake.
Presenter And would her eyes have been open?
Professor Yes, sleepwalkers usually have their eyes open. That's why sometimes it's difficult to know if someone is sleepwalking or not.
Presenter Is sleepwalking very common?
Professor Yes. Research shows that about 18% of the population have a tendency to sleepwalk. In fact, it's much more common in children than in teenagers or adults. And curiously it's more common among boys than girls. Adults who sleepwalk are normally people who used to sleepwalk when they were children. Adult sleepwalking often happens after a stressful event, for example, after a road accident.
Presenter People always say that you should never wake a sleepwalker up when they're walking. Is that true?
Professor No, it isn't. People used to think that it was dangerous to wake up a sleepwalker. But in fact this isn't the case. You *can* wake a sleepwalker up without any problem, although if you do, it is quite common for the sleepwalker to be confused, so he or she probably won't know where they are for a few moments.
Presenter So if we see someone sleepwalking, should we wake them up?
Professor Yes, you should remember that another of the myths about sleepwalkers is that they cannot injure themselves while they are sleepwalking. But this isn't true. If a sleepwalker is walking around the house, they can trip or fall over a chair or even fall down stairs. The other day there was a case of a nine-year-old girl who opened her bedroom window while sleepwalking and fell ten metres to the ground. Luckily, she wasn't seriously injured. So you see it is definitely safer to wake a sleepwalker up.
Presenter How long does sleepwalking last?
Professor It can be very brief, for example, a few minutes. The most typical cases are people getting up and getting dressed, or people going to the bathroom. But it can occasionally last much longer, maybe half an hour or even more.
Presenter And what happens when sleepwalkers wake up? Do they remember the things they did while they were sleepwalking?
Professor No, a sleepwalker usually doesn't remember anything afterwards. So, for example, the girl who climbed up the crane will probably have no memory of the incident.
Presenter So, is a sleepwalker responsible for his or her actions?
Professor A very good question, actually. A few years ago a man from Canada got up in the middle of the night and drove 20 kilometres from his home to the house where his parents-in-law lived and, for no apparent reason, he killed his mother-in-law. The man was charged with murder but he was found not guilty because he had been asleep at the time he committed the crime.

5.15 The best thing about my job is that I get to go to the best restaurants in England and sometimes abroad, and I don't get a bill at the end of the evening. I get the chance to eat the most wonderful, exquisite food in restaurants that I wouldn't normally be able to afford and I can order the most expensive dishes and wines without worrying about what it's costing me.

The other great side of the job is that I can take a friend with me so it's a good way of catching up with old friends who I may not have seen for a while. And everyone loves a free meal in a posh restaurant so I rarely have to eat on my own.

The downside? Well, there are several. I often have to eat a lot when I'm not really hungry. To do my job properly, I have to try all the courses – you know starter, main course, dessert, and sometimes I don't feel like eating so much, but I have to do it. I also have a problem with my weight now – it's very easy to put on weight when you eat out several times a week. In fact, most restaurant critics have a weight problem. Another problem is that if I write a bad review of a meal I have, it's difficult for me to ever go to that restaurant again, because the owner of the restaurant will probably recognize me. Another disadvantage of the job is that because I do it so often, eating out has lost a lot of its attraction for me. When the weekend comes I prefer to eat at home rather than go out for a meal.

5.16 Nearly all foreign correspondents and war reporters that I've met are people who were looking for adventure. They're not the kind of people who would be happy with a nine-to-five job. They are people who got into the job precisely because it has very weird hours and involves going to difficult places. I mean to some extent the things which are difficult and potentially dangerous about the job are also the things that made you want to do the job in the first place and the reason why the job is so exciting.

Something else I really like about the job is that I work as part of a team – you sit down and have dinner together at the end of the day and talk things through with other journalists and photographers and you're talking to people who have experienced the same things as you, and seen the same things as you. And that's very important in this kind of work. One of the problems of the job is seeing a lot of horrific things and then going back home to normality. I remember a few years ago coming back from a war zone where I had been for a long time and I'd seen a lot of death and destruction and I went to a friend's wedding in London. It was a beautiful day, everyone was drinking champagne and talking about unimportant things, and I wanted to say, 'Why can't you see that there is something awful happening in the world?'

Another major worry about my job these days is the risk of being killed. Journalists used to get killed by accident, but now there are more and more cases of journalists being killed simply because they are journalists, and they are also becoming the target of kidnappers. Two of my colleagues have been kidnapped recently and a very good friend of mine was killed last year.

5.17 **Interviewer** Sir Nicholas Kenyon was the director of a festival of concerts called the Proms for 12 years. How did the Proms start?

Nicholas The promenade concerts started way back in 1895 when a brilliant impresario wanted to use a newly-built concert hall in London, the Queen's Hall, for a series of popular concerts that really brought classical music to the widest possible audience. There were important classical concerts during the year, but in the summer people tended to go away, society life finished and so he had the brilliant idea of taking away all the seats on the floor of the hall, where the expensive people usually sat and letting people come in and stand there and walk around and have a very informal experience of concert-going. The name 'Proms' is an abbreviation of 'Promenade concerts' and it basically means that people are able to walk around and stand during the music

Interviewer How long do the Proms last?

Nicholas The Proms lasts for two months in the summer, from the middle of July to the middle of September and during that period there's one concert every day. Two concerts on many days,

three concerts on some days. So it's a very very intense period of music-making and people buy season tickets in order to be able to attend all the concerts, whether they do or not, very few people attend actually all of them, except me, and they come and they queue during the day in order to get the best places in the floor of the hall where they stand.

Interviewer World-class musicians perform at the Proms for much lower fees than they would expect to receive. Why do you think that is?

Nicholas I think the Proms has an absolutely unique atmosphere that's what orchestras and conductors and performers who come here say. And so people do want to come and perform. What you get at the Proms is a wonderful mixture of total informality and total concentration. So that although people don't dress up to come to the Proms, they behave how they want, they actually absolutely listen to the music and that is a feature that so many conductors and orchestras really comment on – the level of concentration is absolutely amazing.

5.18 **Interviewer** There must have been many truly memorable concerts during your time as director of the Proms – Could you tell us about one of them?

Nicholas The death of Princess Diana was particularly difficult because of course she lived just across the road in Kensington Palace from where the Proms happened in the Royal Albert Hall. We changed some programmes to make them more appropriate. On the day of her funeral, we put in Fauré's Requiem to the programme. Very oddly we had programmed two or three requiems in that last two weeks of the season and they fitted very very well. We then lost another major figure of the musical world, the conductor Sir Georg Solti, who was to have conducted the Verdi Requiem on the last Friday of the season and he had been a very good friend of Princess Diana and indeed had rung me up just after Diana's death to say that he wanted to dedicate this Verdi Requiem to her memory. As it turned out, he died just a week later and so another conductor, Colin Davies, took over that Verdi Requiem and dedicated it to both of them and it was a fantastically charged atmosphere in the hall. I can't remember such an electric occasion as that.

Interviewer I understand there was also another spooky coincidence in the programme at the time of Diana's death? Could you tell us about it?

Nicholas A wonderful American composer called John Adams had written an absolutely wonderful piece which we were going to do on the last night of the Proms in 1997. Unfortunately, I mean it could have been called absolutely anything this piece, it's a whirling abstract piece of fanfare music. Unfortunately he had called it *Short ride in a fast machine*. And so it was perfectly obvious from the first moment that we had to take that piece out and change the programme.

Interviewer Are there any embarrassing or amusing experiences you remember?

Nicholas One of the things that was a real challenge to the Proms was the arrival of the mobile phone, because in the beginning people didn't know how to use them, when to switch them off and the Albert Hall is a very very big space and mobile phones would go off in concerts and it could be very embarrassing. Usually, because they were in the middle of the music, conductors just ignored them and people got embarrassed and switched them off. But there was one particular incident that was just so awful because Stravinsky's *The Rite of Spring* starts with a very very exposed quiet bassoon solo and Simon Rattle and the Berlin Philharmonic making one of their first appearances together at the Proms had just begun that piece when a mobile phone went off very loudly in the stalls and Simon Rattle stopped the bassoonist and turned round and glared at this person in the stalls and there was a round of

applause and everything. So anyway, it restarted and the performance was a spectacular success and it was wonderful. But this was such an incident, that he had actually stopped it, that it became the subject of a lot of media attention and there were paragraphs in the papers and I had to go and be interviewed the next day at home for a Radio 4 programme about mobile phones going off in concerts, and in the middle of this interview, my own phone went off and it's a wonderfully classic little bit of tape. My embarrassment at the same thing happening to me.

5.20 **Interviewer** Have you ever been to a music festival?

Anne Yes. Isle of Wight in the 70s.

Interviewer What was it like?

Anne There were just thousands and thousands of people just chilling out doing whatever you wanted to do. And it was just great fun – there was music, dancing, a great memory actually.

Interviewer Have you ever been to a music festival?

Jordan Yes, we have a rock festival back home in Ohio that we go to, a lot of my friends and I go to.

Interviewer What was it like?

Jordan I don't know what it's called but it's just like a whole bunch of alternative music, it's like two days long and you all go and it's just a fun time – all outside. There's a ton of people and they're all usually younger, from like college age usually, and they have a whole bunch of stages set up, and there's just bars in different places, and you can just go and hang out and listen to some music.

Interviewer Have you ever been to a music festival?

Mike Yes, I went to Glastonbury.

Interviewer What was it like?

Mike Incredibly muddy, incredibly muddy, but great fun, absolutely so much fun, I didn't get any sleep at all.

Interviewer Have you ever been to a music festival?

Ray Yes, not for many years. When I was much younger I went to Bath, Bath Music Blues festival, I've been to Reading Music Festival, I can't remember which other ones I've been to, but yes, in the 1970s, early 80s I went to quite a few.

Interviewer What were they like?

Ray From a 57-year-old's point of view? Well, at the time they were really exciting. I can remember a long journey down to Bath, sleeping in a field, I can remember expensive food, waiting up all night to the see the band that you wanted to see and then falling asleep. I can remember being taken back to sleep in somebody's tent then waking up and realizing we were in the wrong tent, and had no idea whose tent we were in the next morning. I can remember feeling slightly sort of sick and hungry all the time I was there, but yeah, it was good, it was exciting.

Interviewer Have you ever been to a music festival?

Harley No. Oh, yeah, actually. The Big Chill? Yeah, we went to the Big Chill.

Interviewer What was it like?

Harley Yeah, it was really good. I went with my dad and my sister, and we went in a camper van. So we camped and yeah, it was good.

6.5

1 I was giving a talk to about two hundred people in a large hotel room in Poland. About halfway through the talk, I realized that something was flying around the room. At first I just ignored it, as I thought it was probably a bird that had come in through the window, but after a while I noticed that the women in the audience were following its movements with their eyes and were not looking very happy. It was then that I realized that it was a large bat. The next moment I could see from the audience's eyes that it was directly above my head. I'm really frightened of bats, and I just panicked. I tried to carry on, but I couldn't concentrate and I kept forgetting what I was going to say. So I hurried through the last part of the talk and then as soon as I finished, I rushed out of the room. It was awful, I'll never forget it!

2 I get invited to talk to teachers all around the world, and this time I was in Mexico giving a talk to some English teachers. Though I say it myself, I think I'm a good speaker and usually the audiences enjoy my talks and are interested in what I'm saying. But after about ten minutes, I realized that something was wrong. The audience weren't laughing at my jokes and some people were looking very unhappy. Then I saw several people get up and walk out of the hall. I just couldn't work out what was going on. I'd given a presentation there the year before and the audience had been really enthusiastic. In the end, I just stopped and asked them. 'Is anything the matter? You don't seem to be enjoying this.' And one teacher said 'Actually the problem is that you gave exactly the same talk last year, so we've heard it all before'. I didn't really know what to do at this point. I just apologized profusely and invited the people who had already heard the talk to leave, which, unfortunately, was almost everybody.

3 I was giving a presentation to a rather serious group of businessmen in Germany. They listened politely for 45 minutes, and at the end I asked for any questions. Nobody said anything. Then a young man stood up and said to me, 'Sir, you are open.' I looked down at my trousers and realized that I was.

4 I had to give a talk to some students at Imperial College in London. It's the science and technology department of London University, so I didn't think there would be any problems with the equipment. I'd seen the auditorium before and it was a nice room, good sound and screen, etc. But as soon as I began my talk, people started complaining that they couldn't see the slides – there was something wrong with the projector and the screen was too dark. So I started touching keys on my laptop, and I don't know what I did, but I managed to delete the whole presentation. So there I was with no presentation notes at all, nothing, and I had to improvise from what I could remember. It was all very embarrassing, I must say.

5 I had to give a business presentation to a company in Paris, and after I'd got there and checked into my hotel, I thought I'd go for a walk as it was such a beautiful day and I had plenty of time. My talk wasn't until one o'clock and I was well prepared. I was strolling along by the river enjoying the sunshine when I noticed that several people at the cafés were already having lunch. I thought it was a bit early for lunch and I checked my watch – it was only a quarter to twelve. And then I suddenly realized that I'd forgotten to change my watch. The UK is one hour behind France, so that meant it was in fact quarter to *one*. My presentation was supposed to start in 15 minutes' time. I desperately looked for a taxi to take me first back to my hotel and then to the company's offices where I was going to give the presentation. I finally arrived 20 minutes late and very stressed – and the worst thing of all was that the title of the talk I was giving was 'How to manage your time better!'

6.9 Interviewer What advice would you give to someone visiting London for the first time?
Sebastian It's often said that London is a city of villages, for example, Hampstead, even Chelsea, were all villages in the past; so take some time to get to know the village you are staying in before you start to explore the famous sights.
Interviewer What's the one thing you would say someone visiting London should do or see?
Sebastian Outdoors: walk up Parliament Hill – you get far and away the best view over the city. Indoors: the British Museum. When you see what the people of ancient times were capable of, it makes you feel humble about the achievements of our own age.
Interviewer And what's the best place to have your photo taken?
Sebastian I've always liked the classic view of the Houses of Parliament either from Westminster Bridge or from the other side of the river.

Interviewer What's your favourite landmark?
Sebastian St Paul's Cathedral. It is so hidden-away that when you catch your first sight of it, it's always a thrill. You just turn a corner and suddenly there it is.
Interviewer What's the best place to watch the sunset?
Sebastian Well, the views from the bridges are always spectacular. I imagine the London Eye, by Waterloo Bridge, would be a good spot, but I'm ashamed to say I have never been on it. And on a summer evening I like the roof garden of The Trafalgar Hotel just off Trafalgar Square – you can watch the city lights come on as the sun sets.
Interviewer What's the best place to be at dawn?
Sebastian In the summer, almost anywhere. I love the city when it's completely deserted in the early morning light. One of my favourite places to be at that time is the all-night bagel shop on Brick Lane. I love queuing on the pavement outside for a salmon and cream cheese bagel in the early morning, because then it means I must have been out all night doing something fun or interesting. But in winter the best place to be at dawn is in bed – definitely!
Interviewer What would be a good thing to do on a scorching hot day?
Sebastian Getting a boat on the Serpentine or in Battersea Park is one of my favourite things, and another of my favourite places, the London Aquarium, is somewhere where you can escape from the heat into a world of water and air conditioning.
Interviewer What's a good thing to do which is absolutely free?
Sebastian Walking in the parks. London's parks deserve their fame. I love walking in Hyde Park. It always reminds me of my childhood – I have memories of feeding the squirrels there.
Interviewer What do you think is the most romantic place in London?
Sebastian In Kensington, Knightsbridge, and Chelsea, residential squares have enclosed gardens. They're magical places at any time of day, like secret gardens, but at night you can often hear nightingales singing – they're the only birds that sing at night. It's very romantic.

6.11 Presenter And tonight on the book programme we're reviewing a book called *Did you spot the gorilla?* by Dr Richard Wiseman, who's an expert on creative thinking. With us tonight to talk about this book is Steven Hutchinson, a freelance journalist. So Steven, what exactly is Dr Wiseman's main message?
Steven Well, Dr Wiseman's theory is that most people don't think creatively because they concentrate so hard on the small, specific job that they are working on that they don't see the bigger picture. That's what the gorilla experiment proves.
Presenter What was the gorilla experiment?
Steven Well, a study was carried out by Daniel Simons and Christopher Chabris at Harvard University in 1999. He got volunteers to watch a 45-second film of people playing basketball. There were two teams. One team were wearing black T-shirts and the other team were wearing white ones. He gave the volunteers a simple task: they just had to count the number of passes made by the white team. Afterwards, he asked them how many passes they had counted and most people got the answer right. Then he asked them if they had seen anything unusual and at least half of them said no. And that's really amazing. Because during the film, while the two teams were playing basketball, a woman dressed as a gorilla walked onto the court and she beat her chest at the camera, and then slowly walked off the court. And half the volunteers just didn't see it!
Presenter That's incredible. Why not?
Steven Because they were so busy trying to count the passes that they didn't notice the gorilla! Dr Wiseman repeated this experiment many times and the result was always the same. In fact, he

actually tried it on a group of top British scientists and not one of them saw the gorilla.
Presenter How extraordinary!

6.12 Steven The gorilla experiment is a perfect demonstration that we normally only focus on what we're looking for, and don't see outside it, so we sometimes miss really important discoveries which are right in front of us, we just don't see them. That's why when something is invented people often say, 'Why didn't anybody think of that before?' – well, they didn't because they didn't think creatively.
Presenter Dr Wiseman gives some examples of people who he says *are* creative thinkers, doesn't he?
Steven Yes, people like the man who invented Post-it™ notes. He was actually trying to develop a really strong kind of glue, but he could only manage to make a very weak one. But instead of just thinking, 'Oh that's no good' he actually thought of a way of using the weak glue to make Post-it™ notes, notes that would stick to something but not too much. Or the man who set up IKEA, the furniture company – I mean for years people had been wanting cheap furniture that was well designed, but nobody did it. Or the idea of cheap air travel. People just accepted that it was impossible. But then somebody said 'It *is* possible, and I'm going to do it'. And that's how we got low-cost airlines like easyJet™.
Presenter Can we make ourselves creative thinkers?
Steven Yes, Dr Wiseman has lots of tips on how we can become more creative. One of the things he recommends is to try to do the *opposite* of what you normally do. For example, he told a group of journalists to try to think of articles that *nobody* would find interesting – he said that from that, possibly a brilliant idea for something interesting will come up. His book is full of tips – it's really worth reading.
Presenter Has he had any 'Eureka' moments himself?
Steven Yes, actually he's thought up a great idea for book lovers. His idea is to print a book which contains the first chapters of 15 other different books. This book has a book token in the back, a voucher that you can use to buy another book. The idea is that you read the beginnings and then choose which book you want to read more of and buy it with the book token.
Presenter What a great idea! That's creative thinking for you.

6.16 Interviewer John Bigos is the managing director of London Duck Tours Limited. This company use Ducks, renovated World War II amphibious vehicles, which can travel on land and water. What makes a Duck tour better than a normal sightseeing tour?
John What makes Duck tours more interesting in terms of the tour as opposed to other tours is the ability to be able to go on the land and the river in one tour at the same time. That has a great benefit for all our clients. We also have a very small vessel which only takes 30 people and that allows you to have a much more intimate relationship with your clients, which makes it a wonderful experience, which you don't get when you go on ordinary, pre-determined computerized tours.
Interviewer Some people might say that taking tourists on such a busy river is a bit dangerous. Have you ever had any accidents?
John In terms of accidents, we have had breakdowns, that means that we have to drop the anchor in the river which is similar to having to use the brake on the land and we've had to recover both our boat and our passengers, but that fortunately is quite a rare thing, but it adds to the fact that the tour is unique and no one else can do it. It's an experience, which can include being recovered by another Duck.
Interviewer Do you ever have to rescue other people on the river?

John When we are on the river, we are one of the most frequent users of this part of the river and people will often fall or jump off Westminster Bridge, Lambeth Bridge … or indeed Vauxhall Bridge and therefore we will be within the vicinity and often have to rescue people who have either fallen off accidentally or deliberately tried to commit suicide, so in terms of the river it is a very serious river with a very fast-flowing tide and we treat it with the utmost respect.

Interviewer Do you have many difficult customers?

John We do have people who come in a very unprepared manner, for example a lady in a mink coat who then gets wet and she asks for the mink coat to be specifically cleaned, which would cost us a whole day's revenue, the coat was very expensive and the good news is that she was travelling abroad back to her homeland and unfortunately we were unable to get it cleaned within the time that she asked, and in the circumstances, it didn't cost us any money. So those sort of people can be difficult as well as your normal customers who either don't think they've had the service they requested or the tour was not up to a standard that they thought they would like, probably because they're afraid of water.

6.17 **Interviewer** What are the most popular sights?

John The most popular sights that get people really excited are Parliament Square, where we have the new Nelson Mandela statue, and that's the first statue that I'm aware of that has been erected whilst someone is still alive, and that's very exciting. Additionally we have a number of heroes in our country and Trafalgar Square with all the fountains and Nelson and Nelson's Column, really excite people, and finally we obviously have MI6, which is where our vessels go into the water and it is also where the films *The Living Daylights* and *The World is not Enough* started when the boat came out of a second-floor window and as a 'Duck' we replicate that in our own style.

Interviewer What are your personal favourite sights on the tour?

John I personally like the Houses of Parliament, because I think it is a beautifully designed building and it's got some very, very interesting features. I also favour the statue of Emmeline Pankhurst because that is quite interesting in so much as it was only in 1928 that women were given the vote and yet it seems so many years ago and then in terms of large sights, obviously things like Buckingham Palace and Horse Guards are very interesting as well, because of the history.

Interviewer What do you think is the best and worst thing about London for a tourist?

John I think the best thing is the fantastic variety and depth of culture that we have in our capital city here. We have over 200 different cultures and nations who live here in the centre of London, and it makes for a fantastic cosmopolitan city with so much variety that it is impossible to get bored. It is a fabulous capital to come to as a tourist.

In terms of the worst things for tourists in London, I don't think our capital has yet reached the standards of service that a lot of other cities have, where you don't get good quality food at a reasonable price on time quite often and you have a lot of delays in terms of travel and congestion and therefore there are many things that can still be done to improve the quality of service for a fantastic capital city.

6.19 **Interviewer** What's your favourite city?

Theresa I would have said Prague actually, but I've recently been to Stockholm a couple of times and I loved it. Stockholm is fantastic. It's built on 14 islands, lots of water, which I love, lots of interesting museums, Stockholm's lovely.

Interviewer Which city would you most like to visit?

Theresa I went to Cape Town earlier on this year and we were only there for five days and there was

so much that I didn't see that I would love to go back to Cape Town and see Robben Island and some of the apartheid museums and learn more about Nelson Mandela.

Interviewer What's your favourite city?

Anne Probably Delhi, because of the difference in culture and the monuments that are there and the people, and looking at the cultural differences of how we live and how they live. And I just find everyone so nice and so friendly.

Interviewer Which city would you most like to visit?

Anne I would most like to visit Barcelona because I've heard the shopping's very good.

Interviewer What's your favourite city?

Agne It would be New York. I like the hustle and bustle and the 'busyness' and just the overall feeling of being in that city – it's just really nice, it just makes you feel really alive all the time, lots and lots of things to do and it just goes on, it just doesn't stop.

Interviewer Which city would you most like to visit?

Agne I'd like to go to Sydney, see what that's like.

Interviewer What's your favourite big city?

Matandra My favourite big city. I risk sounding partial but it would have to be my home town, it would have to be Rome. I think it's, you know, a lot of the reasons are… no need to explain. But I think it's very happening, more than people think and it's the right compromise between a laid-back lifestyle and a, you know, the positive aspects of living in a metropolis.

Interviewer Which city would you most like to visit?

Matandra Either Casablanca or a place like that. I'm just fascinated with that part of the world.

Interviewer What's your favourite city?

Harley Em. London. Because it's got all the shops. So I can come here and go shopping.

Interviewer Which city would you most like to visit?

Harley Any, really, any, I'd like to go to Australia, anywhere hot, anywhere with shops. Anywhere.

7.3

1 When I was a young man, about 17, I was working in Spain as an electrician for the German car company, Mercedes. A man from the engineering company, Bosch, visited Mercedes and he liked the way that I worked and he offered me a job in Germany. I suppose it is what you would call 'an apprenticeship'. I would have learnt to become an engineer. I really wanted to do it, but my parents didn't want me to leave home and go and work in a foreign country. In those days not many people did that. So in the end I didn't go. But I really wish that I'd taken that job because I think it would have opened doors for me and my professional life would have been more fulfilling.

2 Three years ago I was going to take part in a dance competition. I was a bit pale so I decided to go to a suntan studio the day before the competition. As I didn't have much time and I wanted to get a nice tan really quickly, I stayed under the lamp about 20 minutes. Unfortunately, that was too long and I got burnt. The top and skirt I wore the next day for the competition were really skimpy and so everyone in the audience could see how red my skin was. I felt really stupid and really wished I hadn't done it.

3 I really wish I'd been able to know my grandmother better. She died when I was 12, and since then I've discovered that she must have been a fascinating person, and there are so many things I would love to have been able to talk to her about. She was Polish but she was in Russia, in St Petersburg, during the Russian Revolution and she knew all sorts of interesting people at the time, painters, writers, people like that. I was only a child so I never asked her much about her own life. Now I'm discovering all about her through reading her old letters and papers, but I wish she

had lived longer so that I could have talked to her about those times face-to-face.

4 The only thing I really regret is not having had the courage to chat up a guy who I saw at a party last summer. I really fancied him – he was very good-looking – but I just wasn't brave enough to start a conversation. I wish I'd tried. I'm absolutely positive we would have got on well. And now it's too late – he's engaged to another girl!

5 My biggest regret is how I spent my time at university. I studied English Literature, which was something I was quite interested in, but it certainly wasn't the most important thing in my life. I played a lot of sport, I played in a band, and listened to a lot of music, but I also spent most of my time either socializing or asleep. And in terms of studying, I just did the bare minimum – I read what I had to, but never anything more. I only went to the compulsory lectures, never the optional ones and I left all my essays until the last minute and kept them as short as I could. OK, I passed my exams and I got my degree in the end, but I've always regretted not taking more advantage of those three years. I wish I'd realized at the time that this was a unique opportunity to read lots of novels, to learn about great writers, and to listen to people who really knew what they were talking about. Now I'm working and have small children, I don't have time to read anything.

7.5 When Paul Feldman started his business, you know, he really thought that at least 95% of the people would pay for their bagels. This was presumably because that was the payment rate that he got in his own office. But in fact this rate wasn't representative at all. I mean in his office, most people paid probably just because Feldman worked there himself, and they knew him personally, and probably liked him.

So when Feldman sold his bagels in other offices, he had to accept less. After a while, he considered that a company was 'honest' if over 90% of the people paid. Between 80 and 90% was what he considered to be normal, you know, the average rate. He didn't like it, but he had to accept it. It was only if a company habitually paid less than 80% – which luckily not many did – that he would feel he had to do something. First he would leave a note, sort of giving them a warning, and then, if things didn't improve, he would simply stop selling there. Interestingly, since he started the business, the boxes he leaves to collect the cash have hardly ever been stolen. Obviously in the mind of an office worker, to steal a bagel isn't a crime – but to steal the money box is.

So what does the bagel data tell us about the kind of offices that were not honest, the ones that *didn't* pay? Well, first of all, it shows that smaller offices are more honest than big ones. An office with twenty to thirty employees generally pays 3 to 5% more than an office with two to three hundred employees. This seems to be because in a smaller community people are more worried about being dishonest – probably because they would feel worse if they were caught.

The bagel data also suggests that your mood, how you feel, affects how honest you are. For example, the weather is a really important factor. When the weather is unusually good, more people pay, but if it's unusually cold or rainy, fewer people pay. And people are also affected by public holidays, but in different ways – it depends *which* public holiday. Before Christmas and Thanksgiving, people are less honest, but just before the 4th of July and Labour Day they are *more* honest. This seems to be because holidays like the 4th of July, are just a day off work, and people always look forward to them. But Christmas and Thanksgiving are holidays where people often feel quite stressed or miserable. So their bad mood makes them less honest.

The other thing Feldman believes affects how honest people are is the morale in an office. When employees like their boss and like their job, then the office is more honest. He also thinks that the higher people are promoted, the less honest they are. He reached this conclusion because over several years he'd been delivering three baskets of bagels to a company that was on three floors. The top floor was the executive floor, and the lower two floors were people who worked in sales, and service, and administrative employees. Well, it turned out that the least honest floor was the executive floor! It makes you wonder whether maybe these guys got to be executives because they were good at cheating!

But in general the story of Feldman's bagel business is a really positive one. It's true that some people *do* steal from him, but the vast majority, even though no one is watching them, are honest.

7.7 **Presenter** Now it's time for our regular Wednesday afternoon spot about words and their origins. And I have with me, as usual, our English language expert, Sally Davies. So what are the three words you are going to tell us about today, Sally?

Sally Hello, John. My three words today are 'ketchup', 'orange', – that's the fruit, the colour came later, and 'tennis'.

Presenter Let's start with 'ketchup' then.

Sally Yes, well, the Chinese invented a sauce called 'ke-tsiap', spelled K-E-hyphen-T-S-I-A-P in the 1690s. It was made from fish and spices, but absolutely no tomatoes. By the early eighteenth century, its popularity had spread to Malaysia, and this is where British explorers first found it, and obviously really liked it. By 1740 the sauce was part of the English diet – people were eating a lot of it and it was also becoming popular in the American colonies. And they renamed the sauce 'ketchup', because it was a bit easier for the English to pronounce. Then about fifty years later, in 1790, some American colonists in New England mixed tomatoes into the sauce and it became known as 'tomato ketchup'.

Presenter So it is American after all?

Sally Well, tomato ketchup is.

Presenter So, tell us about orange?

Sally Well, it's very interesting that neither 'orange' in English nor 'naranja' in Spanish or 'arancia' in Italian, come from the Latin word for 'orange', which was 'citrus aurentium'. Instead they, they all come from the ancient Sanskrit word 'narangah'. There is also an interesting story about where this word, 'narangah', comes from. It's said that it comes from 'naga ranga', which literally means 'poison for elephants'.

Presenter Poison for elephants?

Sally Yes, apparently, one day in around the 7th or 8th century BC an elephant was passing through the forest, when he found a tree which he had never seen before. This tree was full of beautiful, tempting oranges; as a result, the elephant ate so many that he died. Many years later a man came to the same spot and noticed the remains of the elephant with some orange trees growing from what had been its stomach. The man then exclaimed, 'These fruit are naga ranga' that is, 'poison for elephants'.

Presenter So is this true?

Sally Well, I don't know, but it's a nice story!

Presenter And finally our last word is 'tennis'.

Sally This is my favourite one, and it shows that the English have always had their own special way of pronouncing foreign languages. Tennis is a sport which first developed in France. The name was originally 'tenez' which is from the French verb 'tenir' which means, in this case, something like 'Here you are'. Players used to say 'tenez' when they hit the ball meaning something like 'There, try to get this one'. But the sport lost popularity in France and gained popularity in England at the same time. So, English people were still using the word 'tenez' each time they hit the ball, but they were saying it with the English accent which sounded more like 'tennis', and eventually it took this new spelling. Then the sport gained popularity worldwide and was taken up by many nationalities, including the French – but they now had to call it 'le tennis'!

Presenter Fascinating! Well, thank you very much for those three words, Sally, and we'll look forward to next week's programme.

7.9 **Interviewer** Susie Dent is a well-known English lexicographer who also appears in the popular British TV Quiz *Countdown*. Could you give us an estimate of how many new words come into the English language each year?

Susie A lot of people ask me how many new words are born in any particular year and the quick answer to that is no one knows, because thousands and thousands and thousands of new words are made up every second. What we do know is that in the twentieth century about 900,000 new words went into the *Oxford English Dictionary*, which is the vast vast dictionary that Oxford keeps going, basically constantly, tracking current language and historical language, so that means on average about 900 words each year made it in that in a significant enough way to get into the dictionary.

Interviewer How does a new word or expression get into the dictionary?

Susie Normally dictionary makers will wait about five years to see whether or not a word will survive before they put it in. So they have quite strict criteria. There are exceptions to that and 'bling' is a prime example. It went into the dictionary very very soon.

'Bling' is a wonderful word that is used by journalists particularly to sum up the sort of celebrity obsessed, very materialistic opening years of the 21st century, but in fact is was coined in 1999 and it was coined by a rapper and I think it's an absolutely beautiful word because it's from US black slang particularly and hip hop and rap have had a major influence on British slang particularly today, and it was used by the rapper Baby Gangsta or BG and it was probably suggestive of light flashing off jewellery so it was 'bling' and that's how it was taken up and it went into the mainstream incredibly quickly.

7.10 **Interviewer** Where do new words come from?

Susie One of the main processes by which new words come about today is one called 'blending' where you put two words together to form a new one. And one of my favourites is 'chofas' which is a cross between a chair and a sofa and 'waparazzi' as well which I think is really clever and 'waparazzi' is basically citizen journalists, if you like, going around snapping celebrities with their WAP (W-A-P) enabled phone, and so people thought, 'Oh, we'll call them the 'waparazzi'. So that's quite a good example of how new words are coming about. 'Mandals' is another one, male sandals or 'man sandals' is another one that has been doing the rounds in Britain anyway.

Another process by which new words are born is by bringing older words back. And so, 'cool' for example was around probably in the late nineteenth century, then it was popularized by jazz circles, Charlie Parker and people like that and now it's just, you know, it's used by young people everywhere.

Another way in which new words are coined if you like is when old words come back and take on a slightly different meaning. So again they're not completely new at all but we've adapted them to our new environment. A great example of this is 'wireless'. Whereas our grandparents certainly in Britain used to listen to the wireless and it meant a portable radio, today 'wireless' has everything to do with broadband and the way that we use our computers in a cable-free way.

Interviewer Any other ways?

Susie English has long been a 'hoover', really, of foreign languages and it is made up of so many different words from different cultures, right back from Latin and Greek to modern influences now. Food is a wonderful example of that where we just take different cuisines from around the world and we introduce obvious examples, like 'sushi', 'sashimi', that sort of thing, into our language. Brand names, another key way in which we generate new words if you like. If you think about Kleenex or Hoover as I mentioned. Those used to be brand names, they are still brand names, but we've somehow imported them so that we know exactly what we're talking about and they mean anything generic.

Interviewer Do you have any favourite new words of the last few years?

Susie I have so many favourites from the last few years, ever since I've been first writing the *Language reports*, I have to collect my favourite new words of the year. I loved the idea of a 'marmalade dropper', which was basically a news item that made you drop your toast in the morning. In America it was called a 'muffin choker'.

7.12 **Interviewer** Are there any English words that are used in your language?

Mateusz Yes, for example, hamburger. It is used I think worldwide, but in Poland we say *hamburger*. Yes, maybe computer, in Poland *komputer*, there are plenty of words like that, plenty of words that are about cuisine, *hot dog*, hot dog in Polish. Really, plenty of words like that.

Interviewer Do you think it would be better to use your own words?

Mateusz No, I don't think so, because they are used everywhere in this world and why not in Poland?

Interviewer Are there any English words that are used in your language?

Victoria Erm yes. Well, no I don't think there are a lot of English words, but there are a lot of French words that sound English like *parking* which actually doesn't make sense in English. It's a car park and we call it *parking* and it's not French at all. But we have a lot of things like that because English is cool and so we try to make our words sound English.

Interviewer Do you think it would be better to use your own words?

Victoria No, we should … I like the idea that there are words that you can understand in every country, it brings nations, people closer, you know.

Interviewer Are there any English words that are used in your language?

Matandra An English word that is used in the Italian language well, everything to do with technology, everything to do with the Internet, and Internet itself, well someone could argue that Internet is actually Latin but … say *download*, we've given up saying the Italian version of downloading which is *scaricare* and most people just go with *downloadare* which sounds very odd to the Italian ear, but we, we're going with it.

Interviewer Do you think it would be better to use your own words?

Matandra I don't think it's necessary to to set off on a crusade to defend language in so much as, you know, as specific areas which are just the domain of another language. Italian is the main domain in say music. No one complains around the world because you say *pianissimo* when you have to play softly.

Interviewer Are there any English words that are used in your language?

Volke Too many, too many, I must say. We forget a lot of German words and replace them by English words and I mean they are pronounced in the same way. I miss that, because I like Spanish as well and they have so many, they have lots, words for computer or skateboard and things like that which we don't have and we take all the English words. And if there are new inventions or stuff like that we don't invent new words – we just take them and I think it's a pity not to do the opposite.

Interviewer Do you think it would be better to use your own words?

Volke It's part of culture and I think we should maintain that. You can be open to other languages and cultures but at the same time you should keep your own one, I think.

1

1A   question formation

> 1 **Can you** drive? Why **are you** crying?
> 2 Where **do you** live? **Did you** go out last night?
> 3 Why **didn't you** like the film? **Isn't this** a beautiful place?
> 4 **What** are they talking **about**? **Where** is she **from**?
> 5 **Who lives** in this house? **How many people came** to the party?
> 6 Could you tell me **where this bus goes**?
>   Do you know **if he's coming**?

1 To make questions with modal verbs and with tenses where there is an auxiliary verb (*be, have,* etc.) invert the subject and the modal / auxiliary verb.
2 With the present and past simple, add *do / does* or *did* before the subject.
3 We often use negative questions to show surprise or when we expect somebody to agree with us.

4 If a verb is followed by a preposition, the preposition comes at the end of the question, e.g. *What are you talking about?* NOT *About w̶ are you talking?*
• We often just use the question word and the preposition, e.g. **A** *I'm thinking.* **B** *What about?*
5 When *who / what / which,* etc. is the **subject** of the question, don't use *do / did,* e.g. *Who wrote this?* NOT *Who did write this?*
6 Use indirect questions when you want to ask a question in a more polite *Where does she live?* (direct) *Could you tell me where she lives?* (indirec
• In indirect questions the order is subject + verb.
  Can you tell me where it is? NOT *Can you tell me where is it?*
• Don't use *do / did* in the second part of the question. *Do you know where he lives?* NOT *does live.*
• You can use *if* or *whether* after *Can you tell me, Do you know,* etc., e.g. *C you tell me if / whether he's at home?*

1B   auxiliary verbs

> 1 **A Do** you speak French?   **B** Yes, **I do.** Quite well.
> 2 I like dogs, but my husband **doesn't.** Jim's coming, but Anna **isn't.**
> 3 **A** I loved the film.   **B So did I.**
>   **A** I haven't finished yet.   **B Neither have I.**
>   He's a doctor and **so is his wife.**
> 4 **A** I went to a psychic yesterday. **B Did you?**
>   **A** I'll make the dinner.   **B Will you?** That's great!
> 5 **A** You didn't lock the door!   **B** I **did** lock it, I promise.
>   **A** Silvia isn't coming.   **B** She **is** coming. I've just spoken to her.
> 6 You won't forget, **will you?** Your wife can speak Italian, **can't she?**

Use auxiliary verbs (*do, have,* etc.) or modal verbs (*can, must,* etc.):
1 in short answers, instead of answering just *Yes / No.*
2 to avoid repeating the main verb / verb phrase, e.g. *I like dogs but my husband doesn't* (~~like dogs~~).
3 with *so* and *neither* to say that something is the same. Use *so* + auxiliary + subject after a positive verb, and *neither* (or *nor*) + auxiliary + subject after a negative verb.

4 to make 'echo questions', to show interest.
5 to show emphasis in a positive sentence. Wit the present / past simple, add *do / does / did* before the main verb. With other auxiliaries stress the auxiliary verb.
6 to make question tags. Use a positive questio tag with a negative verb and a negative question tag with a positive verb.
• Question tags are often used simply to ask another person to agree with you, e.g. *It's a nice day, isn't it?* In this case the question tag is said with falling intonation, i.e. the voice goes down.
• Question tags can also be used to check something you think is true, e.g. *She's a painter, isn't she?* In this case the question ta is said with rising intonation, as in a normal yes / no question.

1C   present perfect (simple and continuous)

present perfect simple: *have / has* + past participle

> 1 **I've been** to Australia. **Have you ever broken** your leg?
> 2 We've **just phoned** the doctor.
>   I've **already finished** my lunch.
> 3 It's the best book **I've** ever **read.**
>   It's the first time **we've done** this.
> 4 My sister**'s had** a baby! Look, **I've cut** my finger.
> 5 **I've known** her **since** I was a child.
>   **She's had** the job **for** six months.
> 6 **How many** of his books **have you read?**
>   **She's been out** twice this week.

Use the present perfect simple:
1 to talk about past experiences when you don't say when something happened.
2 with *already, just,* and *yet.*
3 with superlatives and *the first, second, last time,* etc.
4 for finished actions (no time is specified) which are connected in some way with the present.
5 with *How long?* and *for / since* with **non-action** verbs (= verbs not usually used in the continuous form, e.g. *be, have, know, like,* etc.) to say that something started in the past and is still true now.
6 when we say / ask *how much / many* we have done or *how often* we have done something up to now.

present perfect continuous: *have / has* + *been* + verb + *-ing*

> 1 **How long have you been feeling** like this? **I've been working** here **for** two months.
> 2 **I haven't been sleeping** well recently. **It's been raining** on and off all day.
> 3 **I've been shopping** all morning. I'm exhausted.
>   **A** Take your shoes off. They're filthy.
>   **B** Yes, I know. **I've been working** in the garden.

Use the present perfect continuous:
1 with *How long?* and *for / since* with **action** verbs to say that an action starte the past and is still happening now.
2 for repeated actions, especially with a time expression, e.g. *all day, recently.*
3 for continuous actions which have just finished (but which have present re

present perfect simple or continuous?

> 1 **We've lived / We've been living** in this town since 1980.
>   **We've been living** in a rented flat for the last two months.
> 2 **We've painted** the kitchen. **We've been** painting the kitchen.

1 With *How long…?* and *for / since* you can often use the present perfect simple or continuous. However, we often prefer the present perfect continuous for shorter, more temporary actions.
2 The present perfect simple emphasizes the completion of an action (= the painting is finished). The present perfect continuous emphasizes the continuation of an action (= the painting is probably not finished).

1A

a Order the words to make questions.

friend known long best have How you your
How long have you known your best friend?

1 you messages send ever text Do
2 party was a time you to the When last went
3 if Could bank here a you me near tell is there
4 dinner usually Who the cooks
5 shopping do going Who like you with
6 at don't weekend you What doing the like
7 car to would What you kind like buy of
8 you time concert know finishes Do what the

b Complete the questions.

Where ___*did you go*___ on holiday last year? (you / go)

1 How often _____ exercise? (you / do)
2 Who _____ *Crime and Punishment*? (write)
3 Could you tell me how much _____? (this book / cost)
4 What _____ at the end of the film? (happen)
5 _____ your trip to Paris last weekend? (you / enjoy)
6 What kind of music _____? (Tim / usually listen to)
7 Who _____ Mia's handbag? (steal)
8 Do you know when _____? (the swimming pool / open)
9 Where _____ your boyfriend tonight? (you / meet)
10 Can you remember where _____? (she / live)

1B

a Complete the mini-dialogues with an auxiliary.

A You didn't remember to buy coffee. **B** I __*did*__. It's in the cupboard.

1 **A** It's cold today, _____ it? **B** Yes, it's freezing.
2 **A** So you didn't go to the meeting?
  B I _____ go to the meeting, but I left early.
3 **A** What did you think of the film?
  B Tom liked it, but I _____. I thought it was awful.
4 **A** I wouldn't like to be famous. **B** Neither _____ I.
5 **A** Emma doesn't like me.
  B She _____ like you. She thinks you're very nice.
6 **A** Sarah's had a baby.
  B _____ she? I didn't know she was pregnant!
7 **A** Will your boyfriend be at the party?
  B No, he _____. He's away this week.
8 **A** I can't come tonight.
  B _____ you? Why not?

b Complete the conversation with auxiliary verbs.

A You're Tom's sister, _*aren't*_ you?
B Yes, I [1] _____.
A It's a great club, [2] _____ it?
B Yes, it [3] _____. But I don't like the music much.
A [4] _____ you? I love it!
B Really? [5] _____ you been here before?
A No, I [6] _____.
B Neither [7] _____ I.
A So you [8] _____ go out much, then?
B Well, I [9] _____ go out, but I [10] _____ go to clubs very often.
A Oh, I [11] _____. I love clubbing.
B I'd love a drink.
A So [12] _____ I. Let's go to the bar.

1C

a Circle the correct form of the verb. Tick (✓) if both are correct.

Have you ever (tried) / *been trying* caviar?

1 *She's lived / She's been living* here for years.
2 Your boss *has phoned / has been phoning* three times this morning!
3 The kids are exhausted because *they've played / they've been playing* outside all day.
4 *He hasn't seen / He hasn't been seeing* the new James Bond film yet.
5 *I've never met / I've never been meeting* his wife. Have you?
6 *We've studied / We've been studying* English all our lives.
7 *I've tidied / I've been tidying* the garage all afternoon. I've nearly finished.
8 He'll be here soon. *He's just left / He's just been leaving* work.
9 How long *have you had / have you been having* your car?
10 Oh no! Someone *has broken / has been breaking* the window.

b Complete the sentences with the present perfect simple or continuous.

I've bought _____ a new car. Do you like it? (buy)

1 We _____ Jack and Ann for years. (know)
2 You look hot. _____? (you / run)
3 Rose _____ her homework so she can't go out. (not do)
4 Did you know _____? They live in Torquay now. (they / move)
5 How long _____ together? Five months? (Daisy and Adam / go out)
6 I _____ time to cook dinner. Shall we get a pizza? (not have)
7 We _____ for hours. I think we're lost. (walk)
8 _____ my chocolates? There are only a few left! (you / eat)

2

2A adjectives as nouns, adjective order

nationalities

> 1 **The English** are famous for drinking tea. **The Dutch** make wonderful cheeses. **The Chinese** invented paper.
> 2 **The Argentinians** invented the tango. **The Greeks** are very extrovert.
> 3 **The Turks** drink a lot of coffee. **The Poles** play a lot of basketball.

1 You can use *the* with the nationality adjectives which end in *-sh, -ch, -ss,* or *-ese*. Don't add *s* to these words, or use them without *the*.
2 Nationality words which end in *-an* and a few others, e.g. *Greek* and *Thai,* are both adjectives and nouns. To talk about the people from that country use a plural noun ending in *-s*.
3 Some nationalities have a special noun for the people which is different from the adjective, e.g. *Polish* = adjective, *Pole* = noun. To talk about the people you can either use *the* + adjective or *the* + plural noun, e.g. *the Polish* or *the Poles*.

> ⚠ With any nationality, you can also use the adjective + *people*, e.g. *French people*.
>
> ⚠ To talk about <u>one</u> person from a country you can't use *a / an* + adjective alone:
> 1 *a Japanese man / woman / person, an Englishman / Englishwoman / English person*, NOT ~~a Japanese, an English,~~ etc.
> 2 *an Italian, a Greek,* etc.
> 3 *a Turk, a Pole,* etc.

specific groups of people

> **The poor** are getting poorer and **the rich** are getting richer. The government needs to create more jobs for **the unemployed**.

- You can use *the* + some adjectives to talk about specific groups in society, e.g. *the young, the blind, the homeless, the old, the elderly, the sick*. These expressions are always plural.

one, ones

> **A Which one** would you like? **B The red one**, please. Two ice creams, please. **Big ones**.

- When we don't want to repeat a noun after an adjective because it is already clear what we are talking about, we use the adjective + *one* (singular) or + *ones* (plural).

adjective order

> We've got **a lovely old cottage** just outside Bath.
> She has **long fair** hair.
> I bought a **beautiful Italian leather** belt.

- You can put more than one adjective before a noun (often two and occasionally three). These adjectives go in a particular order, e.g. NOT ~~an old lovely cottage~~.
- Opinion adjectives, e.g. *beautiful, nice, lovely*, usually go <u>before</u> fact adjectives, e.g. *big, old, round*.
- If there is more than one fact adjective, they go in this order:

size	age	shape / style	colour / pattern	nationality	material	nou
big	new	long	pink, striped	Italian	silk	scar

2B narrative tenses: past simple, past continuous, past perfect, past perfect continuous

narrative tenses

> 1 We **arrived** at the airport and **checked in**.
> 2 We **were having dinner** when the plane hit some turbulence.
> 3 When we arrived at the airport, we suddenly realized that **we had left** one of the suitcases in the taxi.
> 4 **We'd been flying** for about two hours when the captain told us to fasten our seat belts because we were flying into some very bad weather.

1 Use the **past simple** to talk about consecutive actions in the past, i.e. for the main events in a story.
2 Use the **past continuous** (*was / were* + verb + *-ing*) to describe a longer continuous past action, which was in progress when another action happened.
3 Use the **past perfect** (*had* + past participle) to talk about the 'earlier past', i.e. things which happened <u>before</u> the main event(s).
4 Use the **past perfect continuous** (*had been* + verb + *-ing*) to talk about a longer continuous action that was going on before the main events happened. Non-action verbs are not normally used in the past continuous or the past perfect continuous.

past perfect simple or continuous?

> She was crying because **she'd been reading** a very sad book.
> She didn't want to see the film, because **she'd read the book**.

The past perfect continuous emphasizes the <u>continuation</u> of an activity. The past perfect simple emphasizes the <u>completion</u> of an activity.

2C adverbs and adverbial phrases

> 1 I don't understand you when you speak **quickly**. The driver was **seriously** injured.
> 2 I **never** have breakfast. He's **always** late.
> 3 They'll be here **soon**. It rained **all day yesterday**.
> 4 I've **nearly** finished. We're **incredibly** tired. He works **a lot**.
> 5 **Unfortunately**, we arrived half an hour late. **Ideally**, we should leave at 10.00.

- Adverbs can describe an action (*he walked slowly*) or modify adjectives or other adverbs (*it's incredibly expensive, he works very hard*). They can either be one word (*often*) or a phrase (*once a week*).
1 **Adverbs of manner** (how somebody does something) usually go after the verb or phrase. However, with passive verbs they usually go in mid-position (before the main verb but after an auxiliary verb).
2 **Adverbs of frequency** go before the main verb but after the verb *to be*.

> ⚠ *sometimes / usually / normally* can go at the beginning of a sentence too.

3 **Adverbs of time** usually go at the end of a sentence or clause.

4 **Adverbs of degree** (which describe how much something is done or modify an adjective).
- *extremely, incredibly, very*, etc. are used with adjectives and adverbs and go before them.
- *much* and *a lot* are often used with verbs and go after the verb or verb phrase.
- *a little / a bit* can be used with adjectives or verbs, e.g. *I'm a bit tired. She sleeps a bit in the afternoon.*
5 **Comment adverbs** (which give the speaker's opinion) usually go at the beginning of a sentence or clause. Other common comment adjectives are *luckily, clearly, obviously, apparently,* etc.

> ⚠ Most other adverbs go in mid-position, e.g. *I **just** need ten more minutes. She didn't **even** say goodbye.*

2A

a Rewrite the underlined phrase using *the* + an adjective.

<u>The people who live in Spain</u> go to bed very late.   *the Spanish*

1 <u>The people from the Netherlands</u> are very good at languages.
2 <u>The people who had injuries</u> were taken to hospital.
3 The system of reading for <u>people who can't see</u> is called Braille.
4 <u>The people from France</u> enjoy eating good food.
5 A nurse's job is to look after <u>the people who aren't well</u>.
6 I think <u>the people from Switzerland</u> are very punctual.
7 The worst season for <u>people without a home</u> is winter.
8 There is a discount for students and <u>people without a job</u>.

b Write the adjectives in brackets in the right place.

a big car park (empty)   *a big empty car park*

1 an attractive man (young)
2 dirty shoes (old)
3 a leather jacket (purple / stylish)
4 a tall woman (thin)
5 a sandy beach (long)
6 a new floor (lovely / wooden)
7 a smart suit (Italian)
8 beautiful eyes (big / dark)
9 an old dog (black / friendly)

2B

a Put the verb in brackets in the past perfect simple (*had done*) or continuous (*had been doing*). If you think both are possible, use the continuous form.

His English was very good. He *'d been learning* it for five years. (learn)

1 My feet were aching. We _____ for hours. (queue)
2 She went to the police, because someone _____ her bag. (steal)
3 The streets were wet. It _____ all morning. (rain).
4 She got to work late because she _____ an accident on the way. (have)
5 I almost didn't recognize him. He _____ a lot since I last saw him. (change)
6 They were very red. They _____ all morning but they _____ any sun cream. (sunbathe, not put on)
7 I could see from their faces that my parents _____. (argue)
8 Jess had a bandage on her arm. She _____ off her bike the day before. (fall)

b Circle the correct verb form.

Meg and Liam McGowan (got) / *were getting* a nasty surprise when they [1]*had checked in / were checking in* at Heathrow airport yesterday with their baby Shaun. They [2]*had won / won* three free plane tickets to Rome in a competition and they [3]*were looking forward to / had been looking forward to* their trip for months. But, unfortunately, they [4]*had been forgetting / had forgotten* to get a passport for their son and so Shaun couldn't fly. Luckily they [5]*had arrived / were arriving* very early for their flight so they still had time to do something about it. They [6]*had run / ran* to the police station in the airport to apply for an emergency passport. Meg [7]*was going / went* with Shaun to the photo machine while Liam [8]*had filled in / was filling in* the forms. The passport was ready in an hour, so they [9]*hurried / were hurrying* back to check-in and finally [10]*caught / had caught* their flight.

2C

a <u>Underline</u> the adverb(s) or adverbial phrase(s) and correct the sentences which are wrong.

We're going to be <u>unfortunately</u> late.   ✗ *Unfortunately, we're going to be late.*

We <u>rarely</u> go to bed <u>before 11.30</u>.   ✔

1 She likes very much the theatre.
2 Dave was late for work yesterday.
3 Immediately the ambulance arrived.
4 They go usually jogging after work.
5 I was extremely tired last night.
6 They won easily the match because they played brilliantly.
7 I forgot your birthday almost.
8 We luckily had taken an umbrella.
9 She always eats healthily.
10 He's been apparently sacked.

b Put the adverbs in brackets in the normal position in these sentences.

Sadly   *very*
ʌI don't speakʌgood English. (sadly, very)

1 The building was damaged in the fire. (badly, last week)
2 We need to do something. (obviously, quickly)
3 Ben is at his friend's house. (often, in the evening)
4 She walked out and she didn't say goodbye. (just, even)
5 He drives fast. (always, extremely)
6 She danced at the ballet. (beautifully, last night)
7 She wasn't injured when she fell. (luckily, seriously)
8 He broke his leg when he was skiing. (apparently, nearly)
9 My father sleeps in the afternoon. (usually, a bit)

3A passive (all forms), *it is said that…, he is thought to…*, etc.

the passive (all forms)

present simple	Murderers **are** usually **sentenced** to life imprisonment.
present continuous	The trial **is being held** at the moment.
present perfect	My car **has been** stolen.
past simple	Jim **was arrested** last month.
past continuous	The cinema **was being rebuilt** when it was set on fire.
past perfect	We saw that one of the windows **had been broken**.
future	The prisoner **will be released** next month.
	The verdict **is going to be given** tomorrow.
infinitive with *to*	People used **to be imprisoned** for stealing bread.
infinitive without *to*	You can **be fined** for parking on a yellow line.
gerund	He paid a fine to avoid **being sent** to jail.

- Use the passive when you want to talk about an action but you are not so interested in saying who or what does / did the action.
- If you also want to mention the person or thing that did the action (the agent), use *by*, e.g. *Prison sentences are decided by judges*. However, in the majority of passive sentences the agent is not mentioned.

it is said that…, he is thought to…, etc.

active	passive
1 They say that the company may close.	**It is said that** the company may close.
People think that prices will go up.	**It is thought that** prices will go up.
2 People say the man is in his 40s.	**The man is said to be** in his 40s.
The police believe he has left the country.	**He is believed to have left** the country.

- This formal structure is used especially in news reports and on TV with the verbs *know, tell, understand, report, expect, say* and *think*. It mak[e] the information sound more impersonal.
1 You can use *It is said, believed*, etc. + *that* + claus[e].
2 You can use *He, The man*, etc. (i.e. the subject of the clause) + *is said, believed*, etc. + *to* + infinitive (e.g. *to be*) or perfect infiniti[ve] (e.g. *to have been*).

3B future perfect and future continuous

future perfect: *will have* + past participle

I'll have finished the article by Friday, so I'll email it to you then.
They'll have built the new terminal in six months' time.

- Use the future perfect to say something will be finished before a certain time in the future.
- This tense is frequently used with the time expressions *by Saturday / March / 2030*, etc. or *in two weeks / months*, etc.
- *By* + a time expression = at the latest. With *in*, you can say *in six months* or *in six months' time*.

future continuous: *will be* + verb + *-ing*

Don't phone between 7.00 and 8.00 as **we'll be having** supper then.
This time next week **I'll be lying** on the beach.

- Use the future continuous to say that an action will be in progress at a certain time in the future.

  ⚠ We sometimes use the future continuous, like the present continuous, to talk about things which are already planned or decided, e.g. *I'll be going to the supermarket later*.

3C conditionals and future time clauses (with all present and future forms)

zero conditional

If **you want** to be fit, **you have to** do exercise every day.
If your muscles **ache** every day, **you are** probably **doing** too much exercise.
If you **haven't been** to London, you **haven't lived**.

- To talk about something which is always true or always happens as a result of something else, use *if* + present simple, and the present simple in the other clause.
- You can also use the present continuous or present perfect in either clause.

first conditional

If the photos **are** good, **I'll send** them to you.
If **you're not going, I'm not going to go** either.
If **I haven't come back** by 9.00, **start** dinner without me.
I'll have finished in an hour if **you don't** disturb me.

- You can use any present tense in the *if* clause (present simple, continuous or perfect) and any future form (*will, going to*, future perfect, future continuous) or an imperative in the other clause.

future time clauses

I'll be ready **as soon as I've had** a shower.
We'll probably be watching the Cup Final **when you arrive**.
We're not going to go out **until** the rain **has stopped**.
I'm not going to work overtime **unless I get paid**.
Take your umbrella **in case it rains**.

- When you are talking about the future, use a present tense after these expressions *as soon as, when, until, unless, before, after*, and *in case*. This can be any present tense, e.g. present simple, present continuous, present perfect.
- We use *in case* when we do something in order to be ready for future situations / problems. Compare the use of *if* and *in case*:
  I'll take a jacket if it's cold. = I won't take one if it's not cold.
  I'll take a jacket in case it's cold. = I'll take a jacket anyway because it might be cold.

3A

a Rewrite the sentences in the passive (without *by*…).

The police caught the burglar immediately.
The burglar *was caught immediately*.

1 Police closed the road after the accident. | The road…
2 Somebody has stolen my handbag. | My handbag…
3 The painters are painting my house. | My house…
4 They'll hold a meeting tomorrow. | A meeting…
5 The inspector fined them for travelling without a ticket. | They…
6 The police can arrest you for drink-driving. | You…
7 Miranda thinks someone was following her last night. | Miranda thinks she…
8 They had sold the house five years earlier. | The house…

b Rephrase the sentences to make them more formal.

People think the murderer is a woman.
It *is thought that the murderer is a woman.*
The murderer *is thought to be a woman.*

1 Police believe the burglar is a local man.
   It…   The burglar…
2 People say the muggers are very dangerous.
   It…   The muggers…
3 Police think the robber entered through an open window.
   It…   The robber…
4 Police say the murderer has disappeared.
   It…   The murderer…
5 Lawyers expect that the trial will last three weeks.
   It…   The trial…

3B

a Complete the sentences using the future perfect or future continuous.

The film starts at 7.00. I will arrive at the cinema at 7.15.
When I arrive at the cinema, the film _will have started_. (start)

1 The plane to Paris takes off at 9.00 and lands at 10.30.
   At 10.00 they _____ to Paris. (fly)
2 I save €200 a month.
   By the end of this year, I _____ €2,400. (save)
3 I leave home at 7.30. It takes an hour to drive to work.
   At 8.00 tomorrow I _____ to work. (drive)
4 Our meeting starts at 2.00 and finishes at 3.30.
   You can't ring me at 2.30 because we _____ a meeting. (have)
5 Sam is paying for his car. The last payment is in November.
   By December he _____ for his car. (pay)
6 Their last exam is on May 31st.
   By the end of May they _____ their exams. (finish)

b Complete the dialogue with verbs in the future continuous or future perfect.

A Well, it looks like the weather's going to be different in the 22nd century.
B What do you mean?
A Well, they say we *'ll be having* _____ much higher temperatures here in London, as high as 30°. And remember, we [1]_____ on the beach, we [2]_____ in 30°, which is quite different. And islands like the Maldives [3]_____ by 2150 because of the rise in the sea level. They say the number of storms and tsunamis [4]_____ by the middle of the century too, so even more people [5]_____ to the cities looking for work. Big cities [6]_____ even bigger by then. Can you imagine the traffic?
B I don't think there will be a problem with the traffic. Petrol [7]_____ by then anyway, so nobody will have a car. Someone [8]_____ a new method of transport, so we [9]_____ around in solar powered cars or something.

have

not lie
work
disappear

double
move
grow

run out
invent
drive

3C

a Circle the correct form.

Don't worry. Rob (will have passed) / has passed the exam if he's studied enough.

1 If *I'm not feeling* / *I won't be feeling* better tomorrow, I'm going to go to the doctor's.
2 Kerry *won't be going* / *doesn't go* to work next week if her children are still ill.
3 Don't call Chloe now. If it's eight o'clock, she'll *bath* / *will be bathing* the baby.
4 You can be fined if you *aren't wearing* / *won't be wearing* a seat belt in your car.
5 If we're lucky, *we'll have sold* / *we've sold* our house by Christmas.
6 If plants aren't watered, they *die* / *will have died*.

b Complete the sentence with a time expression from the list.

after   ~~as soon as~~   before   if   in case (x2)   unless   until   when

I'll call you _as soon as_ I get back from my holiday.

1 He's going to pack his suitcase _____ he goes to bed.
2 They're setting off early _____ there's a lot of traffic.
3 Sophie will be leaving work early tomorrow _____ her boss needs her.
4 I'm meeting an old friend _____ I go to London.
5 I'll call you _____ I find out my results.
6 _____ I'm late tomorrow, start the meeting without me.
7 Lily will have packed some sandwiches _____ we get hungry.
8 They'll be playing in the park _____ it gets dark.

4

4A unreal conditionals

second conditional sentences: *if* + past simple, *would* / *wouldn't* + infinitive

> 1 **If** there **was** a fire in this hotel, it **would be** very difficult to escape.
> I **wouldn't live** in the country **if** I **didn't have** a car.
> 2 **If** you **weren't making** so much noise, I **could concentrate** better.
> 3 **If** I **were** you, I**'d make** Jimmy wear a helmet when he's cycling.

1 Use second conditional sentences to talk about hypothetical or improbable situations in the <u>present</u> / <u>future</u>.
2 In the *if* clause you can also use the past continuous. In the other clause you can use *could* or *might* instead of *would*, e.g. *If you* **weren't making** *so much noise, I* **could concentrate** *better.*
3 With the verb *be* you can use *was* or *were* for *I*, *he*, and *she* in the *if* clause, e.g. *If he was / were here, he would know what to do.* However, in conditionals beginning *If I were you...* to give advice, always use *were*.

third conditional sentences: *if* + past perfect, *would* / *wouldn't have* + past participle

> 1 **If** you **had studied** more, you **would have done** better in the exams.
> I **wouldn't have been** late **if** I **hadn't** overslept.
> 2 He **would have died if** he **hadn't been wearing** a helmet.
> If they **had known** you were coming, they **might have** stayed longer.

1 We use third conditional sentences to talk about a hypothetical <u>past</u> situation and its consequence.
2 You can also use the past perfect continuous in the *if* clause. You can use *could have* or *might have* instead of *would have* in the other clause.

second or third conditional?

> 1 If you **studied** more, you **would** probably **pass** the exam.
> 2 If you **had studied** more, you **would** probably **have passed** the exam.

• Compare the two conditionals. 1 = You don't study enough. You need to study more. 2 = You didn't study enough, so you failed.

> ⚠ We sometimes mix second and third conditionals if a hypothetical situation in the past has a present / future consequence, e.g. *He wouldn't be so relaxed if he hadn't finished his exams.*

4B past modals

must / might / can't, etc. + have + past participle

> 1 I **must have passed** the exam. I'm sure I got all the answers right.
> You **must have seen** something. You were there when the robbery happened.
> 2 Somebody **might have stolen** your wallet when you were getting off the train.
> He still hasn't arrived. I **might not have given** him the right directions.
> 3 They **can't have gone** to bed yet. It's only ten o'clock.
> They **can't have seen** us. It was too dark.

• Use *must / may / might / can't / couldn't* + have + past participle to make deductions or speculate about past actions.
1 Use *must have* when you are almost sure that something happened or was true.

> ⚠ The opposite of *must have* is *can't have* NOT ~~mustn't have~~.

2 Use *might / may have* when you think it's possible that something happened or was true. You can also use *could have* with this meaning, e.g. *They could have stolen your wallet when you were getting off the train.*
3 Use *can't have* when you are almost sure something didn't happen or that it is impossible. You can also use *couldn't have*.

should + have + past participle

> It's my fault. I **should have told** you earlier that she was coming.
> We've gone the wrong way. We **shouldn't have turned** left at the traffic lights.

• Use *should* + have + past participle to say that somebody didn't do the right thing.
• You can use *ought to have* as an alternative to *should have*, e.g. *I ought to have told you earlier.*

4C verbs of the senses

look / feel / smell / sound / taste

> 1 She **looks tired**. That **smells good**! These jeans don't **feel comfortable**.
> 2 He **looks like his father**. This material **feels like silk**. This **tastes like tea**, not coffee.
> 3 She **looks as if she's been crying**. It **smells as if something's burning**. It **sounds as if it's raining**.

1 Use *look, feel*, etc. + adjective.
2 Use *look, feel*, etc. + *like* + noun.

> ⚠ *feel like* can also mean 'want / would like', e.g. *I don't feel like going out* = I don't want to go out.

3 Use *look, feel*, etc. + *as if* + clause.
• You can use *like* or *as though* instead of *as if*, e.g. *It sounds* **like / as though** *it's raining.*

4A

a Complete with a suitable form of the verb in brackets.

If he _hadn't broken_ his leg, he would have played. (not break)

1 I _____ you a present if I'd known it was your birthday. (buy)
2 If you _____ to bed earlier, you wouldn't have been so tired. (go)
3 I _____ you some money if I had any. (lend)
4 If I _____ someone's wallet, I'd keep it. (find)
5 Joe wouldn't have crashed if he _____ so fast. (not drive)
6 We would have a dog if we _____ in the country. (live)
7 If you'd looked after the plants, they _____ (not die)
8 You _____ the news if you'd been watching the TV. (hear)
9 They wouldn't have bought the flat if they _____ what the neighbours were like. (know)
10 If she _____ more sociable, she'd have more friends. (be)

b Complete using a second or third conditional.

I didn't wait another minute. I didn't see you.
If I'd waited another minute, *I would have seen you.*

1 Luke missed the train. He was late for the interview.
If Luke hadn't missed the train, …
2 Rebecca drinks too much coffee. She sleeps badly at night.
If Rebecca didn't drink so much coffee, …
3 It started snowing. We didn't reach the top of the mountain.
If it hadn't started snowing, …
4 Millie didn't buy the jacket. She didn't have enough money.
Millie would have bought the jacket if…
5 I don't drive to work. There's so much traffic.
I'd drive to work if…
6 Matt doesn't speak German fluently. He won't get the job.
If Matt spoke German fluently, …

4B

a Rewrite the **bold sentence** sentence with *must / might (not) / can't + have +* verb.

I'm sure I left my umbrella at home. I don't have it now.
I must have left my umbrella at home.

1 **I'm sure Ben has read my email.** I sent it yesterday.
2 Holly's crying. **Perhaps she's had an argument with her boyfriend.**
3 **I'm sure Sam and Ginny haven't got lost.** They had a map.
4 **You saw Ellie yesterday?** That's impossible. She was in bed with flu.
5 **Perhaps John didn't hear you.** You know he's a bit deaf.
6 **I'm sure Lucy has bought a new car.** I saw her driving a Mercedes!
7 **I'm sure Alex wasn't very ill.** He was only off for one day.
8 They didn't come to our party. **Maybe they didn't receive the invitation.**

b Respond to the first sentence using *should / shouldn't have* + a verb in the list.

buy ~~eat~~ go (x2) invite learn save

A Sue is in bed with a stomach ache.
B She _shouldn't have eaten_ so much chocolate cake.
1 **A** We couldn't understand anybody in Paris.
B You _____ some French before you went.
2 **A** Tom told me his phone number but I've forgotten it.
B You _____ it on your mobile phone.
3 **A** Rob was late because there was so much traffic.
B He _____ by car. The train is much faster.
4 **A** Amanda was rude to everyone at my party.
B You _____ her. She's always like that.
5 **A** I haven't got any money left after going shopping yesterday.
B You _____ so many shoes. Did you need three pairs?
6 **A** You look really tired.
B I know. I _____ to bed earlier.

4C

a Circle the correct form.

Your boyfriend *looks /* (*looks like*) a rugby player.

1 You've gone completely white. You *look / look as if* you've seen a ghost!
2 What's for dinner? It *smells / smells like* delicious!
3 I think John and Megan have arrived. That *sounds / sounds like* their car.
4 Have you ever tried frogs' legs? Apparently they *taste like / taste as if* chicken.
5 Are you OK? You *sound / sound as if* you've got a cold.
6 Can you put the heating on? It *feels / feels like* really cold in here.
7 You *look / look like* really happy. Does that mean you got the job?
8 Your new bag *feels / feels like* real leather.
9 Let's throw this milk away. It *tastes / tastes like* a bit strange.
10 Can you close the window? It *smells / smells as if* someone is having a barbecue.

b Match the two halves of the sentence.

1 That group sounds like *F*
2 Those boys look
3 She looks like
4 That guitar sounds
5 He looks as if
6 Your car sounds as if
7 Your new jacket feels
8 This apple tastes
9 It smells as if
10 Your perfume smells like
11 This rice tastes as if

A her mother.
B completely out of tune.
C very soft.
D someone has been smoking in here.
E really sweet.
F ~~REM.~~
G too young to be drinking beer.
H it's been overcooked.
I roses.
J it's going to break down.
K he's run a marathon.

5

5A gerunds and infinitives

verbs followed by the gerund and verbs followed by the infinitive

> 1 I **enjoy listening** to music. I **couldn't help laughing**.
> 2 I **want to speak** to you. They **can't afford to buy** a new car.
> 3 It **might rain** tonight. I **would rather eat in** than go out tonight.

- When one verb follows another, the first verb determines the form of the second. This can be the gerund (verb + -ing) or the infinitive (with or without to).
1 Use the **gerund** after certain verbs and expressions, e.g. *admit, avoid, can't help, can't stand, carry on, deny, enjoy, fancy, finish, give up, keep on, imagine, involve, mind, miss, postpone, practise, risk, stop, suggest.*
2 Use the **infinitive (with *to*)** after certain verbs and expressions, e.g. *agree, appear, be able to, can't afford, can't wait, decide, expect, happen, have (got), help, learn, manage, offer, plan, pretend, promise, refuse, seem, teach, tend, threaten, want, would like.*
3 Use the **infinitive (without *to*)** after modal verbs, e.g. *can, may, might, must, should, had better, would rather,* and after the verbs *make* and *let.*

> ⚠ In the passive, *make* is followed by the infinitive with *to*. Compare *My boss **makes us work** hard. At school we were **made to wear** a uniform.*
>
> ⚠ Some verbs can be followed by the gerund or infinitive (with *to*) with no change of meaning, e.g. *begin, start, continue.*
>
> ⚠ *like, love, hate,* and *prefer* can also be used with either, but the gerund is more common when you are talking generally, and the infinitive when you talk about a specific occasion. Compare *I like skiing* (in general). *I like to ski in February or March* (specific).

verbs that can be followed by either gerund or infinitive with a change of meaning

> 1 **Remember to lock** the door.
>   I **remember going** to Venice as a child.
> 2 Sorry, I **forgot to do** it.
>   I'll never **forget seeing** the Taj Mahal.
> 3 I **tried to open** the window.
>   **Try calling** Miriam on her mobile.
> 4 You **need to clean** the car.
>   The car **needs cleaning**.

- Some verbs can be followed by the gerund or infinitive (with *to*) with a change of meaning
1 *Remember* + infinitive = you remember first, then you do something. *Remember* + gerund = you do something then you remember it.
2 *Forget* + infinitive = you didn't remember to do something. *Forget* + gerund = you did something and you won't forget it. It is more common in the negative.
3 *Try* + infinitive = make an effort to do something. *Try* + gerund = experiment to see if something works.
4 *Need* + gerund is a passive construction, e.g. *The car needs cleaning* = The car needs to be cleaned. NOT *needs to clean.*

5B used to, be used to, get used to

used to / didn't use to + infinitive

> I **used to drink** five cups of coffee a day, but now I only drink tea.
> When I lived in France as a child I **used to have** croissants for breakfast.
> I didn't recognize him. He **didn't use to have** a beard.

- Use *used to / didn't use to* + infinitive to talk about past habits or repeated actions or situations / states which have changed.

> ⚠ *used to* doesn't exist in the present tense. For present habits, use *usually* + the present simple, e.g. *I usually walk to work.* NOT *I use to walk to work.*

- You can also use *would* to refer to repeated actions in the past. *When I lived in France as a child I would always eat croissants for breakfast.* But you can't use *would* with non-action verbs. NOT *I didn't recognize him. He wouldn't have a beard.*

be used to / get used to + gerund

> 1 Carlos has lived in London for years. He's **used to driving** on the left.
>   I'm **not used to sleeping** with a duvet. I've always slept with blankets.
> 2 **A** I can't **get used to working** at night. I feel tired all the time.
>   **B** Don't worry. You'll soon **get used to it**.

1 Use *be used to* + gerund to talk about a new situation which is now familiar or less strange.
2 Use *get used to* + gerund to talk about a new situation which is **becoming** familiar or less strange.
- You can't use the infinitive after *be / get used to.* NOT *He's used to drive on the left.*

5C reporting verbs

structures after reporting verbs

> 1 Jude **offered to drive** me to the airport.
>   I **promised not to tell** anybody.
> 2 The doctor **advised me to have** a rest.
>   I **persuaded my sister not to go out** with George.
> 3 I **apologized for being** so late.
>   The police **accused Karl of stealing** the car..

- To report what other people have said, you can use *say* or a specific verb, e.g. *'I'll drive you to the airport.'*
  Jude **said** he would drive me to the airport.
  Jude **offered** to drive me to the airport.

- After specific reporting verbs, there are three different grammatical patterns.

1 + to + infinitive		2 + person + to + infinitive		3 + -ing form	
agree		advise		apologize for	
offer		ask		accuse sb of	
refuse	**(not) to do**	convince	**somebody**	admit	**(not) doing**
promise	**something**	encourage	**(not) to do**	blame sb for	**something**
threaten		invite	**something**	deny	
		persuade		insist on	
		remind		recommend	
		tell		regret	
		warn		suggest	

- In negative sentences, use the negative infinitive (*not to be*) or the negative gerund (*not being*), e.g. *He reminded me **not to** be late. She regretted **not going** to the party.*

5A

a Complete with the gerund or infinitive of a verb from the list.

~~call~~ not come do get go go out know talk tidy wait work

I suggested ___calling___ a taxi so we wouldn't be late.

1 I'm exhausted! I don't fancy _____ tonight.
2 If you carry on _____, you'll have to leave the room.
3 We'd better _____ some shopping if we want to cook tonight.
4 I'm very impatient. I can't stand _____ in queues.
5 She tends _____ angry when people disagree with her.
6 My parents used to make me _____ my room every morning.
7 I'd rather _____ tonight. I need to study.
8 I can't wait _____ on holiday!
9 I don't mind _____ late tonight if I can leave early tomorrow.
10 Do you happen _____ her phone number?

b Circle the correct form.

Your hair needs (cutting) / to cut. It's really long!

1 I'll never forget to see / seeing the Grand Canyon for the first time.
2 He needs to call / calling the helpline. His computer has crashed.
3 Have you tried to read / reading a book to help you sleep?
4 I must have my keys somewhere. I can remember to lock / locking the door this morning.
5 We ran home because we had forgotten to turn / turning the oven off.
6 Their house needed to paint / painting so they called the painters.
7 Did you remember to send / sending your sister a card? It's her birthday today.
8 We tried to learn / learning to ski last winter but we were hopeless!

5B

a Right (✔) or wrong (✘)? Correct the wrong phrases.

She isn't used to have a big dinner in the evening. ✘
isn't used to having

1 Nowadays I use to go to bed early.
2 When we visited our friends in London we couldn't get used to drink tea with breakfast.
3 Sorry, I'm not used to staying up so late. I'm usually in bed by midnight.
4 There used to be a cinema in our village, but it closed down three years ago.
5 Paul used to having a beard when he was younger.
6 A I don't think I could work at night.
    B It's not so bad. I use to it now.
7 Did you used to wear a uniform at your school?

b Complete with used to, be used to, or get used to and the verb in brackets.

He's Spanish so he *'s used to driving* on the right. (drive)

1 When Nathan started his first job, he couldn't _____ at 6 a.m. (get up)
2 If you want to lose weight, then you'll have to _____ less. (eat)
3 I don't like having dinner at 10.00 – I _____ a meal so late. (not / have)
4 When we were children we _____ all day playing football in the park. (spend)
5 Jasmine has been a nurse all her life so she _____ nights. (work)
6 I've never worn glasses before, but I'll have to _____ them. (wear)
7 I didn't recognize you! You _____ long hair, didn't you? (have)
8 Amelia is an only child. She _____ her things. (not / share)

5C

a Complete with the gerund or infinitive of the verb in brackets.

They advised me ___to buy___ a new car. (buy)

1 Jamie insisted on _____ for the meal. (pay)
2 Lauren agreed _____ with him at the weekend. (go out)
3 I warned Jane _____ through the park at night. (not walk)
4 Jacob admitted _____ the woman's handbag. (steal)
5 The doctor advised Lily _____ coffee. (give up)
6 Our boss persuaded Megan _____ the company. (not leave)
7 Freya accused me of _____ her pen. (take)
8 I apologized to Evie for _____ her birthday. (not remember)

b Complete using a reporting verb from the list and the verb in brackets.

deny invite ~~offer~~ remind refuse suggest threaten

She said to me, 'I'll take you to the station.'
She *offered to take* (take) me to the station.

1 Ryan said, 'Let's go for a walk. It's a beautiful day.'
   Ryan _____ (go) for a walk.
2 'I won't eat the vegetables,' said my daughter.
   My daughter _____ (eat) the vegetables.
3 Sam's neighbour told him, 'I'll call the police if you have any more parties.'
   Sam's neighbour _____ (call) the police if he had any more parties.
4 The children said, 'We did not write on the wall.'
   The children _____ (write) on the wall.
5 Simon said to me, 'Would you like to have dinner with me on Friday night?'
   Simon _____ (have) dinner with him on Friday night.
6 Molly said to Jack, 'Don't forget to go to the dentist.'
   Molly _____ (go) to the dentist.

6A articles

basic rules: *a / an / the*, no article

> 1 My neighbour has just bought **a dog**.
> **The** dog is **an** Alsatian.
> He got into **the** car and drove to **the** Town Hall.
> 2 **Men** are better at parking than **women**.
> I don't like **sport** or **classical music**.
> I stayed at **home last** weekend.

1 Use *a / an* when you mention somebody / something for the first time or say who / what somebody / something is.
   Use *the* when it's clear who / what somebody / something is (e.g. it has been mentioned before or it's unique).
2 Don't use an article to speak in general with plural and uncountable nouns, or in phrases like *at home /work, go home / to bed, next / last (week)*, etc.

institutions (*church, hospital, school*, etc.)

> My father's **in hospital**. They are building **a new hospital** in my town.

• With *prison, church, school, hospital*, and *university*, etc. don't use an article when you are thinking about the institution and the normal purpose it is used it for. If you are just thinking about the building, use *a* or *the*.

geographical names

> 1 Tunisia is in North Africa.
> 2 Selfridges, one of London's biggest department stores, is in Oxford Street.
> 3 Lake Victoria and Mount Kilimanjaro are both in Africa.
> 4 **The** River Danube flows into **the** Black Sea.
> 5 **The** National Gallery and **the** British Museum are London tourist attractions.

• We **don't normally use** *the* with:
1 most countries, continents, regions ending with the name of a country / continent, e.g. *North America, South East Asia*, islands, states, provinces, towns, and cities (exceptions: *the USA, the UK / United Kingdom, the Netherlands, the Czech Republic*)
2 roads, streets, parks, shops, and restaurants (exceptions: motorways and numbered roads, *the M6, the A25*).
3 individual mountains and lakes.
• We **normally use** *the* with:
4 mountain ranges, rivers, seas, canals, deserts, and island groups.
5 the names of theatres, cinemas, hotels, galleries, and museums.

6B uncountable and plural nouns

uncountable nouns

> 1 The **weather** was terrible, but at least there wasn't much **traffic**.
> The **scenery** is beautiful here, but it's spoiled by all the **rubbish** people leave.
> 2 We bought **some new furniture** for the garden. That's **a lovely piece of furniture**.
> 3 **Iron** is used for building bridges.
> I need to buy **a new iron**. My old one's broken.

1 The following nouns are always uncountable: *behaviour, traffic, weather, accommodation, health, progress, scenery, rubbish, work, politics* (and other words ending in *-ics*, e.g. *athletics, economics*).
• They always need a singular verb, they don't have plurals, and they can't be used with *a / an*.
2 These nouns are also uncountable: *furniture, information, advice, homework, research, news, luck, bread, toast, luggage, equipment*. Use *a piece of* to talk about an individual item.
3 Some nouns can be either countable or uncountable, but the meaning changes, e.g. *iron* = the metal, *an iron* = the thing used to press clothes. Other examples: *glass, business, paper, light, time, space*.

plural and collective nouns

> 1 Your **clothes** are filthy! Put a pair of / some clean trousers on.
> 2 Our **staff are** very efficient.

1 *Arms* (=guns, etc.), *belongings, clothes, manners, outskirts, scissors, trousers / shorts* are plural nouns with no singular. They need a plural verb and can't be used with *a / an*.
• If they consist of two parts, e.g. *scissors, trousers, shorts*, they can be used with *a pair of* or *some*.
2 *Crew, police, staff*, etc. are collective nouns and refer to a group of people. They need a plural verb.

6C quantifiers: *all / every*, etc.

all, every, most

> 1 **All** animals need food. **All** fruit contains sugar.
> **All (of) the** animals in this zoo look sad.
> The animals **all** looked sad.
> 2 **Everybody** is here. **Everything** is very expensive.
> 3 **Most people** live in cities.
> **Most of the** people in this class are women.
> 4 **All of** us work hard and **most of** us come to class every week.
> 5 **Every** room has a bathroom. I work **every** Saturday.

1 Use *all* or *all (of) the* + a plural or uncountable noun.
   All = in general, *all (of) the* = specific.
   All can be used before a main verb (and after *be*).
2 *All* can't be used <u>without</u> a noun. Use *everything / everybody*, + singular verb, e.g. *Everything **is** very expensive*.
3 Use *most* to say the majority. *Most* = general; *Most of* = specific.
4 We often use *all / most of* + an object pronoun, e.g. *all of us, most of them, all of you, most of it*.
5 Use *every* + singular countable noun to mean 'all of a group'.

> ⚠ *every* and *all* + time expressions: *Every day* = Monday to Sunday. *All day* = from morning to night.

no, none, any

> 1 Is there any milk? Sorry, there is **no** milk. There **isn't any** (milk).
> 2 Is there any food? No, **none**. / There is **none**.
> But **none of us** are hungry.
> 3 Come **any** weekend! **Anyone** can come.

1 Use *no* + a noun and a ⊞ verb, or *any* + noun + ⊟ verb to refer to zero quantity. *Any* can also be used without a noun.
2 Use *none* in short answers, or with a ⊞ verb to refer to zero quantity. You can also use *none* + *of* + pronoun / noun.
3 Use *any* (and *anything, anyone*, etc.) and a ⊞ verb to mean it doesn't matter when, who, etc.

both, neither, either

> 1 **Both** Pierre **and** Marie Curie were scientists. **Neither** Pierre **nor** Marie was / were aware of the dangers of radiation.
> Marie Curie wanted to study **either** physics **or** mathematics. In the end she studied **both** subjects at the Sorbonne in Paris.
> 2 She and her husband **both** won Nobel prizes.
> 3 **Neither of them** realized how dangerous radium was.

• Use *both, either*, and *neither* to talk about two people, things, actions, etc. *both* = A **and** B; *either* = A **or** B; *neither* = **not** A **and not** B.
1 Use a ⊞ verb. The verb is plural with *both*, and either singular or plural with *neither*.
2 When *both* refers to the subject of a clause it can also be used before a main verb.
3 We often use *both / either / neither + of* + object pronoun, e.g. *us, them*, etc. or *+ of the* + noun.

6A

a Circle the correct article.

James bought (*a*)/ *the* / (–) *new suit* at the weekend.

1 The weather was awful so we stayed at *a* / *the* / (–) home.
2 *A* / *The* / (–) dishwasher we bought last week has stopped working already.
3 I love reading *a* / *the* / (–) historical novels.
4 Sarah had had an exhausting day so she went to *a* / *the* / (–) bed early.
5 My boyfriend drives *a* / *the* / (–) very cool sports car.
6 The teachers are on strike so the children aren't going to *a* / *the* / (–) school.
7 Turn left immediately after *a* / *the* / (–) church and go up the hill.
8 My neighbour's in *a* / *the* / (–) prison because he didn't pay his taxes.
9 People are complaining because the council have refused to build *a* / *the* / (–) new hospital.
10 Visitors will not be allowed to enter *a* / *the* / (–) hospital after 7.00 p.m.

b Complete with *the* or (–).

They're going to ___*the*___ USA to visit family.

1 I think _____ Sicily is the largest island in _____ Mediterranean.
2 Cairo is on _____ River Nile.
3 We didn't have time to visit _____ Louvre when we were in Paris.
4 _____ south-west England is famous for its beautiful countryside and beaches.
5 _____ Mount Everest is in _____ Himalayas.
6 The largest inland lake is _____ Caspian Sea.
7 We stayed at _____ Palace Hotel while we were in Madrid.
8 *Romeo and Juliet* is on at _____ Globe Theatre.
9 _____ Channel Islands are situated between England and France.
10 I've always wanted to visit _____ India.

6B

a Right (✔) or wrong (✘)? Correct the wrong phrases.

Our accommodation isn't satisfactory. ✔
The news are good. ✘ *The news is*

1 We had a beautiful weather when we were on holiday.
2 They've got some lovely furnitures in their house.
3 My brother gave me a useful piece of advice.
4 The police has arrested two suspects.
5 I need to buy a new trousers for my interview tomorrow.
6 The staff is very unhappy about the new dress code.
7 Your glasses are really dirty. Can you see anything?
8 The homeworks were very difficult last night.

b Circle the correct form. Tick (✔) if both are correct.

The traffic (*is*)/ *are* awful during the rush hour.

1 Athletics *is* / *are* my favourite sport.
2 I bought *a pair of* / *some* jeans.
3 Harvey's clothes *look* / *looks* really expensive.
4 The flight crew *work* / *works* hard to make passengers comfortable.
5 I found out *some* / *a piece of* useful information at the meeting.
6 Is that vase made of *a glass* / *glass*?
7 I think I'll have *a* / *some* time after lunch to help you with that report.
8 I've got *a* / *some* good news for you about your job application.
9 We've made a lot of *progresses* / *progress* in the last two weeks.
10 My eyesight is getting worse. I need a new *glasses* / *pair of glasses*.

6C

a Circle the correct word(s).

We've eaten (*all the*)/ *all* cake.

1 *Most of* / *Most* my closest friends live near me.
2 I'm afraid there's *no* / *none* room for you in the car.
3 *All* / *Everything* is ready for the party. We're just waiting for the guests to arrive.
4 *Most* / *Most of* people enjoy the summer, but for some it's too hot.
5 She goes dancing *all* / *every* Friday night.
6 We haven't got *any* / *no* onions for the soup.
7 *Any* / *None* of us want to go out tonight. We're all broke.
8 *Nobody* / *Anybody* can go to the festival. It's free.

b Complete the second sentence so that it means the same as the first. Use the **bold** word.

I like meat. I like fish too.   I like *both meat and fish.*   **both**

1 We could go to Greece. We could go to Italy.   **either**
   We could go _____.

2 I didn't stay very long. You didn't stay very long.   **neither**
   _____ stayed very long.

3 I think her birthday is on the 6th of May – but perhaps it's the 7th.   **either**
   Her birthday is on _____.

4 One of my children could read when he was four. So could the other one.   **both**
   _____ when they were four.

5 My brothers don't smoke. My sisters don't smoke.   **neither**
   _____ smoke.

7

7A structures after *wish*

wish + past simple, *wish* + *would / wouldn't*

> 1 I wish **I was** taller!
>   My brother wishes **he could** speak English better.
> 2 I wish the bus **would come.** I'm freezing.
>   I wish you **wouldn't leave** your shoes there. I almost fell over them.

1 Use *wish* + past simple to talk about things you would like to be different in the present / future (but which are impossible or unlikely).
• After *wish* you can use *was* or *were* with *I*, *he*, *she*, and *it*, e.g. *I wish I were taller.*
2 Use *wish* + person / thing + *would* to talk about things we want to happen, or stop happening because they annoy us.

> ⚠ You can't use *would* for a wish about yourself, e.g. NOT *I wish I would…*

wish + past perfect

> I wish **you had told** me the truth.
> I wish **I hadn't bought** those shoes.

Use *wish* + past perfect to talk about things that happened or didn't happen in the past and which you now regret.

> ⚠ You can also use *If only* instead of *I wish* with these tenses, e.g. *If only the bus would come. If only I hadn't bought those shoes.*

7B clauses of contrast and purpose

clauses of contrast

> 1 **Although** the weather was terrible, we had a good time.
>   I went to work **even though** I was ill.
>   I like Ann **though** she sometimes annoys me.
> 2 **In spite of** / **Despite** his age, he is still very active.
>   being 85, he is still very active.
>   the fact that he's 85, he is still very active.

1 Use *although, though, even though* + a clause.
• *Although* and *even though* can be used at the beginning or in the middle of a sentence.
• *Even though* is stronger than *although* and is used to express a big or surprising contrast.
• *Though* is more informal than *although*. It can only be used in the middle of a sentence.
2 After *in spite of* or *despite*, use a noun, a verb in the *-ing* form, or *the fact that* + subject + verb.

> ⚠ Don't use *of* with *despite* NOT *Despite of the rain…*

clauses of purpose

> 1 I went to the bank **to**
>   **in order to** talk to my bank manager.
>   **so as to**
> 2 I went to the bank **for** a meeting with my bank manager.
> 3 I went to the bank **so that** I could take out some money.
> 4 I wrote it down **so as not to** forget it.

• Use *to, in order to, so as to, for* and *so that* to express purpose.
1 After *to, in order to,* and *so as to* use an infinitive.
2 Use *for* + a noun, e.g. *for a meeting.*

> ⚠ You can also use *for* + gerund to describe the exact purpose of a thing, e.g. *This liquid is for cleaning metal.*

3 After *so that*, use a subject + modal verb (*can, could, would,* etc.).
4 To express a negative purpose use *so as not to* or *in order not to* NOT *not to.* You can also use *so that* + subject + *wouldn't,* e.g. *I wrote it down so that I wouldn't forget it.*

7C relative clauses

defining relative clauses

> 1 She's the woman **who / that lives next door.** That's the book **which / that won a prize.**
> 2 That's my neighbour **whose dog never stops barking.**
> 3 James is the man **(who) I met at the party.** That's the shop **(which) I told you about.**
> 4 My sister's the only person **to whom I can talk.** My sister's the only person **(who)** I can talk **to.**
>   That's the drawer **in which** I keep my keys.
> 5 She told me **what she had seen. What I like best about London** is the parks.

• Use *who, which, whose, whom,* and *what* to introduce a defining relative clause, i.e. a clause which gives essential information about somebody or something.
1 You can use *that* instead of *who / which.*
2 Use *whose* to mean 'of who' or 'of which'.
3 When *who* or *which* are the <u>object</u> of the verb in the relative clause, you can leave them out.
4 After a preposition, use *whom* for a person and *which* for a thing. In informal English, it is more common to leave out the relative pronoun and put the preposition after the verb.
5 Use *what* as a relative pronoun to mean 'the thing' or 'things which'.

non-defining relative clauses

> 1 My aunt, **who doesn't like cats**, was given a kitten for Christmas.
>   The palace, **which was built in the 12th century**, is visited by thousands of tourists.
> 2 Adriana hasn't come to class for two weeks, **which is a bit worrying**.

1 A non-defining relative clause gives extra, non-essential information about a person or thing.
• In written English, this kind of clause is separated by commas, or between a comma and a full stop.
• You can't use *that* instead of *who / which.*
2 *Which* can also be used to refer to the whole of the preceding clause.

7A

a Circle the correct form.

I wish I (was) / would be thinner! My clothes don't fit me!

1 I wish I *had* / *would have* blonde hair!
2 She wishes her parents *lived* / *would live* nearer.
3 You're driving too fast. I wish you *would drive* / *drove* more slowly.
4 I wish it *stopped* / *would stop* raining. I want to go out for a walk!
5 Ben's been wearing the same clothes for years. I wish he *bought* / *would buy* some new clothes.
6 Chloe wishes she *knew* / *would know* how to play the guitar.
7 I'm cold. I wish my flat *had* / *would have* central heating.
8 Their TV is really loud. I wish they *turned* / *would turn* it down.

b Write a sentence with *I wish* + past perfect.

I spent all my money last night and now I'm broke.
I wish I hadn't spent all my money last night

1 I left my camera in the car and someone stole it.
2 I didn't set my alarm clock, so I was late for work.
3 I bought a house in the country, but I really miss the city centre.
4 I dropped my phone in the bath and now it doesn't work.
5 Unfortunately, I couldn't go to your party.
6 I didn't have a holiday last year and now I'm really stressed.

7B

a Complete the sentences with *one* word.

We're happy in our new house, __though__ there's a lot to do.

1 We enjoyed our holiday _____ the weather.
2 Carl doesn't like spending money _____ though he's very rich.
3 They went to the airport _____ catch a plane.
4 Sandy made a note of his number so _____ not to forget it.
5 My mother called the doctor's in _____ to make an appointment.
6 Guy passed the exam in _____ of the fact that he hadn't studied much.
7 Angela took a jacket so _____ she wouldn't get cold.
8 _____ the service was poor, the meal was delicious.
9 I went home _____ a shower before I went out.
10 _____ being late, he stopped for a coffee.

b Rewrite the sentences.

Despite playing badly, they won the match.
Even though *they played badly, they won the match.*

1 We took a taxi so as not to arrive late.
  We took a taxi so that…
2 Despite earning a fortune, she drives a very old car.
  Although…
3 Everyone saw the film even though the reviews were terrible.
  Everyone saw the film in spite of…
4 The plane managed to land despite the very thick fog.
  The plane managed to land even though…
5 I told her I liked her jacket so that I wouldn't offend her.
  I told her I liked her jacket so as…
6 The manager called a meeting so as to explain the new policy.
  The manager called a meeting in order…

7C

a Right (✔) or wrong (✗)? Correct the wrong sentences.

That's the man I met on the bus. ✔
She's the woman who her daughter works with me. ✗
whose daughter works

1 This is the programme I was telling you about.
2 Is this the train that it goes to the mountains?
3 She told her boss she'd overslept, that was absolutely true.
4 My son, that is very tall, enjoys playing basketball.
5 The employee to who I spoke gave me some incorrect information.
6 Everyone in my family always eats that I cook.
7 The Canary Islands, which are situated off the coast of Africa, are a popular tourist destination.
8 The woman who suitcase disappeared is a friend of mine.
9 Did you hear I just said?
10 The bag what I bought last week is already broken!

b Join the sentences with a relative pronoun. Be careful with the punctuation.

I've just failed my driving test. It's a pity.
I've *just failed my driving test, which is a pity.*

1 His girlfriend is very intelligent. She's an architect.
  His girlfriend…
2 They gave us a present. This was a complete surprise.
  They…
3 He was saying something. I didn't understand it.
  I didn't understand…
4 A car crashed into mine. It was a Mini.
  The car…
5 I spoke to a police officer. She was working on the reception desk.
  The police officer…
6 We bought our computer two months ago. It keeps on crashing.
  Our computer…
7 I left some things on the table. They aren't there any more.
  The things…
8 It's too hot in my flat. This makes it impossible to sleep.
  It's…

Personality

1 Adjectives and phrases to describe personality

Match the adjectives with phrases 1–20.

~~ambitious~~ ~~arrogant~~ ~~assertive~~ bad-tempered calm /kɑːm/
cheerful conscientious /ˌkɒnʃiˈenʃəs/ easy-going
eccentric /ɪkˈsentrɪk/ funny immature impulsive ~~insecure~~
insincere loyal open-minded ~~optimistic~~ possessive reserved
~~self-confident~~ stubborn /ˈstʌbən/ vain ~~well-balanced~~ wise

---

She's the kind (sort) of person who…   **She's / He's…**

1. always looks at herself in every mirror she passes.   _____
2. takes care to do things carefully and correctly.   _____
3. is prepared to accept new and different ideas.   _____
4. doesn't say what she really thinks.   _____
5. other people often find different or unusual.   _____
6. is fairly relaxed about most things.   _____
7. is emotionally in control, not moody.   *well-balanced*
8. never changes her opinion even when she's clearly wrong.   _____
9. expresses her ideas or opinions with confidence.   *assertive*
10. is always in a good mood.   _____
11. feels sure about her ability to do things   *self-confident*
12. isn't very sure about herself.   *insecure*
13. is determined to be successful   *ambitious*

He's good at…

14. supporting his friends.   _____
15. giving people advice because of his knowledge and experience.   _____
16. keeping his head in a crisis.   _____

She's not very good at…

17. letting other people share her friends.   _____
18. showing her feelings or expressing her opinions.   _____

He tends to…

19. behave like a child.   _____
20. act without thinking.   _____
21. get angry very easily.   _____
22. think he is better and more important than other people.   *arrogant*
23. expect good things to happen   *optimistic*

She has / has got…

24. a great sense of humour.   _____

Can you remember the words on this page?
Test yourself or a partner.

◐ p.9

2 Adjective suffixes

a Many adjectives are formed by adding a suffix to a noun or verb. Look at the typical suffixes in the chart.

-ible	-able	-ful	-y
responsible	*sociable*	*helpful*	*bossy*

-ive	-ous	-al	-ic
assertive	*ambitious*	*practical*	*ironic*

b Add one adjective to each column in **a** by adding a suffix to the nouns / verbs in the list. You may need to make other small changes. (Be careful with *sense* which can have two different endings and meanings.)

---
adventure   critic   forget   mood
pessimist   rely   sense

---

c Think of definitions for the adjectives you made in **b**.

3 Idioms

a Look at the highlighted idioms and try to guess their meanings.

1. My boss is rather a cold fish. I don't even know if he likes me or not.
2. She has a heart of gold. She'll always help anyone with anything.
3. She's as hard as nails. She doesn't care who she hurts.
4. I hope Jack doesn't come tonight. He's such a pain in the neck.

b Match the idioms with their meanings.

A annoying, difficult
B very kind, generous
C distant, unfriendly
D shows no sympathy or fear

1 Symptoms

a Match the words and pictures.

He has / He's got…

☐ a <u>temperature</u> /ˈtemprətʃə/.
☐ a cough /kɒf/.
☐ a <u>headache</u> (<u>ear</u>ache, <u>stom</u>ach ache, etc.).
☐ a rash.
1 a <u>blis</u>ter.
☐ a pain (in his chest).

☐ He's being sick.
☐ She's <u>sneez</u>ing a lot.
☐ Her finger is <u>bleed</u>ing.
☐ His ankle is <u>swol</u>len.
☐ Her back hurts / aches.

b Match the sentences.

1 She's un<u>con</u>scious /ʌnˈkɒnʃəs/. ☐
2 She has a sore throat. ☐
3 She has diar<u>rhoea</u> /ˌdaɪəˈrɪə/. ☐
4 She feels sick. ☐
5 She <u>faint</u>ed. ☐
6 She feels <u>dizz</u>y. ☐

A She's been to the toilet five times this morning.
B She's breathing but her eyes are closed and she can't hear or feel anything.
C She wants to be sick / vomit.
D It was so hot on the train that she lost consciousness.
E She feels that everything is spinning round.
F It hurts when she talks or swallows food.

2 Illnesses and injuries

Match the illnesses / conditions with their causes or symptoms.

1 He has **flu**. ☐
2 He's **caught a cold**. ☐
3 He is **allergic** to cats. ☐
4 He has **asthma** /ˈæsmə/. ☐
5 He has **high** (low) **blood pressure** /ˈblʌdˈpreʃə/. ☐
6 He's had **a heart attack**. ☐
7 He's had **a stroke**. ☐
8 He has **food poisoning**. ☐
9 He's **twisted / sprained** his ankle. ☐
10 He's **burnt** himself. ☐
11 He has **a bruise** on his toe. ☐

A It's 150 over 100.
B He was overweight, a smoker, and very highly stressed.
C His right side is paralysed and he can't speak.
D He ate some prawns that weren't fresh.
E He's sneezing a lot and he has a cough.
F He dropped a chair on it and now there's a blue mark.
G He has difficulty breathing.
H He starts sneezing as soon as he's near one.
I He's got a temperature and his body aches.
J He touched the iron when it was on.
K He fell badly and now it's swollen.

3 Treatment

Write the missing word in the treatment column.

<u>ban</u>dage /ˈbændɪdʒ/   injection   <u>med</u>icine   ope<u>ra</u>tion   rest   <u>spec</u>ialist   stitches   <u>X</u>-ray

Go to the doctor's (GP). He / she may tell you to…   treatment

1 take some ▒▒▒ e.g. **antibiotics** /æntibaɪˈɒtɪks/ or **painkillers**.   _____
2 stay at home and ▒▒▒.   _____
3 go to hospital to see a ▒▒▒.   _____

Go to hospital / to A & E (Accident and Emergency). You may have to…

4 have an ▒▒▒ or **scan** to see if anything is broken.   _____
5 have ▒▒▒ if you have a very **deep cut**.   _____
6 have an ▒▒▒, when a **drug** is put into your body through a **needle**.   _____
7 have a ▒▒▒ put on to keep the **wound** /wuːnd/ clean.   _____
8 have an ▒▒▒, when part of your body is cut open to remove or repair a damaged part.   _____

Can you remember the words on this page? Test yourself or a partner. **p.12**

Clothes and fashion

1 Describing clothes

a Match the adjectives and pictures.

Fit
- ☐ tight
- ☐ loose /luːs/

Style
- ☐ sleeveless
- ☐ long- (short-) sleeved
- ☐ hooded /ˈhʊdɪd/
- ☐ V-neck

Pattern
- ☐ spotted
- ☐ plain
- ☐ striped
- ☐ checked
- ☐ patterned

b Match the phrases and pictures

Materials
- ☐ a cotton vest
- ☐ a silk scarf
- ☐ leather sandals
- ☐ nylon /ˈnaɪlɒn/ stockings
- ☐ a linen /ˈlɪnɪn/ suit
- ☐ a Lycra™ /ˈlaɪkrə/ swimsuit
- ☐ suede /sweɪd/ slippers
- ☐ a denim backpack
- ☐ a velvet bow /bəʊ/
- ☐ a fur /fɜː/ collar
- ☐ a woollen /ˈwʊlən/ cardigan

c Write the missing word in the **Opinion** column.

old-fashioned   scruffy   smart   stylish   trendy

	Opinion
1 She's very ▭. She always wears the latest fashions.	_____
2 The Italians have a reputation for being very ▭ – both men and women dress very well.	_____
3 He looks really ▭. His clothes are old and a bit dirty and he hasn't shaved.	_____
4 You ought to wear a ▭ suit for your job interview.	_____
5 That tie's very ▭. People don't wear such wide ones any more.	_____

2 Verb phrases

a Match the sentences.

1 I'm going to **dress up** tonight.	☐	A Don't leave it on the chair.
2 Please **hang up** your coat.	☐	B I've just spilt coffee on my dress.
3 These jeans don't **fit** me.	☐	C I'm going to a party.
4 That skirt really **suits** you.	☐	D Breakfast is on the table.
5 Your bag **matches** your shoes.	☐	E It's bath time.
6 I need to **get changed**.	☐	F They're too small.
7 Hurry up and **get undressed**.	☐	G They're exactly the same colour.
8 Get up and **get dressed**.	☐	H You look great in it.

b Cover sentences 1–8. Look at A–H. Try to remember 1–8.

3 Idioms

a Look at the highlighted idioms and try to guess their meanings.

1 What a dress! You're really dressed to kill tonight.
2 That suit fits her like a glove. Did she have it especially made for her?
3 He will have to pull his socks up if he wants to pass the exam.
4 That sounds like a difficult situation. I wouldn't like to be in your shoes.

b Match the idioms to their meanings.

A start trying harder ☐
B in your place ☐
C wearing clothes that people will notice / admire ☐
D is exactly the right size ☐

Can you remember the words on this page? Test yourself or a partner.

⟲ p.22

1 Crimes and criminals

Match the examples to the crimes in the chart.

A A gang took a rich man's son and asked the family for money.

B She went to her ex-husband's house and shot him dead.

C A passenger on a flight made the pilot land in the desert.

D After the party the man made the woman have sex against her will.

E We came home from holiday and found that our TV had gone.

F Someone tried to sell me some marijuana during a concert.

G When the border police searched his car, it was full of cigarettes.

H Someone threw paint on the statue in the park.

I He said he'd send the photos to a newspaper if the actress didn't pay him a lot of money.

J An armed man walked into a bank and shouted, 'Hands up!'

K A man transferred company money into his own bank account.

L A builder offered the mayor a free flat in return for a favour.

M Two men left a bomb in the supermarket car park.

N Somebody stole my car last night from outside my house.

O A man held out a knife and made me give him my wallet.

		Crime	Criminal	Verb
1	I	blackmail	blackmailer	to blackmail
2		bribery	–	to bribe
3		burglary /'bɜːgləri/	burglar	to break in / burgle
4		drug dealing	drug dealer	to sell drugs
5		fraud /frɔːd/	–	to commit fraud
6		hijacking /haɪdʒækɪŋ/	hijacker	to hijack
7		kidnapping	kidnapper	to kidnap
8		mugging	mugger	to mug
9		murder* /'mɜːdə/	murderer	to murder
10		rape	rapist	to rape
11		robbery	robber	to rob
12		smuggling	smuggler	to smuggle
13		terrorism	terrorist	to set off bombs, etc.
14		theft	thief /θiːf/	to steal
15		vandalism	vandal	to vandalize

* manslaughter /'mænslɔːtə/ = killing somebody illegally, but unintentionally
assassination = murder of an important person, usually for political reasons (verb *assassinate*).

2 What happens to a criminal

Complete the sentences. Write the words in the column.

arrested   caught   charged   ~~committed~~   investigated   questioned

The crime

1 Carl and Adam ▢ a crime. They murdered a man.   *committed*

2 The police ▢ the crime. _____

3 Carl and Adam were ▢ on the way to the airport. _____

4 They were ▢ and taken to a police station. _____

5 The police ▢ them for ten hours. _____

6 Finally they were ▢ with murder. _____

acquitted   court   evidence   guilty   judge   jury   not guilty
proof   punishment   sentenced   verdict   witnesses

The trial

7 Two months later, Carl and Adam appeared in ▢. _____

8 ▢ told the court what they had seen or knew. _____

9 The ▢ (of 12 people) looked at and heard all the ▢. _____/_____

10 After two days the jury reached their ▢. _____

11 Carl was found ▢. His fingerprints were on the gun. _____

12 The ▢ decided what Carl's ▢ should be. _____/_____

13 He ▢ him to 10 years in prison / jail. _____

14 Adam was found ▢ (they thought he was innocent). _____

15 There was no ▢ that he had committed the crime. _____

16 He was ▢ and allowed to go free. _____

Punishments

- community service (doing some work to help society, e.g painting, cleaning, etc.)
- a (€600) fine
- six months in prison
- a life sentence
- capital punishment (the death penalty)

Can you remember the words on this page? Test yourself or a partner. p.37

Weather

1 What's the weather like?

a Put the words or phrases in the right place in the chart.

below zero   breeze   chilly   cool   damp   drizzling
freezing   gale-force   mild   pouring (with rain)
scorching   showers   warm

b Complete the text with *fog*, *mist*, and *smog*.

When the weather is foggy or misty, or there is smog, it is difficult to see.
_____ is not usually very thick, and often occurs in the mountain
or near the sea.
_____ is thicker, and can be found in towns and in the country.
_____ is caused by pollution and usually occurs in big cities.

1 It's _____. (quite cold, not cold or hot)	5 It's _____. (pleasant and not cold)	8 It's _____. (a bit wet but not raining)	12 There's a _____. (a light wind)
2 It's _____. (unpleasantly cold)	6 It's _____. (a pleasantly high temperature)	9 It's _____. (raining lightly)	
		10 There are _____. (short periods of rain)	
It's cold.	**It's hot.**	**It's raining / wet.**	**It's windy.**
3 It's _____.	7 It's _____ / boiling. (unpleasantly hot)	11 It's _____. (raining a lot)	13 There are _____ (very strong) **winds**.
4 The temperature is _____. (−10°)			

2 Extreme weather

Match the words and definitions.

blizzard   drought /draʊt/   flood /flʌd/
hailstorm   heatwave   hurricane
lightning   monsoon   thunder   tornado

1 _____ (n) a period of unusually hot weather

2 _____ (n) a long, usually hot, dry period when there is little or no rain

3 _____ (n) a storm with small balls of ice that fall like rain

4 _____ (n) a flash of very bright light in the sky caused by electricity

5 _____ (n and v) the loud noise that you hear during a storm

6 _____ (n) a snowstorm with very strong winds

7 _____ (v and n) when everything becomes filled and covered with water

8 _____ (n) a violent storm with very strong winds especially in the western Atlantic Ocean

9 _____ (n) a violent storm with very strong winds which move in a circle

10 _____ (n) the season when it rains a lot in southern Asia

3 Adjectives to describe weather

Complete the weather forecast with these adjectives.

bright   changeable   clear   heavy   icy   settled   strong   sunny   thick

In the north of England and Scotland it will be very cold, with [1] _____ winds and
[2] _____ rain. There will also be [3] _____ fog in the hills and near the coast, though
it should clear by midday. Driving will be dangerous as the roads will be [4] _____.
However, the south of England and the Midlands will have [5] _____ skies and
[6] _____ sunshine, though the temperature will still be quite low. Over the next few
days the weather will be [7] _____, with some showers but occasional [8] _____
periods. It should become more [9] _____ over the weekend.

4 Adjectives and verbs connected with weather

Match the sentences. Can you guess the meaning of the words in **bold**?

1 Be careful! The pavement's very **slippery**.
2 You're **shivering**.
3 I'm **sweating** /ˈswetɪŋ/.
4 I **got soaked** this morning.
5 It's very **humid** /ˈhjuːmɪd/ today.
6 The snow is starting to **melt**.
7 Don't **get sunburnt**!

A Come and sit in the shade.
B It will all be gone by tonight.
C You might fall over.
D It's hot and damp and there's no
E Can we turn the air conditioning c
F Do you want to borrow my jacket
G It poured with rain and I didn't have an umbrella.

Can you remember the words on this page? Test yourself or a partner.   ⟲ p.41

1 Adjectives

a Match the adjectives with the situations.

~~confused~~   disappointed   glad   grateful   homesick   lonely   nervous   offended   relieved   ~~shocked~~

How would you feel if…?

1 two people gave you completely opposite advice   _confused_
2 the police told you that your flat had been burgled   _shocked_
3 a friend helped you a lot with a problem   _____
4 you thought you had lost your passport but then you found it   _____
5 you didn't get a present you were hoping to get   _____
6 you went to study abroad and were missing your family   _____
7 you moved to a new town and didn't have any friends   _____
8 you were about to talk in public for the first time   _____
9 your friend tells you she has just passed her driving test   _____ (or *pleased*)
10 a very good friend didn't invite you to his party   _____

Some adjectives describe a mixture of feelings, e.g.

fed up = bored or frustrated and unhappy (especially with a situation which has gone on too long)
I'm really fed up with my job. I think I'm going to look for something else.

upset = unhappy and worried / anxious
She was very upset when she heard that her cousin had had an accident.

---

b Match the **strong** adjectives with their definitions.

astonished   delighted   desperate   devastated   exhausted /ɪgˈzɔːstɪd/
furious /ˈfjʊəriəs/   miserable   ~~stunned~~   terrified   thrilled

1 very surprised and unable to move or react   _stunned_
2 extremely upset and shocked   _____
3 very pleased   _____
4 really tired   _____
5 very excited   _____
6 extremely scared   _____
7 really angry   _____
8 very surprised   _____ (or *amazed*)
9 with little hope, and ready to do anything
   to improve the situation   _____
10 very unhappy   _____

⚠ Remember you <u>can't</u> use *very*, *extremely*, etc. with strong
adjectives. If you want to use an intensifier, use *absolutely*,
e.g. *absolutely astonished* NOT ~~very astonished~~.

Can you remember the words on this page?
Test yourself or a partner.

🔵 p.53

2 Idioms

a Look at the highlighted idioms and
try to guess their meaning.

1 I'm sick and tired of telling you to
   do your homework. Get on with it!
2 When I saw the burglar I was
   scared stiff .
3 He finally passed his driving test!
   He's over the moon !
4 You look a bit down in the dumps .
   Has life been treating you badly?
5 I'm completely worn out . I just want
   to sit down and put my feet up.
6 When I saw her, I couldn't believe my
   eyes . She looked ten years younger.

b Match the idioms and the feelings.

A exhausted
B (be) very surprised
C fed up
D terrified
E sad, depressed
F very happy

The body

1 Parts of the body and organs

Match the words and pictures.

ankle
calf /kɑːf/
(pl calves)
heel

chest
waist
hip
thigh /θaɪ/

elbow /'elbəʊ/
wrist
nails
palm /pɑːm/

brain
heart /hɑːt/
kidneys
liver
lungs

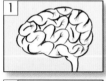
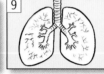
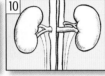

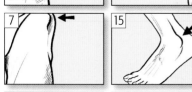
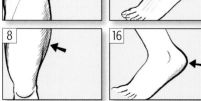

2 Verbs and verb phrases

a Match the verbs with the parts of the body.

arms   eyebrows /'aɪbraʊz/   hair (x2)   hand   hands (x2)
head (x2)   ~~nails~~   nose   shoulders   teeth

1 bite your ___nails___
2 blow your _____
3 brush your _____ / _____
4 clap your _____
5 comb your _____
6 fold your _____

7 hold somebody's _____
8 nod your _____
9 shake your _____ (to say no)
10 raise your _____ (to show surprise)
11 shake _____ (with someone)
12 shrug your _____

b Read the sentences. Write the part of the body related to the **bold** verb.

1 He **winked** at me to show that he was only joking.   ___eye___
2 The steak was tough and difficult to **chew**.   _____
3 When we met, we were so happy we **hugged** each other.   _____
4 Don't **scratch** the mosquito bite. You'll only make it worse.   _____
5 She **waved** goodbye sadly to her boyfriend as the train left the station.   _____
6 Some women think a man should **kneel down** when he proposes marriage.   _____
7 The teacher **frowned** /fraʊnd/ when she saw all the mistakes I had made.   _____
8 The painting was so strange I **stared** /steəd/ at it for a long time.   _____
9 She got out of bed, and **yawned** /jɔːnd/ and **stretched**.   _____ / _____
10 If you don't know the word for something, just **point** at what you want.   _____

3 Idioms

Complete the sentences with a part of the body.

chest   foot   feet   hand   head   heart (x2)   leg   stomach   tongue /tʌŋ/

1 Could you **give me a** ▢ with my homework? It's really difficult.   _____
2 You really **put your** ▢ **in it** when you told Mark that Jane had been married before.   _____
3 You can't be serious. You must be **pulling my** ▢!   _____
4 I can't remember her name but it's **on the tip of my** ▢.   _____
5 I'm not sure I want to go climbing now. I'm starting to **get cold** ▢.   _____
6 The test is on Friday. I've **got butterflies in my** ▢!   _____
7 When Miriam left David, she **broke his** ▢.   _____
8 **I can't get** that song **out of my** ▢. I keep whistling it.   _____
9 You need to **learn** the irregular past tenses **by** ▢.   _____
10 I need to tell somebody about it and **get it off my** ▢.   _____

Can you remember the words on this page? Test yourself or a partner.   ◯ p.62

Music

1 Instruments and musicians

a Match the words and pictures.

	bass /beɪs/ guitar	_____	piano _____
8	cello /ˈtʃeləʊ/	_cellist_	saxophone _____
	drums	_____	trumpet _____
	keyboard	_____	violin /ˌvaɪəˈlɪn/ _____
	organ	_____	

b What do you call the musicians who play each of the instruments above? Write the words next to the name of the instrument? Underline the stressed syllable.

c Match the words and definitions.

bass   choir /ˈkwaɪə/   composer   conductor   DJ (disc jockey)
lead singer   orchestra /ˈɔːkɪstrə/   rapper   singer-songwriter
soloist   soprano   tenor

1 a man who sings with quite a high-pitched voice _____
2 a man who sings with a low-pitched voice _____
3 a woman who sings with a high-pitched voice _____
4 a large group of musicians who play different musical instruments together _____
5 a group of people who sing together, for example in a church service _____
6 somebody who writes and sings his / her own songs _____
7 someone who speaks the words of a song _____
8 somebody who sings or plays an instrument on their own _____
9 the main singer in a band _____
10 the person who directs an orchestra _____
11 somebody who writes music _____
12 the person who chooses, introduces, and plays music on the radio or in a club _____

2 Adjectives and phrases to describe music

Match the sentences.

1 This song has **incomprehensible** lyrics.
2 It's a very **catchy** song.
3 This music is so **moving**.
4 It's a song with a very strong **beat**.
5 I think his voice is very **monotonous**.
6 I don't know what it's called but I recognize the **tune** /tjuːn/.

A The rhythm makes you want to tap your feet.
B It almost sends me to sleep.
C The music sounds familiar.
D I can't understand what it's about.
E I can't get it out of my head.
F It almost makes me want to cry.

3 Idioms

Complete the sentences with the correct music idiom.

A blowing his own trumpet   B face the music   C good ear for music   D music to my ears   E out of tune

1 He has a _____. He can sing a tune as soon as he's heard it.
2 He's not singing the same notes as we are. He's completely _____!
3 He's always _____. He tells everyone how wonderful he is.
4 The others ran away, leaving him to _____. He got punished for what they had all done.
5 When I heard the news it was _____. It was exactly what I wanted to hear.

Can you remember the words on this page? Test yourself or a partner. ⟳ p.70

The media

1 Journalists and people in the media

Match the words and definitions.

commentator   critic   editor   freelance journalist   newsreader   paparazzi /ˌpæpəˈrætsi/
presenter   press photographer   reporter

1 _____   photographers who follow famous people around to get good photos of them to sell to a newspaper
2 _____   a person who writes about the good / bad qualities of books, concerts, plays, films, etc.
3 _____   a person who describes a sports event while it's happening on TV or radio
4 _____   a person who collects and reports news for newspapers, radio, or TV
5 _____   a person in charge of a newspaper or magazine, or part of one, who decides what should be in it
6 _____   a person who introduces the different sections of a radio or TV programme
7 _____   a person who writes articles for different papers and is not employed by a single newspaper
8 _____   a person who reads the news on TV or radio
9 _____   a person who takes photos for a newspaper

2 Sections of a newspaper or news website

Match the words and pictures.

☐ advertisement
☐ cartoon
☐ crossword
☐ front page
☐ horoscope
☐ review /rɪˈvjuː/
☐ small ads
☐ weather forecast

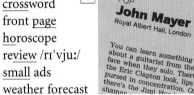

3 Adjectives to describe the media

Match the sentences. Then look at the way the **bold** adjectives are used in context, and guess their meaning.

1 The reporting in the paper was very **sensational**. ☐
2 The news on that TV channel is really **biased** /ˈbaɪəst/. ☐
3 I think *The Observer* is the most **objective** of the Sunday papers. ☐
4 The film review was quite **accurate** /ˈækjərət/. ☐
5 I think the report was **censored**. ☐

A It said the plot was poor but the acting good, which was quite true.
B It bases its stories just on facts, not on feelings or beliefs.
C The newspaper wasn't allowed to publish all the details.
D It made the story more shocking than it really was.
E You can't believe anything you hear on it. It's obvious what political party they favour!

**Can you remember the words on this page?
Test yourself or a partner.**

↪ p.78

4 The language of headlines

Match the highlighted 'headline phrases' with its meaning.

1 ☐ **Famous actress in restaurant bill row**

7 ☐ **Prime minister backs Chancellor in latest scandal**

2 ☐ **United boss to quit after shock cup defeat**

5 ☐ **Prince to wed 18-year-old TV soap star**

8 ☐ **Tarantino tipped for Oscar win**

3 ☐ **Thousands of jobs axed by UK firms**

4 ☐ **Stock market hit by oil fears**

6 ☐ **Police quiz witness in murder trial**

A argument ☐   E is going to marry ☐
B have been cut ☐   F is predicted (to be successful) ☐
C question, interrogate ☐   G has been badly affected ☐
D is going to leave ☐   H supports ☐

1 Buildings, landmarks, and getting around

Write four words in each column.

cable car   chapel   concert hall   cycle lane   football stadium   harbour   hill   law courts /ˈlɔː kɔːts/   mosque
pedestrian street   skyscraper   square /skweə/   statue   synagogue /ˈsɪnəgɒg/   taxi rank   temple   tower

places of worship	other buildings	other landmarks and sights	getting around
cathedral	town hall	bridge	underground

2 Where people live / work

a Match the words and definitions.

1 in **the city / town centre**   A an area and the people who live there
2 in a (friendly) **neighbourhood**   B the area of a town outside the centre
3 in **the suburbs** /ˈsʌbɜːbz/   C the historic part of a town
4 **on the outskirts**   D an area where, e.g. all the banks (or theatres, etc.) are
5 in the (financial) **district**   E the middle
6 in **the old town**   F the furthest part from the centre, on the edge of the town / city

b Describe where you live.

3 City problems

a Complete the **Problems** column with a word from the list.

beggars   homeless people   overcrowding   pollution   poverty   slums   traffic jams   vandalism

Problems

1 There are a lot of   and congestion, especially during the rush hour. _____
2 There are   on the outskirts of the city, where the houses are in very bad condition. _____
3 There is a lot of   , and often phone boxes are destroyed and don't work. _____
4 In some parts of the city there is a lot of   with too many people living in one building. _____
5 There is too much   caused by car fumes and factory emissions. _____
6 There are a lot of   who sleep in the street. _____
7   are poor people who stop you in the street and ask you for money. _____
8 There is a lot of   in this country. Many people are earning less than a dollar a day. _____

b Which of these are problems in your country?

4 Adjectives to describe a town / city

Match the sentences.

1 London is a very **cosmopolitan** city.   A It has many interesting old buildings and monuments.
2 This area of the city is quite **run down**.   B It's full of life and energy.
3 It's a very **industrial** city.   C It's full of people from different cultures.
4 Prague is a very **historic** city.   D People here have a small-town mentality.
5 I think my city is very **provincial**.   E The air is full of toxic chemicals.
6 Buenos Aires is a **vibrant** /ˈvaɪbrənt/ city.   F The buildings are in bad condition.
7 This city is terribly **polluted**.   G There are a lot of factories in and around the city.

Can you remember the words on this page? Test yourself or a partner.

⟳ p.89

Business and advertising

1 Verbs and expressions

a Complete with verbs from the list.

> become   expand   export   import
> launch /lɔːntʃ/   manufacture
> market   merge   set up   take over

1 _____ a company (= start)
2 _____ a product (= make in a factory)
3 _____ a product (= sell using advertising)
4 _____ materials (= buy from another country)
5 _____ your product (= sell to other countries)
6 _____ (= get bigger)
7 _____ the market leader (= be the most successful company)
8 _____ another company (= get control of)
9 _____ a new product, an advertising campaign (= show for the first time)
10 _____ with another company (= combine to make one single company)

b *Do* or *make*? Put the words or phrases in the right column.

> business (with)   a deal
> a decision   a job
> market research
> money   a profit
> somebody redundant

do	make

Can you remember the words on this page? Test yourself or a partner.

⊘ p.105

2 Organizations and people

a **Organizations.** Match the words and definitions.

> a branch   a business / company / firm /fɜːm/   a chain
> head office   a multinational

1 _____ a group of shops, hotels, etc. owned by the same person or company
2 _____ an organization which produces or sells goods or provides a service
3 _____ a company that has offices or factories in many countries
4 _____ the main office of a company
5 _____ an office or shop that is part of a larger organization

b **People.** Match the words and definitions.

> a client /'klaɪənt/   a colleague /'kɒliːg/   a customer
> the (managing) director (MD)   an employee   an employer
> head of department   manager   the owner   the staff

1 _____ the group of people who work for an organization
2 _____ a person who works for somebody
3 _____ a person or company that employs other people
4 _____ someone who buys goods or services e.g. from a shop
5 _____ someone who receives a service from a professional person
6 _____ a person who works with you
7 _____ the person who manages or controls a company or organization
8 _____ the person who owns a business
9 _____ a person who is in charge of a department in a company
10 _____ a person in charge of part of an organization, e.g. a branch

3 Advertising

Match the words / phrases and pictures.

▢ advertisement / advert / ad
▢ commercial
▢ logo /'ləʊgəʊ/
▢ slogan /'sləʊgən/
▢ junk mail
▢ cold-calling

Phrasal verbs in context

FILE 1

Complete the phrasal verbs from File 1 with the correct particle.

> back   down (x2)   up (x3)

1 My brother and his girlfriend **broke** _____ last month.
2 I can't talk now, I'm driving. I'll **call** you _____ in fifteen minutes.
3 This club isn't a very good place to **chat** _____ girls. The music is too loud.
4 The doctor said that I had to **cut** _____ to one cup of coffee a day.
5 Don't **give** _____. If you keep trying, I'm sure you'll find a good job soon.
6 **Slow** _____! There are speed cameras on this road.

FILE 2

Complete the phrasal verbs from File 2 with a verb in the correct form.

> burst   knock   leave   put   turn

1 Everyone _____ **out** laughing when Jimmy arrived wearing a large, white hat.
2 Can you _____ the TV **up**? I can't hear it with the children shouting in the kitchen.
3 Don't _____ anything **behind** when you get off the plane.
4 What a pity! They're going to _____ **down** our local cinema and build a car park.
5 If you take any of my things, please _____ them **back** when you've finished with them.

FILE 3

Match the phrasal verbs from File 3 with a definition A–E.

1 **Watch out**, there are often pickpockets on this station.
2 The company has been **going through** a bad period recently.
3 The police told us to **get out** because the building wasn't safe.
4 If we **carry on** polluting the planet, we're going to destroy it.
5 The restaurant wasn't popular and it **closed down** last year

A continue
B leave
C stop operating
D be careful
E experience or suffer

FILE 4

Complete the phrasal verbs from File 4 with the correct particle.

> down   off (x2)   on   out

1 If there is an emergency, all passengers must **get** ____ of the plane as fast as they can.
2 It was an eight-hour journey so we **set** ____ early in the morning
3 Jessica was getting really angry with Tom so I told her to **calm** _____.
4 **Hold** ____ to me. It's very slippery and you might fall.
5 The teacher **told** me ____ because I hadn't done my homework.

FILE 5

Complete the phrasal verbs from File 5 with the correct verb.

> catch   eat   fall   fill   lie   put

1 I'm exhausted. I'm going to _____ **down** for half an hour.
2 I'm not very good at ice skating. I always _____ **over** at least twenty times!
3 We stopped at a petrol station to _____ **up** with petrol.
4 I'm looking forward to the party. It will be a good chance to _____ **up with** old friends.
5 It's very easy to _____ **on** weight if you _____ **out** several times a week.

FILE 6

Match the phrasal verbs from File 6 with a definition A–E.

1 The teacher **hurried through** the last part of the class.
2 I'll only call you if something interesting **comes up** in the meeting
3 James has **thought up** a brilliant new idea for our new product.
4 An old man was **run over** on the pedestrian crossing.
5 A lorry **crashed into** my car when it was parked outside my house.

A hit someting while moving
B hit and knocked to the ground by a vehicle
C invent
D complete quickly
E occurs or appears unexpectedly

FILE 7

Complete the phrasal verbs with the correct form of the verb.

> end   go   pick   take

1 I don't know what's _____ **on**. Can anyone tell me what's happening?
2 We got completely lost and we _____ **up** miles away from where we wanted to go.
3 I'll _____ you **up** at the station if you tell me what time your train arrives.
4 I've decided to _____ **up** a new hobby – I'm going to learn to dance salsa.

■ short **vowels**

■ **long** vowels

■ diphthongs

■ voiced
■ unvoiced

1 fish /fɪʃ/	11 egg /eg/
2 tree /triː/	12 up /ʌp/
3 cat /kæt/	13 train /treɪn/
4 car /kɑː/	14 phone /fəʊn/
5 clock /klɒk/	15 bike /baɪk/
6 horse /hɔːs/	16 owl /aʊl/
7 bull /bʊl/	17 boy /bɔɪ/
8 boot /buːt/	18 ear /ɪə/
9 computer /kəmpˈjuːtə/	19 chair /tʃeə/
10 bird /bɜːd/	20 tourist /ˈtʊərɪst/

21 parrot /ˈpærət/	33 thumb /θʌm/
22 bag /bæg/	34 mother /ˈmʌðə/
23 key /kiː/	35 chess /tʃes/
24 girl /gɜːl/	36 jazz /dʒæz/
25 flower /ˈflaʊə/	37 leg /leg/
26 vase /vɑːz/	38 right /raɪt/
27 tie /taɪ/	39 witch /wɪtʃ/
28 dog /dɒg/	40 yacht /jɒt/
29 snake /sneɪk/	41 monkey /ˈmʌŋki/
30 zebra /ˈzebrə/	42 nose /nəʊz/
31 shower /ˈʃaʊə/	43 singer /ˈsɪŋə/
32 television /ˈtelɪvɪʒn/	44 house /haʊs/

		usual spelling		⚠ but also
fish	**i**	twisted blister silk fitness sick linen		reliable eccentric bandage business builder symptoms
tree	**ee** **ea** **e**	sneeze feel easy team even recent		believe key people ski
cat	**a**	act glad classic pattern scratch vandal		
car	**ar** **a**	scarf alarm harmful advanced branch staff		palm laugh heart
clock	**o**	opera obvious rob spotted body bossy		cough swallow because knowledge
horse	**or** **al** **aw** **au**	organ explore already talkative law yawn exhausted fraud		brought caught warm course floor board
bull	**u** **oo**	fully push bookcase hooded stood woollen		could would woman
boot	**oo** **u*** **ew**	loose moody flu confused chew news		routine juice suit move soup queue beautiful
bird	**er** **ir** **ur**	reserved allergic firm thirsty burn hurt		earth learn world worse journey
computer	Many different spellings, always unstressed. as<u>ser</u>tive <u>o</u>pinion <u>prac</u>tical <u>tem</u>per <u>doc</u>tor <u>for</u>getful <u>stub</u>born in<u>jec</u>tion <u>ob</u>viously			

* especially before consonant + **e**

		usual spelling		⚠ but also
egg	**e**	energy pessimist credit else rest velvet		leather friend many says said
up	**u** **o**	brush drums lungs scruffy trumpet stunned glove money		flood blood rough enough couple trouble
train	**a*** **ai** **ay**	danger gale vain faint may say		great break neighbour suede survey grey
phone	**o*** **oa** **ow**	lonely choke both throat load elbow blow		soul though shoulders
bike	**i*** **y** **igh**	crime wise style nylon high tight		eyebrow neither buy guy
owl	**ou** **ow**	ground council amount drought frown tower		
boy	**oi** **oy**	disappointed avoid voice choice annoy toy		
ear	**eer** **ere** **ear**	cheerful beer atmosphere sincere appear fear		area ideally diarrhoea series
chair	**air** **are**	airline repair wheelchair square stare		everywhere bear scary
tourist	A very unusual sound. furious assure insecure surely euro plural			
/i/	A sound between /ɪ/ and /iː/. Consonant + **y** at the end of words is pronounced /i/. happy angry thirsty			
/u/	An unusual sound. education usually situation			

Sounds and spelling – consonants

	usual spelling		⚠ but also
parrot	**p**	press plain export hip	
	pp	kidnapping disappear	
bag	**b**	burglar bribe vibrant job	
	bb	stubborn robbery	
keys	**c**	calm ironic	chemist choir ache
	k	kind stroke	
	ck	trick neck	
	qu	mosque queue	
girl	**g**	global guilty drug forget	ghost ghetto
	gg	mugger beggar	
flower	**f**	fed up grateful	tough cough
	ph	photo elephant	
	ff	traffic offended	
vase	**v**	violin vest sleeve review provincial heatwave	of
tie	**t**	trendy terrorist storm strict	worked passed debt doubt receipt
	tt	settled patterned	
dog	**d**	dream denim hand confident	failed bored
	dd	address middle	
snake	**s**	strange responsible	scientist psychologist
	ss	depressing possessive	
	ce/ci	peace celebrity	
zebra	**z**	zero freezing	dessert
	zz	dizzy blizzard drizzle	
	s	miserable museum loves trousers	
shower	**sh**	shocked shy cash selfish	sugar sure brochure moustache anxious pressure
	ti	operation injection (+ vowel)	
	ci	unconcious sociable (+ vowel)	
television	An unusual sound. decision confusion pleasure usually garage		

	usual spelling		⚠ but also
thumb	**th**	theory thrilled healthy truth thief both	
mother	**th**	although with clothes rhythm weather	
chess	**ch**	cheerful chest	cello
	tch	stitches match	
	t (+ure)	immature temperature	
jazz	**j**	jealous injury	soldier
	g	generous original	
	-dge	badge judge	
leg	**l**	launch employ deal blackmail	
	ll	colleague chilly	
right	**r**	relieved reporter breeze critic	wrist wrinkled
	rr	terrified hurricane	
witch	**w**	wave waist windy motorway	one once
	wh	whatever wheel	
yacht	**y**	yoga yawn yoghurt yourself	view
	before u	university human	
monkey	**m**	medicine media damp homeless	thumb comb
	mm	commercial recommend	
nose	**n**	needle nervous kidney monotonous	kneel knew design foreign
	nn	tennis connection	
singer	**-ng**	lightning pouring tongue scorching	
	before k	wink ankle	
house	**h**	hijack horoscope historic incomprehensible unhelpful behave	whoever whose whole

)XFORD
NIVERSITY PRESS

reat Clarendon Street, Oxford OX2 6DP

xford University Press is a department of the niversity of Oxford. It furthers the University's ojective of excellence in research, scholarship, id education by publishing worldwide in

xford New York

ickland Cape Town Dar es Salaam
ong Kong Karachi Kuala Lumpur Madrid
elbourne Mexico-City Nairobi New Delhi
ianghai Taipei Toronto

ith offices in

gentina Austria Brazil Chile Czech Republic
ance Greece Guatemala Hungary Italy Japan
iland Portugal Singapore South Korea
vitzerland Thailand Turkey Ukraine Vietnam

XFORD and OXFORD ENGLISH are registered ade marks of Oxford University Press in the K and in certain other countries

Oxford University Press 2008

ne moral rights of the author have been asserted

atabase right Oxford University Press (maker)

rst published 2008
15
) 19 18

o unauthorized photocopying

l rights reserved. No part of this publication ay be reproduced, stored in a retrieval system, transmitted, in any form or by any means, ithout the prior permission in writing of Oxford niversity Press, or as expressly permitted by law, under terms agreed with the appropriate prographics rights organization. Enquiries oncerning reproduction outside the scope of e above should be sent to the ELT Rights epartment, Oxford University Press, at the ldress above

ou must not circulate this book in any other nding or cover and you must impose this same ondition on any acquirer

ny websites referred to in this publication are the public domain and their addresses are ovided by Oxford University Press for formation only. Oxford University Press sclaims any responsibility for the content.

BN: 978 0 19 451842 0

inted in China

is book is printed on paper from certified and ell-managed sources.

CKNOWLEDGEMENTS

sign and composition by: Stephen Strong

e authors would like to thank all the teachers and students ind the world whose feedback has helped us to shape New glish File. We would also like to thank: Pat Gibson, Richard ll, Alexander Hermon, Sebastian Hope, Gordon Lewis, ke Nugent, John Sloboda, Stephen Turner, Irving ardle, Norman Whitney, Kelly Jennings, Martin Cinert, d Jonathan Pool for agreeing to be interviewed, Frank fford, Hayley Levine, EZ, Sir Nicholas Kenyon, Trevor hite, John Bigos, and Susie Dent for agreeing to appear the DVD, and Sally Wehmeier for helping us check finitions.

e authors would also like to thank: Alicia Monge, Joanna snowska and her students, Krysia Cogollos, Bea Martin d Michael O'Brien for their much appreciated help th ideas and material.

e authors would like to acknowledge their debt to Michael an's Practical English Usage and John Eastwood's Oxford ide to English Grammar.

e authors would also like to thank: all those at Oxford iversity Press (both in Oxford and around the world) d the design team who have contributed their skills d ideas to producing this course.

ally very special thanks from Clive to Maria Angeles, Lucia, d Eric, and from Christina to Cristina, for all their help and couragement. Christina would also like to thank her children iquin, Marco, and Krysia for their constant inspiration.

The publisher and authors would also like to thank the following for their invaluable feedback on the materials: Jane Hudson, Tim Banks, Chris Lima, Brian Brennan, Elena Ruiz, Graham Rumbelow, Kathryn Burn and Robert Anderson.

The authors and publisher are grateful to those who have given permission to reproduce the following extracts and adaptations of copyright material: p.4 'Q & A – Nora Jones' and 'Q & A – Lionel Ritchie' by Rosanna Greenstreet. First published in The Guardian. Reproduced by permission of Rosanna Greenstreet, p.6 'I had only three minutes to get to know the love of my life' by Anushka Asthana, The Observer, 26 January 2003. © Guardian News & Media Ltd. 2003. Reproduced by permission, p.13 'I nearly killed my son through ignorance' by Philippa Heath, The Times, 20 December 2004. © Times Newspapers Ltd. Reproduced by permission, p.15 'Get stressed, stay young – the new health advice' by Sarah Kate Templeton, Times Online, 8 May 2005. © Times Newspapers Ltd. Reproduced by permission, p.22 'Watching the English' by Kate Fox. Reproduced by permission of Hodder and Stoughton Limited, p.24 from 'Air Babylon' by Imogen Edwards-Jones, published by Bantam Press. Reprinted by permission of The Random House Group Ltd, p.26 'We're going to crash' by Andrew Levy, Daily Mail, 28 February 2006. © Daily Mail. Reproduced by permission, p.28 'A Born Loser' by Jean Pressling. 'Winter Cleaning' by Rachael Gardner. 'Tempus Fugit' by James O'Connor. 'Maid to Serve' by Emily Tilton. Taken from 'Mini Sagas' edited by Brian Aldiss (Enitharmon Press, 2001). Reproduced by permission of Enitharmon Press, p.30 'Little Brother ™' by Bruce Holland Rogers, 30 October 2000. www.sff.net/people/bruce/. Reproduced by permission, p.35 'How I conquered my fear of flying' by Sean Langan, Daily Mail, 20 October 2003. © Daily Mail. Reproduced by permission, p.37 'How I learnt to pick a pocket (or two)' by Lottie Moggach, Times Online, 6 October 2005. © Times Newspapers Ltd. Reproduced by permission, p.47 'Fantasy or fact – Japan's children play safe' by Justin McCurry, www.guardian.co.uk, 2 September 2006. © Guardian News & Media Ltd. 2003, p.47 'Risk-taking nursery a breath of fresh air' by Stephanie Condron, www.telegraph.co.uk, 3 April 2006. © The Daily Telegraph. Reproduced by permission, p.51 'Cartoonist makes a mug of hapless bicycle thief' by Ray Marcelo, Times Online, 18 January 2006. © Times Newspapers Ltd. Reproduced by permission, p.57 This is an extract from a column for the New York Times by Amy Sutherland, author of 'What Shamu Taught Me About Life, Love and Marriage' (Random House, February 2008) and 'Kicked, Bitten and Scratched: Life and Lessons at the Premier School for Exotic Animal Trainers' (Viking, June 2006), p.67 'Slimline snaps that help holidaymakers to stretch the truth' by Will Pavia, The Times, 16 August 2006. © Times Newspapers Ltd. Reproduced by permission, p.77 'Back to school for red-faced council', Guardian Unlimited, February 17 2006. Reproduced by permission of The Press Association, p.84 'One small world is one giant sigh of relief for Armstrong' by Jacqui Goddard, The Times, 2 October 2006. © Times Newspapers Ltd. Reproduced by permission, p.92 'Eureka! Thinking outside the bath' by Anjana Ahuja, The Times, 2 August 2004. © Times Newspapers Ltd. Reproduced by permission, p.94 © Bill Bryson. Extracted from 'A Short History of Nearly Everything' by Bill Bryson, published by Black Swan, a division of Transworld Publishers. All rights reserved. Reprinted by permission of the Random House Group Ltd, p.99 'Loud and clear: the message sent by your voice' by Kim Thomas, The Financial Times, 2 November 2005 Reproduced by permission of Kim Thomas, p.102 'Learning curve What I wish I'd known at 21…' by Yvonne Swan, The Daily Mail Weekend Magazine, 5 May 2001. © The Mail Weekend Magazine. Reproduced by permission. p.104 'Freakonomics' by Steven Levitt and Steven J. Dubner (Allen Lane, The Penguin Press 2005) © Steven Levitt & Steven J. Dubner, 2005, p.106 'I slept my way to fitness' from www.oft.gov.uk. Reproduced by permission.

Although every effort has been made to trace and contact copyright holders before publication, this has not been possible in some cases. We apologize for any apparent infringement of copyright and if notified, the publisher will be pleased to rectify any errors or omissions at the earliest opportunity.

The publisher would like to thank the following for their kind permission to reproduce photographs and other copyright material: Advertising Archive p.107, 156 (Bakers dog, Nike); Aurora Photos p.83; Australian Associated Press p.51 (Andrew Brownbill); Alamy pp.21 (Zute Lightfoot/Brazilian flag, FAN Travelstock/girls at Carnival), 23 (Yadid Levy/Punk, Homer Sykes/judges), 32 (Ken Welsh/Emergency Exit), 48 (Andy Day/leaping pavement and leaping roof), 49 (Janine Wiedel), 55 (Jacques Jangoux/aerial view of river), 58 (Ace Stock/Mother and daughter row), 72 (Dominic Burke/road sign), 73 (Yadid Levy), 75 (Patrick Eden), 78 (Rolf Adlercreutz/Guys and Dolls), 90 (Alex Segre/Parliament Hill, Andrew Critchell/Serpentine, Alice De Maria/Beigel Shop), 96 (Alvey & Towers/Duckland, Travelshots/Nelsons column, Banana Pancake/Nelson Mandela Statue, Johnnny Greig Travel/Duck on river), 100 (Rex Argent/dentist, David Stares/cyclist), 101 (Everynight Images/Girls in Sunglasses), 149 (Ian McKinnell); Allstar p.36 (R.P. Productions/Runteam Ltd/Oliver running); Art Institute of Chicago p.120 (Edward Hopper, Nighthawks, Friends of American Art Collection 1942–51. Reproduction, The Art Institute of Chicago, photo by Robert Hashimoto); Camera Press pp.5 (Gamma/Ulf Andersen/William Boyd), 41 (Gamma/Xavier Rossi/Bridges), 79 (Gamma/Catherine Lambermont/paparazzo), 92 (Gamma/Frederic Neema/IKEA); Centre for Alternative Technology p.43 (Arthur Girling/Barbara Haddrill); Corbis pp.8 (Dewitt Jones/Jack Nicholson signature, Einstein signature), 23 (Tony Arruza/sandals and socks), 40 (EPA/Marcel Antonisse/Amsterdam storm), 55 (spotter plane), 62 (Andrew Ross), 71 (EPA/Steffen Schmidt/Metallica, 85 (Bettmann/Martin Luthur King, Keystone/Winston Churchill), 97 (Barry Lewis), 156 (Zefa/Gary Edwards); DK Images pp.16 (Astrology chart), 106 (Man flexing muscles), 110 (taxi, alarm clock); easyJet p.92; Daniel Everett p.115; Peter Ford p.84 (voice analysis); Frank Lane Picture Agency pp.54–55 (Frans Lanting/Jungle); Fraser's Autographs p.8 (Tom Hanks, Victoria Beckham and Orlando Bloom signatures); FremantleMedia Stills Library p.102 (Man about the house); Getty Images pp.5 (Matt Cardy/Natalie Imbruglia), 8 (Gandhi signature) 13 (David Westing/Trisha Goddard), 21 (Christian Science Monitor/Underground, Koji Watanabe/Nissan employees), 27 (Indranil Mukherjee), 35 (Michal Cizek), 36 (Bertram Henry/Break in), 39 (Lynn Saville/forest), (Sean Gallup/Prague floods buildings), 42 (Axiom/Paul Miles/bear), 55 (Minden Pictures/jaguar), 57 (Science Faction/Stephen Frink/dolphin), 58 (Jim Naughten/car), 71 (Hulton Archive/Maria Callas, AFP/Leela James), 72 (Peter MacDiarmid/John Prescott), 79 (Tom Shaw/cricket), 84 (Hulton Archive/Nasa), 85 (Keystone/Hulton Archive/Edward VIII), 88 (Photonica/Jon Jones/Los Angeles), 90 (David Tipling/nightingale, Georgette Douwma/squirrel, Travel Pix/Houses of Parliament), 101 (David Oliver/Underground, Ryuhei Shindo/Girl on phone), 102 (Claire Greenway/Paula Wilcox older), 155 (Jorg Greuel); Pat Gibson p.79; Tim Graham p.23 (Queen); Trafalgar Hotel p.90 (roof garden); Sebastian Hope p.90; Indiapolis Museum of Art p.118 (Edward Hopper, The Hotel Lobby, 1943, William Ray Adams Memorial Collection. Reproduction Indiapolis Museum of Art.; iStockphoto p.55 (man on raft); Landov p.88 (CBS/logo, teenagers); Magnum Photos pp.11 (Tarot stall); Nokia p.156; Oxford University Press pp.104, 110 (wedding cake ornament), 135 (Hemera/cello/drums/bass guitar/keyboard/piano/saxophone/trumpet/violin); Philips Lighting p.43 (light bulb); Photostage p.64 (Coriolanus); Press Association pp.4 (Darko Bandic), 5 (AP/Steffen Schmidt/Lionel Richie), 39 (AP/Tony Dejak/Judge Cicconetti, AP/The Plain Dealer, Marvin Fong/Michelle Murray), 40 (AP/The Fresno Bee/John Walker/oranges and icicles), 47 (AP/Junji Kurokawa/Japan nursery), 52 (AP/Suzanne Plunkett/9/11), 80 (Empics/Albert Hall and Simon Rattle); Punchstock pp.16 (palm of hand), 42 (ice melting), 44 (Life saving ring), 72 (child), 90 (St Paul's), 100 (child), 106 (doctor), 119; Retna pp.5 (Kiera Fyles/Shaznay Lewis); Reuters p.116 (Kai Pfaffenbach); Rex Features pp.5 (Huw John/Danny Jones, Inferno/Everett/Martin Freeman, BEI/Grefory Pace/Helena Christensen), 6, (Richard Saker/bald man, girl with sunglasses), 7, 10 (The Sun/Mystic Meg), 11 (Kevin Foy/Palmistry Sign), 23 (Steve Maisey/suit), 36 (R.P. Productions/Runteam Ltd/Oliver and Fagan), 40 (crowd), 53 (Sipa Press/air crash), 57 (Stewart Cook/chimpanzee), 90 (RHPL/Walter Rawlings/post box), 91 (Andre Segre), 110 (hooligan), 156 (Ray Tang/Advertising Hoarding); Scala Archives p.63 (Edward Hopper: Cape Cod Morning, 1950, Washington DC, Smithsonian American Art Museum); Howard Schatz pp.60, 61; Science Photo Library p.84 (Earthrise, footprint); Daniel J. Simons p.92 (The video depicted in this figure is available as part of a DVD from Viscog Productions); Specialist News Service p.67; Sportsphoto p.23 (Michael Mayhew/plastic macs); Stockbyte p.44 (handgun); Telegraph p.47 (David Burgess/Farley Nursery School); Virgin Atlantic p.26; Irving Wardle p.78; the photograph of the OED on p.112 from Oxford University Press Archives, reproduced by permission to the Secretary of the Delegates of Oxford University Press.

Commissioned photography: by Gareth Boden p.13 (boy with tomatoes), 22 (Goth) 56 (couple at breakfast), 117 (flat); Mark Mason pp.55 (lighter and spray), 110 (tip, jeans), 111, 148, 154 (junk mail)

Illustrations by: Cartoonstock/Ian Baker pp.18, 50, 76–77, 81, 82, 113; Cartoonstock/Neil Bennet p.38; Cartoonstock/Clive Goddard 94; Phil Disley pp.9, 24, 33, 46, 53, 59, 73, 74, 92, 93, 109, 146, 148, 149, 151, 152; Mark Duffin p.85; Marie-Helene Jeeves pp.14, 15, 28; Kath Hextall pp.12, 62, 63, 86, 118; Illustrationweb/Stuart Holmes p.65; Ellis Nadler pronunciation symbols; Annabel Milne pp.13, 43; Thorogood Illustration/Kanoko & Yuzuru pp.30–31; Annabel Wright pp.68–69, 70

Picture research and illustrations commissioned by: Cathy Blackie

Student's Book

'It has all the elements that have made the series such a successful one.'

- Motivating, real-world texts **p.84**
- Grammar Bank with rules and exercises **p.132**
- Illustrated Vocabulary Bank **p.146** and Sound Bank **p.158**
- Colloquial English focus on everyday language **p.32**

English Sounds Pronunciation Chart based on an original idea and design by Paul Seligson and Carmen Dolz

OXFORD
UNIVERSITY PRESS

www.oup.com/elt

New ENGLISH FILE

The course that gets students talking

Fun, motivating lessons that work
The perfect balance of grammar, vocabulary, pronunciation, and skills to help your students use English really effectively.

A complete package for teachers and students
The Teacher's Book gives you the support you need, and all the components work together for more effective learning.

Common European Framework of Reference B2

Oxford › making **digital** sense

For students
- **Student's Book**
- **Workbook with or without key**
- **MultiROM**
  - CD-ROM and audio CD in one
  - Online test and skills practice with oxfordenglishtesting.com
- **www.oup.com/elt/englishfile/upper-intermediate**
  - Extra exercises and downloadable material

For teachers
- **Teacher's Book with photocopiable activities and Test and Assessment CD-ROM**
- **Class audio CDs**
- **Class DVD**
- **iPack**
  - For interactive whiteboards, projectors, and computers
- **www.oup.com/elt/teacher/englishfile**
  - Resources, ideas, and reference materials

Look out for Study Link throughout the course. This shows links between components to make teaching and learning more effective.

for all your testing needs online go to
oxfordenglishtesting.com

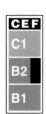
CEF
C1
B2
B1

OXFORD ENGLISH
ISBN 978-0-19-451842-

9 780194 518420